Co**ntents**

QuickTime for Java™
A Developer's Notebook™

Chris Adamson

O'REILLY®

Beijing · Cambridge · Farnham · Köln · Paris · Sebastopol · Taipei · Tokyo

QuickTime for Java™: A Developer's Notebook™
by Chris Adamson

Published by O'Reilly Media, Inc., 1005 Gravenstein Highway North, Sebastopol, CA 95472.

O'Reilly books may be purchased for educational, business, or sales promotional use. Online editions are also available for most titles (*safari.oreilly.com*). For more information, contact our corporate/institutional sales department: (800) 998-9938 or *corporate@oreilly.com*.

Editor:	Brett McLaughlin
Production Editor:	Sarah Sherman
Cover Designer:	Edie Freedman
Interior Designer:	David Futato

Printing History:

January 2005:	First Edition.

 This book uses RepKover,™ a durable and flexible lay-flat binding.

ISBN: 0-596-00822-8
[M]

The Developer's Notebook Series

So, you've managed to pick this book up. Cool. Really, I'm excited about that! Of course, you may be wondering why these books have the odd-looking, college notebook sort of cover. I mean, this is O'Reilly, right? Where are the animals? And, really, do you *need* another series? Couldn't this just be a cookbook? How about a nutshell, or one of those cool hacks books that seems to be everywhere? The short answer is that a developer's notebook is none of those things—in fact, it's such an important idea that we came up with an entirely new look and feel, complete with cover, fonts, and even some notes in the margin. This is all a result of trying to get something into your hands you can actually use.

It's my strong belief that while the nineties were characterized by everyone wanting to learn everything (Why not? We all had six-figure incomes from dot-com companies), the new millennium is about information pain. People don't have time (or the income) to read through 600 page books, often learning 200 things, of which only about 4 apply to their current job. It would be much nicer to just sit near one of the uber-coders and look over his shoulder, wouldn't it? To ask the guys that are neck-deep in this stuff why they chose a particular method, how they performed this one tricky task, or how they avoided that threading issue when working with piped streams. The thinking has always been that books can't serve that particular need—they can inform, and let you decide, but ultimately a coder's mind was something that couldn't really be captured on a piece of paper.

This series says that assumption is patently wrong—and we aim to prove it.

A Developer's Notebook is just what it claims to be: the often-frantic scribbling and notes that a true-blue alpha geek mentally makes when working with a new language, API, or project. It's the no-nonsense code that solves problems, stripped of page-filling commentary that often serves more as a paperweight than an epiphany. It's hackery, focused not on what is nifty or might be fun to do when you've got some free time (when's the last time that happened?), but on what you need to simply "make it work." This isn't a lecture, folks—it's a lab. If you want a lot of concept, architecture, and UML diagrams, I'll happily and proudly point you to our animal and nutshell books. If you want every answer to every problem under the sun, our omnibus cookbooks are killer. And if you are into arcane and often quirky uses of technology, hacks books simply rock. But if you're a coder, down to your core, and you just want to get on with it, then you want a Developer's Notebook. Coffee stains and all, this is from the mind of a developer to yours, barely even cleaned up enough for print. I hope you enjoy it...we sure had a good time writing them.

Notebooks Are...

Example-driven guides

As you'll see in the "Organization" section, developer's notebooks are built entirely around example code. You'll see code on nearly every page, and it's code that *does something*—not trivial "Hello World!" programs that aren't worth more than the paper they're printed on.

Aimed at developers

Ever read a book that seems to be aimed at pointy-haired bosses, filled with buzzwords, and feels more like a marketing manifesto than a programming text? We have too—and these books are the antithesis of that. In fact, a good notebook is incomprehensible to someone who can't program (don't say we didn't warn you!), and that's just the way it's supposed to be. But for developers...it's as good as it gets.

Actually enjoyable to work through

Do you really have time to sit around reading something that isn't any fun? If you do, then maybe you're into thousand-page language references—but if you're like the rest of us, notebooks are a much better fit. Practical code samples, terse dialogue centered around practical examples, and even some humor here and there—these are the ingredients of a good developer's notebook.

About doing, not talking about doing

If you want to read a book late at night without a computer nearby, these books might not be that useful. The intent is that you're coding as you go along, knee deep in bytecode. For that reason, notebooks talk code, code, code. Fire up your editor before digging in.

Notebooks Aren't...

Lectures

We don't let just anyone write a developer's notebook—you've got to be a bona fide programmer, and preferably one who stays up a little too late coding. While full-time writers, academics, and theorists are great in some areas, these books are about programming in the trenches, and are filled with instruction, not lecture.

Filled with conceptual drawings and class hierarchies

This isn't a nutshell (there, we said it). You won't find 100-page indices with every method listed, and you won't see full-page UML diagrams with methods, inheritance trees, and flow charts. What you will find is page after page of source code. Are you starting to sense a recurring theme?

Long on explanation, light on application

It seems that many programming books these days have three, four, or more chapters before you even see any working code. I'm not sure who has authors convinced that it's good to keep a reader waiting this long, but it's not anybody working on *this* series. We believe that if you're not coding within ten pages, something's wrong. These books are also chock-full of practical application, taking you from an example in a book to putting things to work on your job, as quickly as possible.

Organization

Developer's Notebooks try to communicate different information than most books, and as a result, are organized differently. They do indeed have chapters, but that's about as far as the similarity between a notebook and a traditional programming book goes. First, you'll find that all the headings in each chapter are organized around a specific task. You'll note that we said *task*, not *concept*. That's one of the important things to get about these books—they are first and foremost about doing something. Each of these headings represents a single *lab*. A lab is just what it sounds like—steps to accomplish a specific goal. In fact, that's the first heading you'll see under each lab: "How do I do that?" This is the central question of each lab, and you'll find lots of down-and-dirty code and detail in these sections. Many labs offer alternatives and address common questions about different approaches to similar problems. These are the "What about…" sections, which will help give each task some context within the programming big picture.

And one last thing—on many pages, you'll find notes scrawled in the margins of the page. These aren't for decoration; they contain tips, tricks, insights from the developers of a product, and sometimes even a little humor, just to keep you going. These notes represent part of the overall communication flow—getting you as close to reading the mind of the developer-author as we can. Hopefully they'll get you that much closer to feeling like you are indeed learning from a master.

And most of all, remember—these books are…

All Lab, No Lecture

—Brett McLaughlin, Series Creator

Preface

Java has been a huge success in many fields—distributed enterprise applications, mobile phones, web applications—but one field that it has clearly flopped in is media. A sound API, *javax.sound*, suffices for simple playback and mixing of a handful of old formats, and was added to the Java core (the classes any Java runtime must include) in Java 2 Standard Edition (J2SE) 1.3. The optional package for media, Java Media Framework (JMF), fared much worse. After two releases, a 1.0 that provided only playback and a 2.0 that added streaming, transcoding, and some lower-level access, the product was slipped into maintenance mode and has seen little attention since 1999. In fact, the most monumental change to JMF in this time was the *loss* of a feature: MP3 support was removed in 2002, due to licensing concerns. Making things worse, JMF's all-Java version had weak support for popular formats and codecs. Native editions could play more media, but Sun initially created versions only for Windows and Solaris, later providing minimal support to a third-party Linux port and absolutely no support for a Mac version. Setting aside the dubious premise of Solaris as a media production OS, this effectively made JMF practical only on Windows, eliminating Java's cross-platform advantage.

Enter QuickTime, a multimedia framework originally introduced by Apple for the ("Classic") Mac OS in late 1991. QuickTime defines both a file format (the QuickTime *.mov* format) and many APIs for working with time-based media. The provided functions allow applications to create media (either synthetically or via capture), manipulate it, and present it. Media types supported by QuickTime include sound and video, timed text (captions), graphics, interactivity, and a panoramic-image style of virtual reality (VR).

Unfortunately, despite having an industry-leading multimedia framework, in 1998 there was no straightforward means of exposing Quick-Time to Java developers. And whereas most APIs start with an interface and then gain a reference implementation, Apple had an implementation and the native QuickTime libraries, but no Java interface. Compounding the problem, QuickTime was designed to be called from C (sometimes called "straight C" or "procedural C") and thus lacked the object orientation a Java interface would call for.

Enter Biscotti

Apple's "Biscotti" project took a remarkable approach to this problem—not only did the Biscotti designers provide a Java layer to make Quick-Time calls, but they also fashioned an object-oriented API out of a non-OO framework. It helps that QuickTime is made up of a number of fairly elaborate structures, along with functions that work with them. The Biscotti designers saw that these structures could be combined into Java objects. For example, they took the Movie struct and many of the functions that worked with a movie, and fashioned these into the quicktime.std.Movie class. Functions such as StartMovie( ), StopMovie( ), CopyMovieSelection( ), and PasteMovieSelection( ) became the Java instance methods start( ), stop( ), copySelection( ), and pasteSelection( ), respectively. Biscotti, now known as QuickTime for Java, still has its quirks, but it's a lot more Java-like than some other "wrapper" frameworks for Java.

By comparison, the JOGL API, which offers a Java wrapper to the OpenGL graphics library, simply dumps the functions defined in the C header files into pseudo-objects with upward of 2,000 methods each!

Whatever Apple's reasons for creating QuickTime for Java (QTJ), the application has been the beneficiary of many fortuitous advances. The most significant comes from QTJ's nature as a Java wrapper around a native framework: as the native QuickTime grows, so does QTJ. In particular, when QuickTime supports a new format or codec, it is almost always available to QTJ immediately, without requiring any new QTJ development. When QuickTime added MPEG-4 support, QTJ picked it up for free. When Apple started selling songs on the iTunes Music Store, QTJ was able to play the encrypted AAC audio files right away.

Why a QuickTime for Java Book?

The strangest thing about QuickTime for Java might be that if you read Apple's documentation, you get the idea that it was originally aimed not at Java developers, but at QuickTime developers. One of the introductory docs, "Summary of QuickTime for Java," says as much: "QuickTime for

Java came about to meet developers' need for a way to get at QuickTime besides using C calls." It then goes on to define Java concepts like classes, objects, and instance methods...it even has a gentle introduction to the idea of garbage collection.

To a Java developer, this seems wildly backward. The Java developer, evaluating QTJ as a multimedia toolkit, already knows about garbage collection, and instead he needs an introduction to the QuickTime concepts that are taken for granted: the idea of the movie as an "organizing principle" rather than an explicit media stream, the relationship of movies, tracks, and media, and odd legacies left over from the old Mac OS. The existing documentation doesn't help much—the Javadoc for a given method often gives a one-line description (at best), followed by a reference to the underlying C function it calls.

The goal of this book is to offer a guide to QTJ *from a Java point of view*. That means introducing QuickTime concepts as necessary, treating it as essentially new material. Hopefully, this will present QTJ as an end in itself, meaning you can write effective QTJ applications without having to understand the native QuickTime API or constantly consult its documentation. It also means that as a book for Java developers, we'll always adhere to Java coding conventions, taking particular care to note where QTJ's way of doing something might not seem "normal" from a Java perspective.

Assumptions and Definitions

This book assumes that you are comfortable with Java 2 Standard Edition, Version 1.4 (J2SE 1.4). You should understand the core language and packages, particularly AWT and Swing. I use both AWT and Swing extensively—sometimes in the same example, when it's clearer to do it that way—AWT is much faster, but Swing has some space-saving conveniences that keep the examples short and focused.

If you don't think AWT is overly verbose, try building a choice dialog sometime.

You should also have at least a passing familiarity with concepts of digital media. Although the Developer's Notebooks aren't about theory, there are a few terms you should know off the bat.

Movie

In QuickTime, a "movie" isn't just an audio/video file—it is an organization of media elements that can include audio, graphics, video, text, interactivity, etc. For the purposes of this book, anything that can be represented by the Movie class is a "movie," including remote MP3 streams, wired-sprite video games, etc.

Codec

A codec is a piece of code that can encode and/or decode media in a given format. Apple's documentation often breaks this down into *media handlers*, which understand a given encoding, and *compressors* and *decompressors* to compress or extract data.

Container format

File formats like QuickTime *.mov* or Microsoft's AVI are containers that can hold different kinds of content, such as a combination of audio, video, or other kinds of media. Note that parsing the format and parsing its contents are two separate things: QuickTime can handle the format of a given AVI file but might not support a codec used in it (and vice versa for libraries that support the QuickTime file format). Also, a container like QuickTime can refer to remote data, such as media in another file or out on the network, so a given *.mov* file does not necessarily contain all the media needed to play the movie.

Organization

This book is organized into chapters of related material, but as you'll see, this is no "animal book," nor is it an *Inside Macintosh*, for that matter. Each chapter is broken down into tasks, most of which can be understood fairly independently. In some cases, a chapter will start off with a complete running application, like the movie player in Chapter 2 or the editor in Chapter 3, then gradually add features (undo, redo, save, etc.) in successive tasks by indicating only what new code needs to be added to implement the feature. The only exception is a startup/teardown convenience class, QTSessionCheck, introduced in Chapter 1 and used by nearly all the other examples as a means of reducing distracting boilerplate code throughout the book.

Each task exists as a complete example in the downloadable sample code, which is hosted at *http://www.oreilly.com/catalog/quicktimejvaadn*.

About the Examples

When unzipped, the examples will create a directory whose contents look like this:

```
build.xml              my.ant.properties.win
classes/               src/
jars/
```

build.xml is the build file for Ant, the de facto standard for building Java projects. You don't have to use Ant, but considering the classpath challenges in dealing with Java builds, particularly with QTJ (see Chapter 1), you'll probably find it well worth your while. If you don't already have it, you can get Ant from *http://ant.apache.org/*, and you can learn more in *Ant: The Definitive Guide* (O'Reilly).

TIP

The *classes* and *jars* directories are created by Ant, and will not be present when you first unzip the archive.

Using the command line, type ant in this directory to run the default target. In this case, it's the help message:

```
cadamson% ant
Buildfile: build.xml

help:
     [echo] Available targets:
     [echo] chOn -- compile source for chapter n (eg "ch01", "ch02", etc.)
     [echo] all -- compile source for all chapters
     [echo] chOn.jar -- make a .jar file for chapter n
     [echo] qtj-notebook.jar -- compile source for all chapters and make jar
     [echo] all.jar -- synonym for qtj-notebook.jar
     [echo] run-example -- compile and run "example"
     [echo] help-names -- echo all example names for use with run-example
     [echo] clean -- remove .class files
     [echo] help -- this help message (default)
     [echo]

BUILD SUCCESSFUL
Total time: 2 seconds
```

You can look in the *build.xml* file for more information. One important note is that compiling requires the path to the *QTJava.zip* file, as described in Chapter 1. The default is the Mac OS X path, */System/Library/Java/Extensions/QTJava.zip*. If you're using Windows, you need to override this. The provided file *my.ant.properties.win* has a sample path that looks like this:

```
qtjavazip.file=c:\\Progra~1\\Java\\j2re1.4.2\\lib\\ext\\QTJava.zip
```

Edit this so that it refers to the path to *QTJava.zip* on your system, and then rename the file to *my.ant.properties*, so *build.xml* will pick it up. Because any Ant properties are picked up from this file, it also gives you the opportunity to make other Ant tweaks, such as repointing jvm.home to use one of several Java installations on your box, or to change the java.compiler to jikes.

To compile all the book examples into a JAR file, type:

```
ant qtj-notebook.jar
```

This will produce output like the following:

```
cadamson% ant qtj-notebook.jar
Buildfile: build.xml

init:
     [echo] qtjavazip.file = /System/Library/Java/Extensions/QTJava.zip

all:
     [javac] Compiling 53 source files to /Users/cadamson/Documents/O'Reilly/
books/qtj developer's notebook/code/classes

qtj-notebook.jar:
      [jar] Building jar: /Users/cadamson/Documents/O'Reilly/books/qtj
developer's notebook/code/jars/qtj-notebook.jar

BUILD SUCCESSFUL
Total time: 7 seconds
```

You can then run any of the examples by extending the classpath to
include the *qtj-notebook.jar* file, as in:

```
java -cp jars/qtj-notebook.jar com.oreilly.qtjnotebook.ch02.SimpleQTPlayer
```

There are also Ant targets to compile and run every example in the book.
Use `ant help-examples` to see a list of example names.

Conventions Used in This Book

The following typographical conventions are used in this book.

Plain text
> Indicates menu titles, menu options, menu buttons, and keyboard
> accelerators (such as Alt and Ctrl).

Italic
> Indicates new terms, URLs, email addresses, filenames, file exten-
> sions, pathnames, directories, and Unix utilities.

`Constant width`
> Indicates commands, options, switches, variables, attributes, keys,
> functions, types, classes, namespaces, methods, modules, properties,
> parameters, values, objects, events, event handlers, XML tags, HTML
> tags, macros, the contents of files, or the output from commands.

`Constant width bold`
> Shows commands or other text that should be typed literally by the
> user.

Constant width italic

Shows text that should be replaced with user-supplied values.

TIP

This icon signifies a tip, suggestion, or general note.

WARNING

This icon indicates a warning or caution.

Using Code Examples

This book is here to help you get your job done. In general, you may use the code in this book in your programs and documentation. You do not need to contact us for permission unless you're reproducing a significant portion of the code. For example, writing a program that uses several chunks of code from this book does not require permission. Selling or distributing a CD-ROM of examples from O'Reilly books does require permission. Answering a question by citing this book and quoting example code does not require permission. Incorporating a significant amount of example code from this book into your product's documentation does require permission.

We appreciate, but do not require, attribution. An attribution usually includes the title, author, publisher, and ISBN. For example: "*QuickTime for Java: A Developer's Notebook* by Chris Adamson. Copyright 2005 O'Reilly Media, Inc., 0-596-00822-8."

If you feel your use of code examples falls outside fair use or the permission given above, feel free to contact us at *permissions@oreilly.com*.

How to Contact Us

Please address comments and questions concerning this book to the publisher:

O'Reilly Media, Inc.
1005 Gravenstein Highway North
Sebastopol, CA 95472
(800) 998-9938 (in the United States or Canada)
(707) 829-0515 (international or local)
(707) 829-0104 (fax)

We have a web page for this book, where we list errata, examples, and any additional information. You can access this page at:

http://www.oreilly.com/catalog/quicktimejvaadn

To comment or ask technical questions about this book, send email to:

bookquestions@oreilly.com

For more information about our books, conferences, Resource Centers, and the O'Reilly Network, see our web site at:

http://www.oreilly.com

Safari Enabled

 When you see a Safari® enabled icon on the cover of your favorite technology book that means the book is available online through the O'Reilly Network Safari Bookshelf.

Safari offers a solution that's better than e-books. It's a virtual library that lets you easily search thousands of top tech books, cut and paste code samples, download chapters, and find quick answers when you need the most accurate, current information. Try it for free at *http://safari.oreilly.com*.

Acknowledgments

Brett McLaughlin deserves huge thanks for getting this book to you. Not only is he the creator of the *Developer's Notebook* series and the editor of this book, but he also saw that QuickTime for Java was a topic whose need for practical know-how (to navigate the media jargon, obtuse concepts, and teeming "gotchas") was well-suited for this series. Chuck Toporek at O'Reilly was also very helpful in getting people excited about the book. And, of course, I wouldn't even be writing for O'Reilly if I hadn't bumped into Daniel Steinberg at the Mac OS X conference a few years ago, which ultimately led to our working together to edit the ONJava and java.net web sites.

The members of the quicktime-java and quicktime-api mailing lists, and the OpenQTJ project at java.net, have also been extremely helpful in working through problematic material and passing along those nuggets of knowledge that you're somehow "just supposed to know." In particular, the material in Chapter 6 about working around the incomplete state of video capture came in many ways from bits of discussion here and there saying, "you can get it to work by passing in your own GWorld." After I posted an early version of this book's "motion detector" example, some quicktime-java members developed it further into a more general-purpose capture preview. Tech reviewers Rolf Howarth, Anthony "aNt" Rogers, Dmitry Markman, and Sean Gilligan have also been generous with their time, attention, and knowledge, and have made this a far better book than it would have been without them.

I couldn't contact my friends on the QuickTime team while working on this book—another publisher has exclusive access to those developers for QuickTime titles—so they were probably wondering where I was while this book was in silent running. But they've been very supportive in the past and I'm looking forward to being able to work with them again.

I wouldn't even have a programming career if Tammie Childs at Pathfire hadn't taken a chance on me when all I had to speak of for my programming skills were a couple of crazy applets. She also took me back in when Piece Of Crap Wireless Companies No.s 1 and 2 crashed and burned, and still encouraged me to pursue my interests when articles led to editing and then to books.

Finally, I want to thank my wife Kelly, and our son Keagan, for being supportive while I took a big chance on writing a book, and for cutting Daddy some slack when he needed to go downstairs and do more writing. I hope that Keagan hasn't picked up the more extreme expressions that I emitted while working through some of the less stable parts of QuickTime for Java. By the way, you'll notice that Keagan is all over this book for two reasons: first, I don't have to pay license fees on media I own, such as my own iMovies, and second, he's quite cute.

Obligatory O'Reilly music check: this time it was Roxy Music, the Kinks, Nellie McKay, Elvis Costello, Thelonious Monk, a bunch of anime soundtracks (notably *.hack//SIGN, Nadia, FLCL,* and *Cowboy Bebop*), and the streaming audio stations Radio Dupree, Armitage's Dimension, and Gamer Girl Radio.

Getting Up and Running
with QuickTime for Java

Do you need to do anything special to start developing QuickTime for
Java applications? The answer to that question is easily answered by
another question: *are you using Mac OS X?* If so, you have everything
you need: Java, QuickTime, and QuickTime for Java (QTJ). If you're using
Windows, you might have some downloading to do.

Setting Up QTJ on Windows

First, you must have Java installed, presumably the latest developer kit
release from Sun. As of this writing, that would be the J2SE 1.4.2 SDK,
which lives at *http://java.sun.com/j2se/1.4.2/download.html*. Now you
must install and/or update QuickTime.

How do I do that?

If you don't already have QuickTime (or iTunes, which includes Quick-
Time in its install), you can get it from *http://quicktime.apple.com/*.
What's perhaps more common is that you have QuickTime, but you don't
have QuickTime for Java, which is *not* installed by default.

In this case, you can use the QuickTime Updater to update your copy of
QuickTime and install custom pieces like QTJ. If you have the QuickTime
icon down in your System Tray, you can right-click it to launch the
Updater, as seen in Figure 1-1. You can also get to the Updater via Start
→ Programs → QuickTime → QuickTime Updater.

Whether you're updating or installing QuickTime for the first time, you
need to click the Custom button to perform a custom install. This will give
you the opportunity to install nondefault features, most of which are
optional *codecs*, or software components to handle various video and

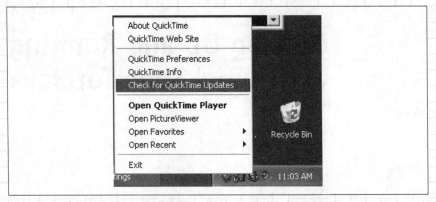

Figure 1-1. Launching the QuickTime Updater from the system tray

audio encoding formats. Scroll down the list and you should see Quick-Time for Java, as shown in Figure 1-2.

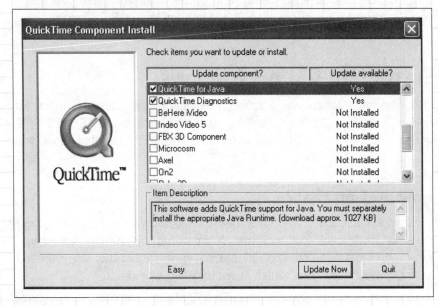

Figure 1-2. Custom install of QuickTime for Java

Continue by clicking Update Now (or Install, if this is a new install) to put the latest version of QuickTime and QuickTime for Java on your PC.

What just happened?

The installer installed QuickTime's various pieces in your system, adding a QuickTime group to your Start Menu, a QuickTime icon in your System

Tray, various pieces in *C:\WINDOWS\System32\QuickTime*, etc. It puts *QTJava.zip* in the *lib/ext* directory of any valid Java installations it finds, adds a systemwide environment variable called QTJAVA with the path to this file, and adds the file's path to the CLASSPATH system environment variable, creating it if necessary. Figure 1-3 shows what this looks like in Windows Explorer.

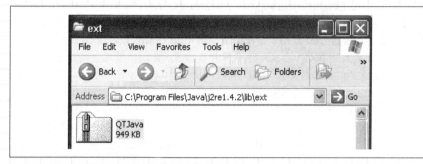

Note that QTJava is a zip file, not a JAR, which gives it this archive-like icon. You don't need, or want, to ever unzip this file.

Figure 1-3. QTJava.zip file installed into a Java 1.4.2 lib/ext folder

It should be obvious that it's important to do the installs in the order shown here: Java first, then QuickTime. That way, QuickTime can find the existing Java directories into which to install *QTJava.zip*. Unfortunately, this can still get messed up if you add another Java Runtime Environment (JRE) later—QuickTime might think QTJ is installed, but the new JRE won't have *QTJava.zip* in its *lib/ext* directory. In this case, copying *QTJava.zip* manually might be the most practical option.

What about...

...installing QTJ on Linux? Sorry. The thing that makes QTJ fast and powerful—the fact that it's a wrapper to an underlying native framework—is also its cross-platform downfall. QuickTime for Java can exist only on platforms that Apple develops QuickTime for, and right now, that means Mac and Windows. On the other hand, if Apple ever did port QuickTime to Linux, bringing QTJ along for the ride probably wouldn't be hard.

And what about installing QTJ on (Classic) Mac OS? Of course. QTJ was originally developed on and for Mac OS 8 and 9. It is part of the standard QuickTime install for Mac OS and thus gets picked up as part of a regular update (which you'd launch with the QuickTime Settings control panel, under the Update Check section). On Classic, the *QTJava.zip* file lives in *System Folder/Extensions/MRJ Libraries/MRJClasses* (yes, there's a space in *MRJ Libraries*, but not in *MRJClasses*).

MRJ means Macintosh Runtime for Java, the name of Classic's JRE. The name and its confusing versioning were dropped for OS X.

However, development of QuickTime for Classic stopped at Version 6.0.3 and does not include the much-changed version of QTJ that this book covers, QTJ 6.1. Furthermore, it's worth remembering that Java on Classic Mac OS never got past Java 1.1.8, which means it doesn't include Swing, Collections, or many other J2SE classes and conveniences that modern Java developers would expect to be present.

Where's the API documentation? Even though *QTJava.zip* is all you need to compile, some documentation and demos would be really helpful, right? The good news is that there is a QTJ SDK that offers Javadocs and demos. Unfortunately, much of what's on Apple's web site as of this writing refers to an earlier version of QTJ that won't work with Java 1.4 on Mac OS X. The most complete SDK right now is labeled as the "QuickTime for Java Windows SDK," and is located at *http://developer.apple.com/sdk/index.html#QTJavaWin*. This package contains a complete set of current Javadocs and demos that have been updated to represent the new API calls in QTJ 6.1. You can also view the Javadoc online at *http://developer.apple.com/documentation/Java/Reference/1.4.1/Java141API_QTJ/index.html*.

TIP

When you look at the Javadoc, many methods will have a boldface reference to their equivalent C function. For example, Movie.start( ), which starts playing a movie (see the next chapter), wraps the native function QuickTime::StartMovie. You can usually find the native documentation by doing a search on Apple's page for the function name or by Googling for it with a search term like site:apple.com StartMovie.

Why would you ever look at the native docs when you're programming in Java? Because a lot of the parameters aren't described in the Javadoc, particularly when methods take behavior flags.

The mailing lists at http://lists.apple.com/ are a great source of information, particularly quicktime-java, quicktime-users (authoring), and quicktime-api (native programming). java-dev is also helpful for figuring out issues with Mac OS X's Java implementation.

Embedding QuickTime in HTML

Every once in a while, a developer new to QuickTime will post to one of the developer lists, saying he needs QTJ to put a QuickTime movie in a web page.

QTJ is great, but this is way, *way* overkill. For this task, you don't need QTJ. In fact, you'd just be creating headaches for yourself by requiring QTJ and dealing with the hassles of applets. Instead, you can just embed QuickTime content in HTML.

How do I do that?

In your HTML page, use an <object> tag, which wraps an <embed>, as shown in Example 1-1.

Example 1-1. Embedding QuickTime in HTML

```
<object classid="clsid:02BF25D5-8C17-4B23-BC80-D3488ABDDC6B"
    width="160" height="136"
    codebase="http://www.apple.com/qtactivex/qtplugin.cab">
      <param name="src" VALUE="buhbuhbuh.mov"/>
      <param name="autoplay" VALUE="true"/>
      <param name="loop" VALUE="true"/>
      <param name="controller" value="true"/>
<embed src="buhbuhbuh.mov" width="160" height="136"
    scale="tofit"
    controller="true"
    autoplay="true"
    loop="true"
    pluginspage="http://www.apple.com/quicktime/download/"/>
</object>
```

The parameters are generally self-explanatory: height, width, and src are the only ones that are actually required. Because I've chosen to include a controller widget, I add 16 to the height parameter and use the scale parameter with the value tofit.

A web page using this tag is shown in Figure 1-4.

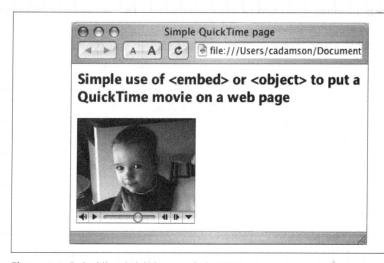

Figure 1-4. Embedding QuickTime movie in HTML

What just happened?

The weird thing about this is, of course, the tag-within-a-tag arrangement. We do this because although most browsers use the <embed> tag to use plug-ins, Internet Explorer on Windows is *special* and insists that we use an <object> tag to talk to a QuickTime ActiveX control.

Because of this arrangement, you have to list all the parameters *twice*, once in each tag. In the <embed> tag they're attributes, and in the <object> tag they're child <param> elements. Each tag also has some boilerplate code, such as the <embed>'s pluginspage and the <object>'s classid and codebase.

What about...

...other options for the plug-in? There are too many to cover here. Check out *http://www.apple.com/quicktime/authoring/embed.html*. There's also some support for controlling a movie via JavaScript in some browsers (including IE and Mozilla derivatives, but not Safari as of this writing), using the attribute enablejavascript.

Preflighting a QTJ Installation

Given the hassle of setting up your own box with a custom QuickTime installation, the idea of having to walk your Windows users through such a process is probably unappealing. Installing the various QuickTime *.dlls* and such by yourself is not an alternative, because you promised not to redistribute QuickTime when you clicked "agree" on that license.

TIP

You know the license I mean—it's the one you didn't read! That's OK, I didn't read it either.

Fortunately, QuickTime 6 offers a "preflighting" feature that allows you to create an XML file that describes what QuickTime features you need, open the file with QuickTime, and have QuickTime download and install your features if they're absent.

How do I do that?

In your favorite text editor, create an XML file, as seen in Example 1-2.

Example 1-2. Preflighting to install QTJ

```
<?xml version="1.0"?>
<?quicktime type="application/x-qtpreflight"?>
<qtpreflight>
  <component type="null" subtype="qtj "/>
</qtpreflight>
```

Save this file with a *.mov* extension to associate it with QuickTime.

Have QuickTime open this file in whatever means is appropriate for your application—embed it in a web page, have an installer script open it with *QuickTimePlayer.exe*, etc. When you do, QuickTime will check to see if QuickTime for Java has been installed; if QTJ hasn't been installed, this will give the user a chance to download and install it, as seen in Figure 1-5.

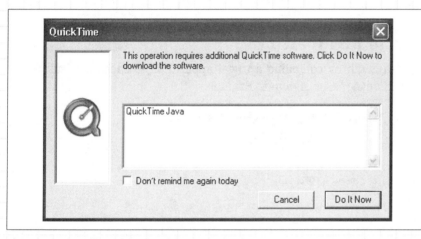

Figure 1-5. Installing QuickTime for Java via preflighting

What just happened?

The XML file specifies a list of QuickTime components that the application knows it needs to run. These components are classified in a type/subtype scheme. For example, to test for MPEG-4 support, you'd use type "imdc" (short for *image decompressor*) and subtype "mp4v". QuickTime for Java is something of a special case, so it gets type "null" and subtype "qtj". The trailing space on the subtype is really important, because all types and subtypes must be *exactly* four characters long.

Chapter 4 has much more information about components and the FOUR_CHAR_CODES that identify them.

If any of the specified components are found to be absent, QuickTime brings up a dialog and offers the user a chance to download and install them on the spot.

Compiling QTJ Code

Once you've installed QuickTime and QuickTime for Java, you have
everything you need to start developing QTJ applications—no separate
SDK is required.

How do I do that?

You can begin by compiling a trivial application to check the QuickTime
and QTJ versions, as shown in Example 1-3.

Example 1-3. Checking the version of QuickTime

```
package com.oreilly.qtjnotebook.ch01;

import quicktime.QTSession;
import quicktime.util.QTBuild;

public class QTVersionCheck {

    public static void main (String[ ] args) {
        try {
            QTSession.open( );
            System.out.println ("QT version: " +
                QTSession.getMajorVersion( ) +
                "." +
                QTSession.getMinorVersion( ));
            System.out.println ("QTJ version: " +
                QTBuild.getVersion( ) +
                "." +
                QTBuild.getSubVersion( ));
            QTSession.close( );
        } catch (Exception e) {
            e.printStackTrace( );
        }
    }

}
```

The compilation is the tricky step here. If you do a straightforward `javac`, bad things happen:

```
cadamson% javac src/com/oreilly/qtjnotebook/ch01/QTVersionCheck.java
src/com/oreilly/qtjnotebook/ch01/QTVersionCheck.java:3:
    package quicktime does not exist
import quicktime.QTSession;
                 ^
src/com/oreilly/qtjnotebook/ch01/QTVersionCheck.java:4:
    package quicktime.util does not exist
import quicktime.util.QTBuild;
                      ^
src/com/oreilly/qtjnotebook/ch01/QTVersionCheck.java:10:
    cannot resolve symbol
symbol  : variable QTSession
location: class com.oreilly.qtjnotebook.ch01.QTVersionCheck
            QTSession.open( );
            ^
```

Here, as in many examples, you should type the entire command on one line. It's broken up in the text for printing purposes.

Instead, you have to explicitly provide the path to *QTJava.zip*, which contains the QTJ classes. On the Mac OS X command line, you would do this as follows:

```
cadamson% javac -classpath /System/Library/Java/Extensions/QTJava.zip
    src/com/oreilly/qtjnotebook/ch01/QTVersionCheck.java
```

On Windows, the path to *QTJava.zip* would point to wherever the Quick-Time installer put the file, which presumably means into your Java installation's *lib/ext*:

```
C:\qtjtests\book stuff\code>javac -classpath
    "c:\Program Files\Java\j2re1.4.2\lib\ext\QTJava.zip"
    src\com\oreilly\qtjnotebook\ch01\QTVersionCheck.java
```

Once the code compiles, running it is a lot easier—you don't need to explicitly put *QTJava.zip* in the runtime classpath to run a QTJ application. Just supply the class name to run, as the following output illustrates:

```
cadamson% java -cp classes com.oreilly.qtjnotebook.ch01.QTVersionCheck
QT version: 6.5
QTJ version: 6.1
cadamson%
```

Using the ant buildfile provided with the downloaded book code (and described in the Preface) makes compiling a lot easier!

What just happened?

As for what this trivial first application actually does, a read-through of the `main( )` method shows it doing four things:

1. Opening the QuickTime session
2. Printing the QuickTime version by making calls to `quicktime.QTSession`

3. Printing the QuickTime for Java version by making calls to `quicktime.util.QTBuild`

4. Closing the QuickTime session

If any of these throws an exception, it's caught and printed to standard-out.

What about...

...the mismatch between the version numbers? QuickTime and Quick-Time for Java versions are somewhat independent, because not every QT update merits a QTJ update. Typically, you'll see both roll out a major version at the same time, but then a number of QuickTime updates will be issued, usually bug-fix updates or minor feature releases, without any changes to QTJ.

The Latest and Greatest

This book covers QTJ 6.1, which was released alongside QuickTime 6.4. If your software reports a lower version, be sure to update with the QuickTime Updater because QTJ 6.1 has massive differences from previous versions, and this book covers only QTJ 6.1.

How different is QTJ 6.1 from its predecessors? Try "every QTJ application broke with 6.1."

The problem was caused by Apple changing the internals of its Java implementation from the Carbon framework to Cocoa for its Java 1.4 implementation. QTJ was heavily dependent on Carbon for its native binding, and a full-blown rewrite for Cocoa was impractical.

However, only the parts involving the AWT/Swing bridge were affected—most of QTJ still worked just fine. So, Apple rolled out a radically simplified GUI layer for QTJ in the new `quicktime.app.view` package. All the incompatible packages, particularly `quicktime.app.display` and its subpackages, were deprecated. A few nice-to-have features, like live-video compositing, weren't ported to 6.1.

QTJ 6.1 can be used on Mac OS X with either Java 1.4 or Java 1.3, and on Windows. Earlier versions work on Windows and with Java 1.3 on Mac OS X, but will throw runtime exceptions with Java 1.4.

Parts of Apple's web site and older books still cover the old API. If you see code that uses `quicktime.app.display`, or any of its classes (like `QTCanvas`, `SGDrawer`, or `SWCompositor`), beware: it won't work on Java 1.4 on Mac OS X and won't be supported going forward. These packages are also in the Javadocs, but they're clearly marked as deprecated.

Opening and Closing the QuickTime Session

All QTJ applications are responsible for managing the QuickTime "session." The call to QTSession.open( ) gives QuickTime an opportunity to initialize itself, and it must be made before any other QTJ call, or you'll get an exception. Similarly, you must call QTSession.close( ) when you're done with QuickTime to give it a chance to clean up.

In general, this means you might want to call QTSession.open( ) as early as possible and QTSession.close( ) as late as possible. The former is easy enough to do: just put it in your application's entry point or even in a static initializer so that it precedes main( ). On the other hand, ensuring that you call QTSession.close( ) gracefully is trickier, because your user could quit your application with a menu item you provide, a Ctrl-C, a Cmd-Q (on Mac), or (heaven forbid) a kill -9 *your-pid* from the command line. Ideally, you'd like to have a fighting chance of properly closing QuickTime in as many cases as possible.

How do I do that?

One way to close QuickTime late is to put QTSession.close( ) in a Java shutdown hook, which will get called as the JVM goes away. There are no guarantees, but it's better than nothing.

You can use the class in Example 1-4 as a general-purpose session handler for QTJ. It is presented here so that none of the other examples in the book will need to explicitly handle opening or closing the QTSession beyond calling this class.

You can also run this example with the provided ant run-ch01-qtversioncheck task.

Example 1-4. Session handler for QuickTime for Java

```
package com.oreilly.qtjnotebook.ch01;

import quicktime.*;

public class QTSessionCheck {

    private Thread shutdownHook;
    private static QTSessionCheck instance;
    private QTSessionCheck( ) throws QTException {
        super( );
        // init
        QTSession.open( );
        // create shutdown handler
        shutdownHook = new Thread( ) {
                public void run( ) {
                    QTSession.close( );
```

Example 1-4. *Session handler for QuickTime for Java (continued)*

```
            }
        };
        Runtime.getRuntime().addShutdownHook(shutdownHook);
    }
    private static QTSessionCheck getInstance() throws QTException {
        if (instance == null)
            instance = new QTSessionCheck();
        return instance;
    }

    public static void check() throws QTException {
        // gets instance.  if a new one needs to be created,
        // it calls QTSession.open() and creates a shutdown hook
        // to call QTSession.close()
        getInstance();
    }
}
```

WARNING

It looks like QTSession.close() hangs on some Windows installations. It might be safer to use QTSession.exitMovies().

What just happened?

The QTSessionHandler class uses a singleton pattern. The idea is that all the work is done in the constructor, which will be called only once (to create the singleton), so you're free to call the static QTSessionHandler.check() method wherever and whenever you like, knowing it will have to run only once.

When you call check(), it makes a trivial call to getInstance(), which creates a new instance if and only if one hasn't been created yet. The constructor calls QTSession.open() to initialize QuickTime, and then sets up a shutdown handler that will call QTSession.close() when Java is shutting down.

What about...

...managing the QTSession myself? Absolutely. If some other arrangement works for your application, go for it. This class is merely a convenience, and is arguably overkill—closing the QuickTime session is handled automatically on Mac OS X when you use the default Quit menu item, and I've never seen a problem that was definitely caused by improperly shutting down QuickTime on Windows. But, as this class shows, getting it right isn't *that* hard.

...making multiple open( ) or close( ) calls? According to QTSession's Javadocs, if you issue multiple open( ) calls, QuickTime won't be shut down until an equal number of close( ) calls are received. There's no benefit (or harm) to multiple open( ) calls, so this is probably just trivia.

Running inside an applet? In an applet, it might make more sense to put your open( ) and close( ) calls in the applet's init( ) and destroy( ) methods, respectively, instead of banking on a particular browser's behavior vis-à-vis taking down the entire JVM and executing shutdown hooks.

Playing an Audio File from the Command Line

To finish this chapter, we'll look at a very simple example of QTJ code that actually plays some media. To keep things simple, I'll completely ignore the GUI, so all this will do is take a file path from the command line—presumably an MP3 or other audio file—and play it in QTJ.

How do I do that?

Compile and run the source for *TrivialAudioPlayer.java*, shown in Example 1-5.

Example 1-5. Playing an audio file from the command line

```
package com.oreilly.qtjnotebook.ch01;

import quicktime.*;
import quicktime.app.time.*;
import quicktime.io.*;
import quicktime.std.*;
import quicktime.std.movies.*;

import java.io.*;

public class TrivialAudioPlayer {

    public static void main (String[ ] args) {
        if (args.length != 1) {
            System.out.println (
                "Usage: TrivialAudioPlayer <file>");
            return;
        }
        try {
            QTSessionCheck.check( );
            QTFile f = new QTFile (new File(args[0]));
            OpenMovieFile omf = OpenMovieFile.asRead(f);
            Movie movie = Movie.fromFile (omf);
```

Example 1-5. Playing an audio file from the command line (continued)

```
                TaskAllMovies.addMovieAndStart( );
                movie.start( );
            } catch (QTException e) {
                e.printStackTrace( );
            }
        }
    }
```

Any dynamic content in QuickTime is going to be a "movie," even if it's an audio-only file, like an MP3. This program also works for AACs, WAVs, iTunes Music Store songs, and anything else QuickTime can open.

Once compiled, run it with the path to an audio file as a command-line argument. Note that if you downloaded the book examples and compiled with the ant buildfile, the classes will be in the classes directory, so you'll need to extend your classpath into there:

```
cadamson% java -classpath classes
     com.oreilly.qtjnotebook.ch01.TrivialAudioPlayer
     ~/mp3testing/Breakaway.mp3
```

What just happened?

This application provides a bare-bones load-and-play example. After checking that there's a valid argument, it does the QTSessionCheck from the previous task to set up the QuickTime session.

The interesting part is in converting the argument to a java.io.File, then to a quicktime.io.OpenMovieFile, from which we can create a quicktime.std.Movie, which represents any kind of playable QuickTime content, in this case our audio file.

The start( ) method begins playing the movie, so once the program is running, you'll hear your MP3 over your speakers or headphones. This program doesn't provide a way to stop playback, so when you want to end the program, you'll need to type **ctrl-c**, use the Windows Task Manager, or hit the Quit menu item that's provided on Mac OS X.

What about...

There's more information on tasking in the next chapter.

...that weird TaskAllMovies call? This is required because our program doesn't have a GUI, which ordinarily gives QTJ some cycles for decoding and playing the audio. Most of the programs in this book have on-screen GUIs, so they don't need to do this.

CHAPTER 2

Playing Movies

Even if you have more elaborate plans for QuickTime for Java, I'm going to assume that your plans will, at some point in time, require reading in a movie or other QuickTime-compatible file, locally or from the network. This chapter presents basic techniques of getting a Movie object, getting it into the Java display space, and adding more sophisticated controls so that your user (or just your code) can know what's happening inside a playing movie and take control.

Building a Simple Movie Player

I'll begin with "the simplest thing that could possibly work:" an application to ask the user for the location of a QuickTime file, which is then opened and put in a Java AWT Frame.

How do I do that?

Example 2-1 shows the code for a simple movie player.

Example 2-1. Simple movie player

```
package com.oreilly.qtjnotebook.ch02;

import quicktime.*;
import quicktime.app.view.*;
import quicktime.std.movies.*;
import quicktime.io.*;

import com.oreilly.qtjnotebook.ch01.QTSessionCheck;

import java.awt.*;

public class BasicQTPlayer extends Frame {
```

Example 2-1. Simple movie player (continued)

```java
public BasicQTPlayer (Movie m) throws QTException {
    super ("Basic QT Player");
    QTComponent qc = QTFactory.makeQTComponent (m);
    Component c = qc.asComponent();
    add (c);
}

public static void main (String[] args) {
    try {
        QTSessionCheck.check();
        QTFile file =
            QTFile.standardGetFilePreview (
        QTFile.kStandardQTFileTypes);
        OpenMovieFile omFile = OpenMovieFile.asRead (file);
        Movie m = Movie.fromFile (omFile);
        Frame f = new BasicQTPlayer (m);
        f.pack();
        f.setVisible(true);
        m.start();
    } catch (Exception e) {
        e.printStackTrace();
    }
}
}
```

If you've downloaded the book code, compile and run with ant run-ch02-basicqtplayer.

Compile this from the command line (remember, as shown in the previous chapter, you must specify QTJava.zip in the classpath; this is the Mac OS X version):

```
cadamson% javac -d classes -classpath
    src:/System/Library/Java/Extensions/QTJava.zip
    src/com/oreilly/qtjnotebook/ch02/BasicQTPlayer.java
```

Then run the program from the command line:

```
cadamson% java -classpath classes
    com.oreilly.qtjnotebook.ch02.BasicQTPlayer
```

When the program starts up, the user will initially see QuickTime's file selector, shown in Figure 2-1.

After the user selects a file (note that I have not provided any error handling if the user clicks Cancel!), the movie will open in a window at its default size and start playing, as seen in Figure 2-2.

Note that this program does not provide any means of quitting the application once the movie finishes playing (or before then, for that matter). Press Ctrl-C from the command line to kill the app. Mac users will also get a "Quit com.oreilly.qtjnotebook.ch02.BasicQTPlayer" menu item.

Figure 2-1. QuickTime file selector

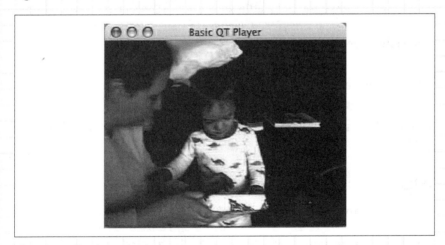

Figure 2-2. Simple movie player

What just happened?

Take a look at the application. The class extends java.awt.Frame and supplies a constructor that takes a quicktime.std.movies.Movie object. Given this Movie, it asks the QTFactory (in package quicktime.app.view) for a QTComponent. From this object, it gets a java.awt.Component, which is added to the Frame.

The main() method starts by doing the QuickTime session check from the last chapter. Then it brings up a file selector dialog, from which it gets a quicktime.io.QTFile, from which it gets an OpenMovieFile, which leads to the creation of a Movie object with Movie.fromFile(). This Movie is then passed to the QTBasicPlayer constructor, and the resulting Frame is pack()ed and shown. Finally, main() calls the Movie's start() method to play the movie.

Notice how practically every line of code in this application either declares that it throws QTException or is wrapped in a try-catch block. That's because pretty much every QuickTime Java call can potentially throw a QTException, which means you either need to catch it or (more frequently) declare that your method throws it to the caller. Presumably at some point further up the call chain, you'll catch the exception and do something responsible with it, such as bringing up an error dialog.

Another point of interest is the QTComponent. This is an interface that exposes methods that allow you to change the movie (or image) displayed by an on-screen widget. asComponent() returns an AWT Component that can be added to an AWT layout just like any other component. Now here's the dirty little secret: all QTComponents received from the QTFactory really are AWT Components, and can be cast safely. That means the asComponent() call:

```
Component c = qc.asComponent();
```

is functionally equivalent to:

```
Component c = (Component) qc;
```

Meaning that asComponent() is really there just for compile-time type safety.

Chapter 4 has more on the FOUR_CHAR_CODE integers used for these "types."

What about...

...using the AWT or Swing file selector? Sure, you can use these—they'll return a java.io.File object, which can then be used to get a QTFile. But the QuickTime file selector is arguably nicer, because on Windows it shows a little preview of the selected movie. Another thing to notice is the odd little constant kStandardQTFileTypes. The standardGetFilePreview() call takes an int[] of up to four "types" of files to allow the user to select. The constant is a very convenient way to specify "just show typical file types that QuickTime can handle." You can also pass in null to show all files.

Adding a Controller

This application isn't particularly user-friendly yet—the user can't start or stop the movie, move through it, or set the volume. Fortunately, it's easy to use a `MovieController` to get the standard QuickTime controller bar, an on-screen control widget that provides a play/pause button, a volume control, and the movie position control (typically called a "scrubber" in QuickTime parlance).

How do I do that?

Create a new class in the source file *BasicQTController.java*. The `main( )` is exactly the same as before, while the constructor adds one new line and changes another, as seen in Example 2-2.

Example 2-2. Getting a movie component with a controller

```
public class BasicQTController extends Frame {

    public BasicQTController (Movie m) throws QTException {
        super ("Basic QT Controller");
        MovieController mc = new MovieController(m);
        QTComponent qc = QTFactory.makeQTComponent (mc);
        Component c = qc.asComponent( );
        add (c);
        pack( );
    }
}
```

Compile and run this example with ant run-ch02-basicqtcontroller.

The result, when run, looks like the application in Figure 2-3. Notice the presence of the classic QuickTime control bar at the bottom of the window.

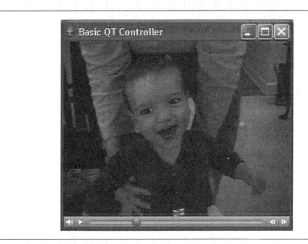

Figure 2-3. Movie with on-screen controller

What just happened?

This time, instead of asking the QTFactory to make a QTComponent from the Movie, the program creates a MovieController object from the Movie and asks the QTFactory to make a QTComponent from that. This eliminates the need for main( ) to call start( ), because the user can start and stop the movie from the play/pause button on the control bar.

Getting a Movie-Playing JComponent

The previous tasks have used the AWT, which seemingly nobody uses anymore. Many developers will want to create a Swing GUI, and thus they need a movie-playing JComponent. QuickTime for Java can provide one.

How do I do that?

Example 2-3 presents a rewrite of the previous BasicQTPlayer that does everything with Swing equivalents (JFrame instead of Frame, JComponent instead of Component, etc.).

Compile and run this example with ant run-ch02- basicswingqtplayer.

Example 2-3. All-Swing simple movie player

```
package com.oreilly.qtjnotebook.ch02;

import quicktime.*;
import quicktime.app.view.*;
import quicktime.std.movies.*;
import quicktime.io.*;

import com.oreilly.qtjnotebook.ch01.QTSessionCheck;

import java.awt.*;
import javax.swing.*;

public class BasicSwingQTPlayer extends JFrame {

    public BasicSwingQTPlayer (Movie m) throws QTException {
        super ("Basic Swing QT Player");
        MoviePlayer mp = new MoviePlayer (m);
        QTJComponent qc = QTFactory.makeQTJComponent (mp);
        JComponent jc = qc.asJComponent();
        getContentPane().add (jc);
        pack();
    }

    public static void main (String[] args) {
        try {
            QTSessionCheck.check();
```

Example 2-3. All-Swing simple movie player (continued)

```
            QTFile file =
                QTFile.standardGetFilePreview (
            QTFile.kStandardQTFileTypes);
            OpenMovieFile omFile = OpenMovieFile.asRead (file);
            Movie m = Movie.fromFile (omFile);
            JFrame f = new BasicSwingQTPlayer (m);
            f.pack();
            f.setVisible(true);
            m.start();
        } catch (Exception e) {
            e.printStackTrace();
        }
    }
}
```

This produces a simple movie-player window—as seen in Figure 2-4—using Swing, but visually indistinguishable from its AWT equivalent.

Figure 2-4. Playing a movie with a Swing JComponent

What just happened?

Creating a QTJComponent (read that as "QT JComponent," not "QTJ Component"—I know, it confused everyone on the developer list at first, too) requires an object called a MoviePlayer, which can be simply created from a Movie. This is passed to QTFactory's makeQTJComponent() method to get a QTJComponent, which in turn can be turned into a Swing JComponent with asJComponent().

What about...

...getting a control bar? Good question. QTJ doesn't provide one for Swing. Remember, the movie's display and the control bar are both native widgets—to display the movie in Swing, the movie has to be drawn to an off-screen region, then painted by Java onto the JComponent so that everything is "lightweight," in Java parlance. QTJ provides this for the movie but not for the control bar (perhaps because it would be difficult for the native QuickTime to keep track of your mouse movements in the Java space), so a developer would need to roll her own Swing widget for controlling the Movie, trapping mouse actions and calling appropriate methods on the Movie or MovieController.

Methods to control a Movie or MovieController are introduced in the next task.

And what about the awful performance? Good catch—depending on your source, the frame rate of this version might be far worse than the AWT equivalent. Think about the earlier paragraph that says the movie needs to be drawn into an off-screen buffer and then reimaged into Swing. Doesn't that sound a little redundant? Think the overhead is going to add up if you need to do it 30 times a second? It is, and it does. Performance of the QTJComponent is *awful* compared to that of the QTComponent. Not only does QTJ have to do extra work, but it also doesn't score hardware-accelerated graphics benefits it might otherwise be able to achieve by using its native rendering pipeline.

So, I'm going to tell you something that clashes with every other Java GUI book you've ever read: *go ahead and mix Swing and AWT widgets*. That's right. It's not going to cause blindness, the end of the world, or a drop in your home's resale value.

To be specific, you can freely mix AWT widgets, like the QTComponent, and Swing widgets in the same container as long as they don't overlap. Unless you're doing something tricky with Swing's "glass pane," or possibly the JLayeredPane, you're probably safe.

The common overlap problem comes from menus, both those that descend from the menu bar and pop-up menus. A lightweight Swing menu will go behind any AWT component, and the result isn't pretty. The way around this is to call setLightweightPopupEnabled(false) on all your menus that might overlap with your QTComponent.

By the way, this problem isn't limited to QTJ. Most Java toolkits that use native drawing spaces for performance reasons run into the same issue. Sun's JMF defaults to heavyweight components, as does the OpenGL-to-Java library JOGL. Getting AWT and Swing to play nice is a common issue for Java multimedia developers.

Controlling a Movie Programmatically

For various reasons, an application might want to control the movie via its own method calls, in lieu of or in addition to the GUI provided by QuickTime's `MovieController`. One example of this is `Movie.start()`. You can programmatically issue many more commands, some of which you can't issue with the default control.

How do I do that?

Example 2-4 shows a new class, `BasicQTButtons.java`. The `main()` is exactly the same as `BasicQTPlayer`, but the constructor has extra work to create some control buttons, and an `actionPerformed()` method implements AWT's `ActionListener`.

Example 2-4. Programmatic control of a movie

```
package com.oreilly.qtjnotebook.ch02;

import quicktime.*;
import quicktime.app.view.*;
import quicktime.std.movies.*;
import quicktime.io.*;

import com.oreilly.qtjnotebook.ch01.QTSessionCheck;

import java.awt.*;
import java.awt.event.*;

public class BasicQTButtons extends Frame
    implements ActionListener {

    Button revButton,
        stopButton,
        startButton,
        fwdButton;

    Movie theMovie;

    public BasicQTButtons (Movie m) throws QTException {
        super ("Basic QT Player");
        theMovie = m;
        QTComponent qc = QTFactory.makeQTComponent (m);
        Component c = qc.asComponent();
        setLayout (new BorderLayout());
        add (c, BorderLayout.CENTER);
        Panel buttons = new Panel();
        revButton = new Button("<");
        revButton.addActionListener (this);
```

Example 2-4. Programmatic control of a movie (continued)

```
        stopButton = new Button ("0");
        stopButton.addActionListener (this);
        startButton = new Button ("1");
        startButton.addActionListener (this);
        fwdButton = new Button (">");
        fwdButton.addActionListener (this);
        buttons.add (revButton);
        buttons.add (stopButton);
        buttons.add (startButton);
        buttons.add (fwdButton);
        add (buttons, BorderLayout.SOUTH);
        pack( );
    }

    public void actionPerformed (ActionEvent e) {
        try {
            if (e.getSource( ) == revButton)
                theMovie.setRate (theMovie.getRate( ) - 0.5f);
            else if (e.getSource( ) == stopButton)
                theMovie.stop( );
            else if (e.getSource( ) == startButton)
                theMovie.start( );
            else if (e.getSource( ) == fwdButton)
                theMovie.setRate (theMovie.getRate( ) + 0.5f);
        } catch (QTException qte) {
            qte.printStackTrace( );
        }
    }

    public static void main (String[ ] args) {
        try {
            QTSessionCheck.check( );
            QTFile file =
                QTFile.standardGetFilePreview (
                    QTFile.kStandardQTFileTypes);
            OpenMovieFile omFile = OpenMovieFile.asRead (file);
            Movie m = Movie.fromFile (omFile);
            Frame f = new BasicQTButtons (m);
            f.pack( );
            f.setVisible(true);
            m.start( );
        } catch (Exception e) {
            e.printStackTrace( );
        }
    }
}
```

Compile and run this example with ant run-ch02-basicqtbuttons.

Run this program to see a display like that shown in Figure 2-5. The buttons call functions to set the rate of the movie. The rate is 0 for a stopped movie, a negative number for a movie playing backward, and a positive number for a movie playing forward. A rate of 1.0 represents normal playing speed, so 0.5 would be half speed, and 2.0 would be double speed. The buttons have the following functions:

< Reduces the rate by 0.5. For a playing movie (rate = 1.0), clicking this once will cut it to half speed (0.5), twice will stop it (0.0), three times will go to half-speed reverse (-0.5), four times to normal-speed reverse (-1.0), etc.

0 Stops the movie, by way of a call to `Movie.stop( )`, which is the same as `Movie.setRate(0)`.

1 Plays the movie forward at normal speed, equivalent to `Movie.setRate(1)`.

> Increases the rate by 0.5.

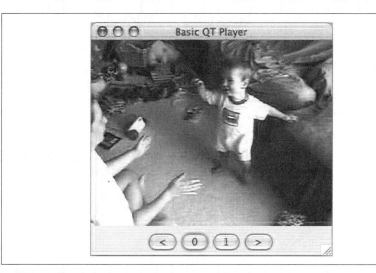

Figure 2-5. Controlling movie play rate with AWT buttons

What just happened?

This is a very simple example of methods that can be called to affect a movie's playback. These are the methods a developer creating his own control widget (i.e., ignoring the warning in the previous section) would need to use.

Another useful method is `setVolume( )`, a self-explanatory method that takes values from 0.0 (silence) to 1.0 (maximum). Also useful is a `setTime( )` method, which changes the current position in the movie.

The next task covers QuickTime's concept of time, which is used as the parameter for setTime( ).

What about...

...using some similar methods in MovieController? A MovieController object, even if it's not used to get an on-screen control widget, provides some methods with equivalent functionality, but with different names and conventions. For example, stop( ), start( ), and setRate( ) are all effectively wrapped by a single method, play( ), which takes a rate argument. MovieController also has some unique functionality, such as only playing the selection, setting "looping" behavior (immediately returning to the beginning when the end is reached, or vice versa), and a method called setPlayEveryFrame( ), which will force the movie to not drop frames, even if that requires it to play more slowly than it should.

Showing a Movie's Current Time

Advanced users, particularly those doing editing, would like to know a movie's current time—i.e., where they are in the movie. The scrubber can provide a general idea of the movie's current time, but certain applications call for an exact value.

How do I do that?

Example 2-5's BasicQTTimeDisplay code extends the BasicQTController by adding a Label to the bottom of the Frame. A Swing Timer calls actionPerformed( ) every 250 milliseconds, and this method checks the current time of the movie and resets the label.

The Swing version of Timer is used to ensure that changing the label occurs on the AWT event-dispatch thread.

Example 2-5. Displaying the current time of a movie

```
package com.oreilly.qtjnotebook.ch02;

import quicktime.*;
import quicktime.app.view.*;
import quicktime.std.movies.*;
import quicktime.io.*;

import com.oreilly.qtjnotebook.ch01.QTSessionCheck;

import java.awt.*;
import java.awt.event.*;

public class BasicQTTimeDisplay extends Frame
    implements ActionListener {
    Movie theMovie;
    Label timeLabel;

    public BasicQTTimeDisplay (Movie m) throws QTException {
        super ("Basic QT Controller");
```

Example 2-5. *Displaying the current time of a movie (continued)*

```
        theMovie = m;
        MovieController mc = new MovieController(m);
        QTComponent qc = QTFactory.makeQTComponent (mc);
        Component c = qc.asComponent();
        setLayout (new BorderLayout());
        add (c, BorderLayout.CENTER);
        timeLabel = new Label ("-:--", Label.CENTER);
        add (timeLabel, BorderLayout.SOUTH);
        javax.swing.Timer timer =
            new javax.swing.Timer (250, this);
        timer.start();
        pack();
    }

    public void actionPerformed (ActionEvent e) {
        if (theMovie == null)
                    return;
        try {
            int totalSeconds = theMovie.getTime() /
                            theMovie.getTimeScale();
            int seconds = totalSeconds % 60;
            int minutes = totalSeconds / 60;
            String secString = (seconds > 9) ?
                Integer.toString (seconds) :
                ("0" + Integer.toString (seconds));
            String minString = Integer.toString (minutes);
            timeLabel.setText (minString + ":" + secString);
        } catch (QTException qte) {
            qte.printStackTrace();
        }
    }

    public static void main (String[] args) {
        try {
            QTSessionCheck.check();
            QTFile file =
                QTFile.standardGetFilePreview (
                    QTFile.kStandardQTFileTypes);
            OpenMovieFile omFile = OpenMovieFile.asRead (file);
            Movie m = Movie.fromFile (omFile);
            Frame f = new BasicQTTimeDisplay (m);
            f.pack();
            f.setVisible(true);
            m.start();
        } catch (Exception e) {
            e.printStackTrace();
        }
    }
}
```

Compile and run this example with ant run-ch02-basicqttimedisplay.

This produces the application seen in Figure 2-6.

Figure 2-6. Displaying the current time of a movie

What just happened?

Obviously, some funky math is happening in the `actionPerformed( )` method, which uses the Movie's `getTime( )` and `getTimeScale( )` methods to figure out the current time in seconds, from which the program calculates the minutes and seconds portions of label.

When we work with editing commands, we'll see that the Movie selection is also represented with time-scale values like these.

QuickTime has a concept of a "time scale," which represents the time-keeping system of a Movie. For a given time scale, *n*, one unit of time in that time scale is $1/n$ seconds. So, if a Movie had a time scale of 1,000, the units would be milliseconds. Movies actually default to a time scale of 600, but the actual value is irrelevant—you just have to be sure to work with whatever value the movie uses. `getTime( )` returns the movie's current time in terms of the time scale, so for a time scale of 600, if `getTime( )` returns 3,600, the current time is exactly 6 seconds into the movie. Other prominent methods that work with the time scale are `setTime( )` and `getDuration( )`.

What about...

...just using milliseconds or nanoseconds or something *normal* instead of this crazy time-scale stuff? Actually, this flexible system of time scales is one of the best things about QuickTime. There needs to be some system of keeping track of time in a Movie, and it's generally desirable for the units to be of a sufficient resolution so that all important times divide evenly—i.e., they can be represented as ints.

Most Java programmers are used to thinking about time in terms of milliseconds, but that's totally inadequate for media. For example, CD audio has 44,100 samples a second, meaning that each sample takes 0.02267… ms. So, that's obviously not going to work. Insisting on some smaller unit (microseconds, nanoseconds, picoseconds, etc.) won't help, because you can never know that it will be good enough for some arbitrary piece of time-based data. QuickTime's system of time scales allows the system of measurement to be ideally suited to the media itself.

An interesting thought about the preceding example is that Movie's default time base of 600 is also inadequate for CD audio. As it turns out, the tracks of a movie (more accurately, the "media" they refer to) can have their own time scales. So, a Movie can have one time scale, its video can have another, and the audio can have a third.

So, why is the default time scale 600? It appears to have originated with the 60 "ticks" per second used for time keeping on the oldest Macs, but it turns out to be a wonderfully common multiple of:

- 24 (frames per second in film)
- 25 (frames per second in PAL and SECAM video, used in Europe, Africa, South America, and parts of Asia)
- 30 (frames per second in NTSC video, used in North America and Japan)

Actually, that last example is not entirely true. NTSC color video is broadcast at an overall rate of 29.97 frames/sec, so to keep things straight, two frame numbers are dropped every minute (except for every 10th minute) to compensate for a synchronization problem in the color signal. QuickTime can handle these "drop-frame" video tracks by making the time scale 2,997 and each frame 100 units long. I told you it was handy!

Listening for Movie State-Changes

One problem with polling to show the current time in the movie is that it's wasteful and inaccurate: it's optimal to check the time only when the movie's playing, and to eliminate latency, it would be nice to be notified when there's a sudden change in the current time, such as when the user slides the scrubber. Fortunately, there's a callback API to notify a program when things like this occur.

How do I do that?

This example revises the BasicQTButtons program. The new version, BasicQTCallback, asks to be notified when the rate changes. When the rate is 0, it will disable the stop button (labeled "0"), and when the rate is 1, it disables the play button (labeled "1"). For space, I'll list only the lines that have changed from BasicQTButtons.

First, there are two new imports: quicktime.std.clocks, which is where callbacks are defined, and quicktime.std, whose StdQTConstants provides constants to specify the callbacks' behavior:

```
import quicktime.std.*;
import quicktime.std.clocks.*;
```

Next, the constructor is changed to pass the Movie to an inner class' constructor:

```
MyQTCallback myCallback = new MyQTCallback (m);
```

And here's the inner class. It has a constructor that takes a Movie argument and an execute( ) method:

```
class MyQTCallback extends RateCallBack {
    public MyQTCallback (Movie m) throws QTException {
        super (m.getTimeBase( ),
               0,
               StdQTConstants.triggerRateChange);
        callMeWhen( );
    }
    public void execute( ) {
        if (rateWhenCalled == 0.0) {
            startButton.setEnabled (true);
            stopButton.setEnabled (false);
        } else if (rateWhenCalled == 1.0) {
            startButton.setEnabled (false);
            stopButton.setEnabled (true);
        }
        // indicate that we want to be called again
        try {
            callMeWhen( );
        } catch (QTException qte) {
            qte.printStackTrace( );
        }
    }
}
```

Compile and run this example with ant run-ch02-basicqtcallbacks.

The result looks like the window in Figure 2-7. Notice how in the screenshot, the stop button ("0") is dimmed, indicating that the movie is already stopped. If the user hits "1," the movie will play and the play button will be disabled.

Figure 2-7. Disabling buttons via callbacks

What just happened?

The inner class creates a QTCallBack, specifically a subclass of RateCallBack. In its constructor, it indicates the conditions under which it wants to be called—by passing the triggerRateChange flag, it asks to be called any time the rate changes. It then invokes callMeWhen( ) to actually register the callback.

QuickTime invokes the callback via the execute( ) method. This implementation checks the rateWhenCalled value, inherited from RateCallBack, to determine if the movie is stopped or started, and enables or disables buttons appropriately. Finally, it issues a new callMeWhen( ) call to ask to get called back on future rate changes—QuickTime callbacks are one-time-only deals, not like the EventListeners that are typical in Java, so programmers have to remember to reregister for new callbacks after every execute( ).

What about...

...that 0 argument to the RateCallBack's constructor? Good question. This is one of those times where all the interesting values are defined only in the native documentation, not the Javadocs. The third argument, used to trigger the callback on any rate change, can be used with the constants triggerRateEquals, triggerRateNotEqual, triggerRateLT ("less than"), triggerRateLTE ("less than or equals"), etc., to define a behavior when the callback is made only when a certain condition is

In the previous lab, a "rate not equal to 0" callback could be used to start or stop the time-label polling thread, so it would run only when the movie has a non-zero rate.

true. When using these triggers, the middle argument specifies the rate to be compared. For example, a callback could be set up to run only when the movie is playing, by passing 0 and triggerRateNotEquals as the second and third arguments, respectively.

Are there other kinds of callbacks? Glad you asked. There are four major callbacks, each with its own class in quicktime.std.clocks:

RateCallBack
: Calls back when the rate changes, as seen in the earlier example.

ExtremesCallBack
: Calls back when playback reaches the beginning or end of the Movie. Behavior is specified with triggerAtStart or triggerAtStop.

TimeCallBack
: Calls back when playback reaches a specific time in the movie. The behavior flag determines if the callback occurs when moving forward (triggerTimeFwd), backward (triggerTimeBwd), or either forward or backward (triggerTimeEither).

TimeJumpCallBack
: Calls back when the movie's current time changes in a way that is not consistent with its current play rate. The typical case here is that the user is grabbing the scrubber to move around the movie. Setting up this callback takes no parameters or behavior flags.

And what about more sophisticated callback setup and teardown? This example doesn't need to clean up anything, but a more sophisticated application, one that opens and closes multiple movies, would need to release callback resources. This is done with a call to the QTCallBack's cancelAndCleanup() method.

There is also a simple cancel() method that can be used to cancel a callback previously registered with callMeWhen(). To change a callback, you must cancel() it, then construct a new callback and register it with callMeWhen().

Moving Frame by Frame

One popular feature for playback is the ability to step forward exactly one frame. It turns out to be trickier than one might initially expect: it's not like there's a Movie.nextFrame() method. Indeed, a Movie might not have a video track at all, if it represents an MP3 or some other audio-only media. So, finding the next frame requires being a little smarter about looking inside the Movie's structure.

How do I do that?

This example builds on the earlier BasicQTButtons code. In this example, the implementations of the forward and back buttons are altered so that instead of changing the play rate, they change the current time to be the next frame before or after the current time. For space, this example shows only the changes from the original BasicQTButtons.

This example needs to import quicktime.std to use StdQTConstants, and quicktime.std.clocks for some time-related classes. It also adds an instance variable visualTrack, which is found with the following call:

```
theMovie = m;
// find video track
visualTrack =
    m.getIndTrackType (1,
                        StdQTConstants.visualMediaCharacteristic,
                        StdQTConstants.movieTrackCharacteristic);
```

If a visual track isn't found, the revButton and fwdButton are disabled later in the constructor.

Finally, a new implementation of actionPerformed( ) does the frame-step logic when the revButton or fwdButton is clicked:

```
if (e.getSource() == revButton) {
    TimeInfo ti =
        visualTrack.getNextInterestingTime (
            StdQTConstants.nextTimeMediaSample,
            theMovie.getTime(),
            -1);
    theMovie.setTime (new TimeRecord (theMovie.getTimeScale(),
                                      ti.time));
}
else if (e.getSource() == stopButton)
    theMovie.stop();
else if (e.getSource() == startButton)
    theMovie.start();
else if (e.getSource() == fwdButton) {
    TimeInfo ti =
        visualTrack.getNextInterestingTime (
            StdQTConstants.nextTimeMediaSample,
            theMovie.getTime(),
            1);
    theMovie.setTime (new TimeRecord (theMovie.getTimeScale(),
                                      ti.time));
}
```

There's no screenshot for this example, because it's difficult to show a frame step in a static medium like a book.

Compile and run this example with ant run-ch02-basicqtstepper.

What just happened?

This program finds the video track with a call to Movie.
getIndTrackType( ), which takes three arguments:

Which instance to find

This is 1-based, so passing 1 means "find the first matching track."

A search criterion

This is a constant from StdQTConstants that can be a media "type"
(videoMediaType, soundMediaType, etc.), or it can be a "characteristic"
(videoMediaCharacteristic, audioMediaCharacteristic). The characteristics are helpful in cases like this when several kinds of media
are acceptable matches ("visual" media includes video, MPEG, Flash,
and more).

Flags to control the search

This should be the value movieTrackMediaType if the previous
argument is a media type or movieTrackCharacteristic if it is a
characteristic.

An alternative way to find a suitable track would be to iterate over the
tracks with Movie.getIndTrack( ), get the Media object from each discovered track, and use instanceof to see if it matches a given media class
(VideoMedia, SoundMedia, etc.).

Assuming you can find such a track, the trick to finding the next frame is to
use the media's getNextInterestingTime( ) method. There are several
kinds of "interesting times," and to indicate interest in the next frame,
which is more accurately the next "sample," you pass the behavior flag
nextTimeMediaSample. The method also takes a parameter representing
the time in the movie where it should start searching for the next frame (in
this case, it's the current time) and the desired search direction (any positive int for a forward search, and any negative int for a backward search).

The value returned by getNextInterestingTime( ) is a TimeInfo object.
This program is interested only in the time field of this object, which is
represented in the Movie's time scale (not the Media's, interestingly
enough). It takes that value and advances the movie to the interesting
time—i.e., the next frame—with a call to Movie.setTime( ).

What about...

...other kinds of times? The native GetMediaNextInterestingTime function offers the following behavior flags:

NextTimeMediaSample

The behavior used in this example.

`NextTimeMediaEdit`

Finds the next group of samples—i.e., the next thing that has been edited into the movie (editing is covered in the next chapter).

`NextTimeSyncSample`

Finds the next "sync sample"—i.e., the next sample that is completely self-contained. Many video compression formats send a sync sample (also known as a "key frame"), which is a complete image, while subsequent samples are just information about what has changed since the sync sample. In other words, these later frames aren't complete and cannot be rendered without information from one or more other samples.

`NextTimeEdgeOK`

Can be OR'ed in with other flags to indicate that it's OK to return the beginning or the end of the media as a valid "interesting time."

What's up with the first track being 1 instead of 0? As a curious legacy, one that feels more like Pascal than Java, most QuickTime methods that do an index-based `get` are one-based, not zero-based. In fact, if you try to `getTrack(0)`, you'll get a `QTException`.

WARNING

The other gotcha is that although this example is written to work with any visual media, it won't work for MPEG-1 or MPEG-2 files. These files multiplex (or "mux") the audio and video into one stream, and QuickTime doesn't de-mux them in memory, so it has no easy way to find the next video sample. This is why there are separate `MPEGMedia` and `MPEGMediaHandler` classes in QTJ; the latter is a subclass of `VisualMediaHandler`, but it is also implementing `AudioMediaHandler`. Fortunately, MPEG-4, whose internal structure is friendlier to QuickTime, appears as separate audio and video tracks just like other QuickTime movies.

Playing Movies from URLs

Along with loading movies from disk, QuickTime can also load them from URLs, and is pretty smart about network latency.

How do I do that?

Example 2-6 shows a totally new class, `BasicQTURLController.java`. This is a significant rethinking of the earlier `BasicQTController` class. This example creates a GUI from an empty "dummy" movie, then asks the user for a URL, gets a `Movie` from that, and replaces the dummy movie. By

---

getting the movie last, it tempts fate to see how well QTJ can deal with loading a movie over the network.

Compile and run this example with ant run-ch02-basicqturlcontroller.

Example 2-6. Loading and playing a movie from a URL

```java
package com.oreilly.qtjnotebook.ch02;

import quicktime.*;
import quicktime.std.*;
import quicktime.app.view.*;
import quicktime.std.movies.*;
import quicktime.std.movies.media.*;
import quicktime.io.*;

import com.oreilly.qtjnotebook.ch01.QTSessionCheck;

import java.awt.*;

public class BasicQTURLController extends Frame {

    QTComponent qc;

    public BasicQTURLController () throws QTException {
        super ("Basic QT DataRef/Controller");
        Movie dummyMovie = new Movie();
        qc = QTFactory.makeQTComponent (dummyMovie);
        Component c = qc.asComponent();
        add (c);
        pack();
    }

    public static void main (String[] args) {
        try {
            QTSessionCheck.check();
            BasicQTURLController f =
                new BasicQTURLController ();
            String url =
                javax.swing.JOptionPane.showInputDialog (f,
                                                "Enter URL");
            DataRef dr = new DataRef (url);
            Movie m = Movie.fromDataRef (dr,
                            StdQTConstants.newMovieActive);
            MovieController mc = new MovieController (m);
            f.qc.setMovieController (mc);
            f.setVisible(true);
            f.pack();
            m.prePreroll(0, 1.0f);
            m.preroll(0, 1.0f);
            m.start();
        } catch (Exception e) {
            e.printStackTrace();
        }
    }
}
```

When this app is first run, the user sees a dialog asking for a URL. Enter a valid URL (notice that again, for simplicity, the examples don't meaningfully check input or handle errors gracefully). Assuming the URL has valid Quick-Time content, the user will see a window like the one shown in Figure 2-8.

Figure 2-8. Movie played from a URL DataRef

What just happened?

Some different techniques are in play in this example, the most important of which is showing that the Movie or MovieController displayed by a QTComponent can be replaced. The constructor creates a QTComponent from the empty dummyMovie, but after creating a Movie from the URL, a MovieController is created for it and is used to replace the contents of the visible QTComponent via the setMovieController( ) call.

Two helper calls, prePreroll( ) and preroll( ), allocate movie-playing resources up front, to reduce jitter and dropped frames when the movie starts playing. These methods take the same two arguments: the movie time and the rate that the program intends to start playing at.

This example uses a MovieController to make a point. As seen in Figure 2-8, the scrubber has an inner bar that is only partially filled in. This is a graphic representation of how much of the movie data has been downloaded. This example goes ahead and plays the movie immediately, trusting that it will download data faster than we can consume it. This isn't a safe assumption at all—dial-up users will stop almost immediately, though the controller gives them the ability to see how much they have and to play when they're ready.

As for getting the Movie, it's a pretty simple process: pass the URL to a DataRef constructor. These DataRef objects are something of a general-purpose media locator in QuickTime, used here for network access. The new Movie is then created with the fromDataRef( ) call.

Notice the second argument to fromDataRef( ). This is an example of using QuickTime *behavior flags*, which are found throughout QuickTime. One of the more interesting concepts about the flags is that these behaviors can be combined. The flags are ints with a single bit turned on (meaning their actual values are powers of 2). The idea is that you can mathematically OR them together to combine multiple behaviors. The constants of the java.awt.Font class, like BOLD and ITALIC, work pretty much the same way. In this case, in addition to making the movie active, the program could set a behavior flag to tell QuickTime not to enable alternate tracks (if there are any), by making a call like this:

```
Movie m = Movie.fromDataRef (dr,
            StdQTConstants.newMovieActive |
            StdQTConstants.newMovieDontAutoAlternate);
```

The other flags mentioned for this call, newMovieDontResolveDataRefs and newMovieDontAskUnresolvedDataRefs, deal with esoteric cases where a movie is not self-contained and some of the media it refers to can't be found.

WARNING

The Javadocs for Movie.fromDataRef( ) advocate using the behavior flag StdQTConstants4.newMovieAsyncOK. That was useful in the old QTJ, but when used in this example in QTJ 6.1, it might allow the QTComponent to decide that your movie has zero height and zero width, because the movie gets handed to the QTComponent before the size metadata gets downloaded. As Figure 2-8 shows, the preceding code does *not* block and wait for the whole movie to be downloaded. Advice for now: don't use it unless you think you're blocking on Movie.fromDataRef( ).

Preventing "Tasking" Problems

All the tasks in this chapter have managed to avoid one of the more obscure hazards in QuickTime. This example tempts fate and exposes the problem by playing a movie that would otherwise freeze up.

How do I do that?

Example 2-7 reprises the command-line audio player from the first chapter, which takes a path to a file as a command-line argument, builds a Movie, and plays it, without getting any kind of GUI.

Example 2-7. Playing audio from the command line

```
package com.oreilly.qtjnotebook.ch01;

import quicktime.*;
import quicktime.app.time.*;
import quicktime.io.*;
import quicktime.std.*;
import quicktime.std.movies.*;

import java.io.*;

public class BasicAudioPlayer {

    public static void main (String[ ] args) {
        if (args.length != 1) {
            System.out.println (
                "Usage: BasicAudioPlayer <file>");
            return;
        }
        try {
            QTSessionCheck.check( );
            QTFile f = new QTFile (new File(args[0]));
            OpenMovieFile omf = OpenMovieFile.asRead(f);
            Movie movie = Movie.fromFile (omf);
            TaskAllMovies.addMovieAndStart( );
            movie.start( );
        } catch (QTException e) {
            e.printStackTrace( );
        }
    }
}
```

Notice the line in bold. Take it out, recompile, and watch what happens. The program will likely hang or immediately exit, playing just a spurt of audio or none at all.

What just happened?

QuickTime movies need to explicitly be given CPU time to do their work: reading from disk or the network, decompressing and decoding, rendering to the screen, or playing to the speakers. This process is called "tasking." Looking at the Javadocs reveals that the Movie class has a task( ) method that could be called to give time to a specific movie, and a static taskAll( ) method that tasks all active movies.

Managing all these calls manually and being sure to call them frequently enough would be, of course, incredibly tedious. That's why QTJ provides TaskAllMovies, a wrapper for a Thread whose job is to call task() on all active movies. This example kicks off TaskAllMovies (assuming nothing else has done so), thereafter allowing it to be blissfully unaware of tasking.

What about...

...all the other examples? Why are we only hearing about this now? Well, TaskAllMovies is so useful that QTJ itself uses it extensively. Any time a program works with QTJ's GUI classes, by getting a Component for a Movie or MovieController, it picks up calls to TaskAllMovies automatically. In fact, it's a little difficult not to pick up automatic tasking calls from QTJ, short of opening audio-only movies with non-QTJ GUI widgets, or no GUI at all, as seen here.

TIP

In the last section, a warning mentioned an edge case where using the newMovieAsyncOK flag might give you a QTComponent with zero size because Movie.fromDataRef() returned immediately, before enough of the movie could be loaded to know how big it was.

Tasking helps you solve this problem. After fromDataRef(), you would go into a while loop, testing whether Movie.getBox() returns non-zero dimensions. If it doesn't, call task() on the movie to give QuickTime a chance to load more of it, maybe do a Thread.sleep() or Thread.yield() to keep Java happy, and go back to the top of the while. Because QuickTime movies usually, but don't always, have metadata early in the file, an alternative to testing the size of the movie would be to call maxLoadedTimeInMovie() on the Movie object and wait for a non-zero value—this would also be better if there's any chance the Movie is audio only.

But seriously, it's not going to happen because you don't need newMovieAsyncOK. Chill.

It's still important to know about tasking in case you stumble into such a case and can't figure out why your application is just sitting there.

In QTJ 6.0 and earlier, there were also URL-loading scenarios where a program might need to task() a few times to download enough of the Movie to read in the metadata and get a valid size, but this behavior seems to have changed in 6.1, making explicit tasking even more of an edge case.

CHAPTER 3

Editing Movies

Playback is nice, but you have nothing to play if you lack tools to create media, and the most critical of these are editing tools. If you've ever used iMovie with your home movies, you know what I'm talking about: there's a huge difference between watching a cute collection of scenes of your kids playing, set to music, and watching the two hours of unedited raw footage you started with. Sometimes, less *is* more.

Copying and Pasting

The most familiar form of editing is copy-and-paste, which many users already are familiar with from the "pro" version of QuickTime Player. The metaphor is identical to how copy-and-paste works in nonmedia applications such as text editors and spreadsheets: select some source material of interest, do a "copy" to put it on the system clipboard, select an insertion point in this or another document, and do a "paste" to put the contents of the clipboard into that target.

In the simplest form of a QuickTime copy-and-paste, the controller bar (from `MovieController`) is used to indicate where copies and pastes should occur. By shift-clicking, a user can select a time-range from the current time (indicated by the play head) to wherever the user shift-clicks (or, if he is dragging, wherever the mouse is released).

How do I do that?

`BasicQTEditor`, shown in Example 3-1, will be the basis for the examples in this chapter. It offers a single empty movie window (with the ability to open movies from disk in new windows or to create new empty movie windows), and an Edit menu with cut, copy, and paste options.

QuickTime Pro costs money ($29.99 as of this writing), but it allows you to exercise much of the QuickTime API from QuickTime Player, which can be a useful debugging tool.

Example 3-1. A copy-and-paste movie editor

```
package com.oreilly.qtjnotebook.ch03;

import quicktime.*;
import quicktime.qd.QDRect;
import quicktime.std.*;
import quicktime.std.movies.*;
import quicktime.app.view.*;
import quicktime.io.*;

import java.awt.*;
import java.awt.event.*;

import com.oreilly.qtjnotebook.ch01.QTSessionCheck;

public class BasicQTEditor extends Frame
    implements ActionListener {

    Component comp;

    Movie movie;
    MovieController controller;
    Menu fileMenu, editMenu;
    MenuItem openItem, closeItem, newItem, quitItem;
    MenuItem copyItem, cutItem, pasteItem;
    static int newFrameX = -1;
    static int newFrameY = -1;
    static int windowCount = 0;

    /** no-arg constructor for "new" movie
     */
    public BasicQTEditor () throws QTException {
        super ("BasicQTEditor");
        setLayout (new BorderLayout());
        QTSessionCheck.check();
        movie = new Movie(StdQTConstants.newMovieActive);
        controller = new MovieController (movie);
        controller.enableEditing(true);
        doMyLayout();
    }

    /** file-based constructor for opening movies
     */
    public BasicQTEditor (QTFile file) throws QTException {
        super ("BasicQTEditor");
        setLayout (new BorderLayout());
        QTSessionCheck.check();
        OpenMovieFile omf = OpenMovieFile.asRead (file);
        movie = Movie.fromFile (omf);
        controller = new MovieController (movie);
        controller.enableEditing(true);
        doMyLayout();
    }
```

Example 3-1. A copy-and-paste movie editor (continued)

```java
/** gets component from controller, makes menus
 */
private void doMyLayout( ) throws QTException {
    // add movie component
    QTComponent qtc =
        QTFactory.makeQTComponent (controller);
    comp = qtc.asComponent( );
    add (comp, BorderLayout.CENTER);
    // file menu
    fileMenu = new Menu ("File");
    newItem = new MenuItem ("New Movie");
    newItem.addActionListener (this);
    fileMenu.add (newItem);
    openItem = new MenuItem ("Open Movie...");
    openItem.addActionListener (this);
    fileMenu.add (openItem);
    closeItem = new MenuItem ("Close");
    closeItem.addActionListener (this);
    fileMenu.add (closeItem);
    fileMenu.addSeparator( );
    quitItem = new MenuItem ("Quit");
    quitItem.addActionListener (this);
    fileMenu.add(quitItem);
    // edit menu
    editMenu = new Menu ("Edit");
    copyItem = new MenuItem ("Copy");
    copyItem.addActionListener(this);
    editMenu.add(copyItem);
    cutItem = new MenuItem ("Cut");
    cutItem.addActionListener(this);
    editMenu.add(cutItem);
    pasteItem = new MenuItem ("Paste");
    pasteItem.addActionListener(this);
    editMenu.add(pasteItem);
    // make menu bar
    MenuBar bar = new MenuBar( );
    bar.add (fileMenu);
    bar.add (editMenu);
    setMenuBar (bar);
    // add close-button handling
    addWindowListener (new WindowAdapter( ) {
            public void windowClosing (WindowEvent e) {
                doClose( );
            }
        });
}

/** handles menu actions
 */
public void actionPerformed (ActionEvent e) {
    Object source = e.getSource( );
```

Example 3-1. A copy-and-paste movie editor (continued)

```java
        try {
            if (source == quitItem) doQuit( );
            else if (source == openItem) doOpen( );
            else if (source == closeItem) doClose( );
            else if (source == newItem) doNew( );
            else if (source == copyItem) doCopy( );
            else if (source == cutItem) doCut( );
            else if (source == pasteItem) doPaste( );
        } catch (QTException qte) {
            qte.printStackTrace( );
        }
    }

    public void doQuit( ) {
        System.exit(0);
    }

    public void doNew( ) throws QTException {
        makeNewAndShow( );
    }

    public void doOpen( ) throws QTException {
        QTFile file =
            QTFile.standardGetFilePreview (QTFile.kStandardQTFileTypes);
        Frame f = new BasicQTEditor (file);
        f.pack( );
        if (newFrameX >= 0)
            f.setLocation (newFrameX+=16, newFrameY+=16);
        f.setVisible(true);
        windowCount++;
    }

    public void doClose( ) {
        setVisible(false);
        dispose( );
        // quit if no windows now showing
        if (--windowCount == 0)
            doQuit( );
    }

    public void doCopy( ) throws QTException {
        Movie copied = controller.copy( );
        copied.putOnScrap(0);
    }

    public void doCut( ) throws QTException {
        Movie cut = controller.cut( );
        cut.putOnScrap(0);
    }

    public void doPaste( ) throws QTException {
        controller.paste( );
```

Example 3-1. *A copy-and-paste movie editor (continued)*

```
        pack( );
    }

/** Force frame's size to respect movie size
    */
    public Dimension getPreferredSize( ) {
        System.out.println ("getPreferredSize");
        if (controller == null)
            return new Dimension (0,0);
        try {
            QDRect contRect = controller.getBounds( );
            Dimension compDim = comp.getPreferredSize( );
            if (contRect.getHeight( ) > compDim.height) {
                return new Dimension (contRect.getWidth( ) +
                                        getInsets( ).left +
                                        getInsets( ).right,
                                        contRect.getHeight( ) +
                                        getInsets( ).top +
                                        getInsets( ).bottom);

            } else {
                return new Dimension (compDim.width +
                                        getInsets( ).left +
                                        getInsets( ).right,
                                        compDim.height +
                                        getInsets( ).top +
                                        getInsets( ).bottom);

            }
        } catch (QTException qte) {
            return new Dimension (0,0);
        }
    }

    /** opens a single new movie window
     */
    public static void main (String[ ] args) {
        try {
            Frame f = makeNewAndShow( );
            // note its x, y for future calls
            newFrameX = f.getLocation( ).x;
            newFrameY = f.getLocation( ).y;
        } catch (Exception e) {
            e.printStackTrace( );
        }
    }

    /** creates "new" movie frame, packs and shows.
        used by main( ) and "new"
     */
    private static Frame makeNewAndShow( )
        throws QTException {
```

With the downloaded book code, compile and run this with ant run-ch03-basicqteditor.

Example 3-1. A copy-and-paste movie editor (continued)

```
        Frame f = new BasicQTEditor();
        f.pack();
        if (newFrameX >= 0)
            f.setLocation (newFrameX+=16, newFrameY+=16);
        f.setVisible(true);
        windowCount++;
        return f;
    }
}
```

Figure 3-1 shows the BasicQTEditor class in action, with two windows open. The window on the left is the original empty movie window, with the user about to paste in some contents. The window on the right is a movie that was opened from a file. Note the small stretch of darker gray in the timeline, under the play head, which indicates the selected segment that was copied from the movie to the system clipboard.

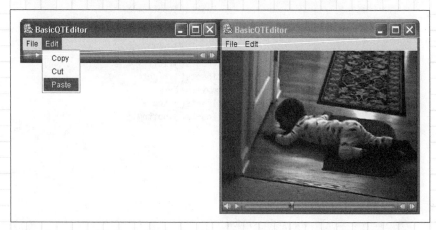

Figure 3-1. BasicQTEditor with two movies open

Also note that when running in Windows, as pictured here, the menus are inside the windows. On Mac OS X, the usage of AWT means the File and Edit menus will be at the top of the screen in the Mac's "One True Menu Bar."

One usability note: for simplicity, I haven't tried to make this particularly smart about what the user "really wants," and that can be bad on the paste. The paste will replace whatever is selected in the target movie, and if there is no selection, it will paste to the beginning of the movie. It's probably more typical to add clips either to the end of the movie, or to the current time as indicated by the play head (i.e., to behave as if a lack of a selection should be interpreted as a zero-length selection beginning and ending at the movie's current time). It's simple enough to add this kind of intelligence to doPaste() and find a behavior that feels better.

What just happened?

This is a big example, so here's an overview.

The no-arg constructor, BasicQTEditor( ), initializes QuickTime with Chapter 1's QTSessionCheck, then creates a new empty Movie, gets a MovieController for it, and calls doMyLayout. A second constructor, BasicQTEditor (QTFile), is essentially identical, except that instead of creating an empty movie, it gets a movie from the provided QTFile. The movie and the controller instance variables are used by many methods throughout the application.

The doMyLayout( ) method sets up the menus and their ActionListeners and reminds us that building GUIs in code is a pain.

actionPerformed (ActionEvent) is used to farm out method calls from clicks on the various menu items.

doQuit( ) is a trivial call to System.exit(0). Remember that the QTSessionCheck call has set up a shutdown handler to close QuickTime when Java goes away.

doNew( ) trivially calls makeNewAndShow( ), which is a convenience method to call the no-arg constructor (which creates an empty Movie), pack the frame, and move it down and to the right 16 pixels from the last place a new window was created.

TIP

Note that there's nothing here to keep new windows from going off-screen if the user creates enough of them. In a more polished application, you'd check the proposed x and y against the screen size reported by the AWT's Toolkit.getScreenSize( ).

---

doOpen( ) brings up a file-open dialog and calls the file-aware constructor. It then pack( )s the window and positions it in the same way makeNewAndShow( ) does.

doClose( ) closes the frame and, if it is the last open window, quits the application via doQuit( ) (yes, this is Windows-like behavior, as opposed to the typical Mac application which can hang around with no open windows).

doCopy( ) and doCut( ) are practically identical, and each needs only two lines to do its thing. They make a call to the MovieController to cut or copy the current selection and return the result as a new Movie. Then they put this movie on the system clipboard with the movie's putOnScrap( ) call.

doPaste( ) is even simpler: it just calls the controller's paste( ) method and then re-pack( )s the window.

The getPreferredSize( ) method overrides the default by indicating that the window needs to be large enough to contain the movie, its control bar, and any insets that might be set. This is why you should pack( ) after each paste: the original empty movie has no size other than its control bar, so when you paste into it, the size of the movie (and thus its controller) changes to accommodate the pasted contents, and you need the frame to adjust to that.

WARNING

This really should be taken care of automatically in Java, because the use of a BorderLayout should allow the contents to achieve their preferred size on a pack( ). Unfortunately, on Mac OS X, the QTComponent exhibits a bizarre behavior where its preferred size is set *once*, when it's packed, and never again. So, a component built from an empty movie always thinks it's supposed to be zero pixels high by 160 pixels wide, even if you paste in contents much larger than that. Fixing this reveals the opposite problem on Windows: sometimes there's a good preferred size and a zero-height controller bound. The version here prefers whichever set of bounds has a greater height.

What about...

...that weird play head? That is odd, isn't it? The call to enableEditing(true) has changed the play head ball to an hourglass shape. Figure 3-2 shows it at an enlarged size.

Figure 3-2. MovieController scrubber bar with editing enabled

My guess is that the shape is supposed to help you select the exact point for making a selection, instead of burying it under the center of the ball. That said, there's a reason you don't see this elsewhere: this default widget isn't terribly well-suited to editing. The QuickTime Player application that comes with QuickTime has a custom controller widget with two little triangles under the timeline to mark in and out points. But that control, like this one, shares the flaw that the accuracy of your edit is limited by the on-screen size of your movie. More serious editing applications, like Premiere and Final Cut Pro, have custom GUI components for editing, usually based on a timeline that can be "zoomed" to an arbitrary accuracy. Of course, one could do the same with AWT or Swing, tracking MouseEvents, paint( )ing as necessary, and making programmatic calls to QTJ to perform actions.

Performing "Low-Level" Edits

Low-level edits are a separate set of editing calls that don't involve the clipboard or selection metaphors. They're called "low level" because instead of operating at the conceptual level of "paste the contents of the clipboard into the user's current selection," they work at the level of "insert a segment from movie M1, ranging from time A to time B, into movie M2 at time C."

By way of comparison, although QuickTime has two sets of editing functions, Sun's Java Media Framework has no editing API at all.

How do I do that?

This version reimplements doCopy( ), doCut( ), and doPaste( ) to use low-level editing calls on the Movie instead of cut/copy/paste-type calls on the MovieController.

First, LowLevelQTEditor needs a static Movie, called copiedMovie, to keep track of what's on its virtual "clipboard" so that it can be shared across the new doCopy( ), doCut( ), and doPaste( ) methods:

```
public void doCopy() throws QTException {
        copiedMovie = new Movie();
        TimeInfo selection = movie.getSelection();
        movie.insertSegment (copiedMovie,
                        selection.time,
                        selection.duration,
                        0);
}

public void doCut() throws QTException {
        copiedMovie = new Movie();
        TimeInfo selection = movie.getSelection();
        movie.insertSegment (copiedMovie,
                        selection.time,
                        selection.duration,
                        0);
        movie.deleteSegment (selection.time,
                        selection.duration);
        controller.movieChanged();
}

public void doPaste() throws QTException {
        if (copiedMovie == null)
            return;
        copiedMovie.insertSegment (movie,
                        0,
```

You can make ant
compile and run
this example with
ant run-ch03-
lowlevelqteditor.

```
                                        copiedMovie.getDuration(),
                                        movie.getSelection().time);
        controller.movieChanged();
        pack();
    }
```

The only thing the user might see as being different or odd in this example is that the cut or copied clip does not get put on the system clipboard because low-level edits don't touch the clipboard.

TIP

For what it's worth, this example was intended originally to be a drag-and-drop demo, for which these low-level, segment-oriented calls are particularly well-suited. Unfortunately, the QTComponent won't generate an AWT "drag gesture." I suppose it would be a little unnatural to drag the current image as a metaphor for copying a segment of a movie. Anyway, if you decide to do your own controller GUI, you can use this low-level stuff for your drag-and-drop.

Time scales are
covered in
Chapter 2, in the
section "Showing a
Movie's Current
Time."

What just happened?

The doCut(), doCopy(), and doPaste() methods all call Movie.insertSegment(); either to put some part of a source movie into the clipboard-like copiedMovie or to put the copiedMovie into the target movie. This method takes four arguments:

- The Movie to insert into
- The start time of the segment, in the movie's time scale
- The end time of the segment, in the movie's time scale
- The time in the target movie when the segment should be inserted

In the case of a cut, the deleteSegment() call removes the segment that was just copied out. This method simply takes the beginning and end times of the segment to delete.

In the doPaste() and doCut() methods, a call to MovieController.movieChanged() lets the controller know that the movie was changed in a way that didn't involve a method call on the controller, and that the controller now needs to update itself to adjust to the changed duration, current time, etc.

What about...

...any other low-level calls? There is an interesting method in the Movie class, called scaleSegment(), which changes the duration of a segment,

---

meaning it either slows it down or speeds it up to suit the specified duration. This could be handy for creating a "slow-motion" or "fast-motion" effect from a normal-speed source, or stretching it out to fit a piece of audio.

Undoing an Edit

Critical to any kind of editing is the ability to back out of a change that had unintended or undesirable effects. Fortunately, controller-based cuts and pastes can be undone with some fairly simple calls.

Compile and run this example with ant run-ch03-undoableqteditor.

How do I do that?

UndoableQTEditor builds on the original BasicQTEditor by adding an "undo" menu item. The doUndo() method it calls has an utterly trivial implementation:

```
public void doUndo() throws QTException {
    controller.undo();
}
```

What just happened?

With a simple call to MovieController.undo(), the program gained the ability to undo a cut or paste, or any other destructive change made through the controller.

What about...

...multiple undoes? Or redoes? Ah, there's the rub. Hit undo again and the cut or paste is redone, in effect undoing the undo.

Sadly, this is your dad's "undo"...the undo from back in 1990, when a single level of undo was a pretty cool thing. Today, when users expect to perform multiple destructive actions with impunity, it's not too impressive.

Undoing and Redoing Multiple Edits

Fortunately, QTJ offers a unique opportunity to combine Swing's thoughtfully designed undo API, javax.swing.undo, with QuickTime's support for reverting a movie to a previous state. Combined, these features provide the ability to support a long trail of undoes and redoes.

How do I do that?

RedoableQTEditor again builds on BasicQTEditor, adding a Swing UndoManager that is used by both the doUndo() and doRedo() methods:

*Compile and run
this example with
ant run-ch03-
redoableqteditor.*

```
public void doUndo() throws QTException {
    if (! undoanager.canUndo()) {
        System.out.println ("can't undo");
        return;
    }
    undoManager.undo();
}

public void doRedo() throws QTException {
    if (! undoManager.canRedo()) {
        System.out.println ("can't redo");
        return;
    }
    undoManager.redo();
}
```

The information about a destructive edit is encapsulated by an inner class called QTEdit:

```
class QTEdit extends AbstractUndoableEdit {
    MovieEditState previousState;
    MovieEditState newState;
    String name;
    public QTEdit (MovieEditState pState,
                   MovieEditState nState,
                   String n) {
        previousState = pState;
        newState = nState;
        this.name = n;
    }
    public String getPresentationName() {
        return name;
    }
    public void redo() throws CannotRedoException {
        super.redo();
        try {
            movie.useEditState (newState);
            controller.movieChanged();
        } catch (QTException qte) {
            qte.printStackTrace();
        }
    }
    public void undo () throws CannotUndoException {
        super.undo();
        try {
            movie.useEditState (previousState);
            controller.movieChanged();
        } catch (QTException qte) {
            qte.printStackTrace();
        }
```

```
    }
    public void die() {
        previousState = null;
        newState = null;
    }
}
```

Finally, doCut() and doPaste() are amended to create suitable QTEdits and hand them to the UndoManager:

```
public void doCut() throws QTException {
    MovieEditState oldState = movie.newEditState();
    Movie cut = movie.cutSelection();
    MovieEditState newState = movie.newEditState();
    QTEdit edit = new QTEdit (oldState, newState, "Cut");
    undoManager.addEdit (edit);
    cut.putOnScrap(0);
    controller.movieChanged();
}

public void doPaste() throws QTException {
    MovieEditState oldState = movie.newEditState();
    Movie pasted = Movie.fromScrap(0);
    movie.pasteSelection (pasted);
    MovieEditState newState = movie.newEditState();
    QTEdit edit = new QTEdit (oldState, newState, "Paste");
    undoManager.addEdit (edit);
    controller.movieChanged();
    pack();
}
```

When clicked, the Undo menu item now undoes a cut or paste. Redo redoes the edit, while a second "undo" will undo the previous edit, etc.

What just happened?

Obviously, the fun parts involve the destructive actions and how they save enough information to be undoable and redoable. In each case, they call Movie.newEditState() to create a MovieEditState, a QuickTime object that contains the information needed to revert the movie to the current state at some point in the future. Then they do the destructive action and create another MovieEditState to represent the post-edit state. These objects are passed to the QTEdit, which is then sent to the UndoManager to join its stack of edits.

When the UndoManager.undo() method is called, it takes the first undoable edit, if there is one, and calls its undo() method. In this case, that means the manager is calling the QTEdit.undo() method, which takes the pre-edit MovieEditState and passes it to Movie.useEditState() to return the movie to that state. Similarly, a post-undo call to QTEdit.redo() also uses useEditState() to get to the post-edit state.

For more on Swing's undo framework, see Chapter 18 of O'Reilly's Java Swing, 2nd Edition, by Mark Loy, Robert Eckstein, Dave Wood, James Elliot, and Brian Cole.

Saving a Movie to a File

Once a user has performed a number of edits and has a finished project, she presumably needs to save the movie to disk. In QuickTime, many different actions can be thought of as "saving" a movie. Perhaps the simplest and most flexible option is to let the user decide.

How do I do that?

Compile and run this example with ant run-ch03-saveableqteditor.

The SaveableQTEditor uses a QTFile to keep track of where a movie was loaded from (null in the case of a new movie). This is used by the doSave() method to indicate where the saved file goes:

```
public void doSave() throws QTException {
    // if no existing file, then prompt for one
    if (file == null) {
        file = new QTFile (new File ("simplemovie.mov"));
    }
    int flags = StdQTConstants.createMovieFileDeleteCurFile |
        StdQTConstants.createMovieFileDontCreateResFile |
        StdQTConstants.showUserSettingsDialog;
    movie.convertToFile (file, // file
                        StdQTConstants.kQTFileTypeMovie, // filetype,
                        StdQTConstants.kMoviePlayer, // creator
                        IOConstants.smSystemScript, // scriptTag
                        flags);
}
```

When the user hits the Save menu item, she'll see the QuickTime Save As dialog as shown in Figure 3-3.

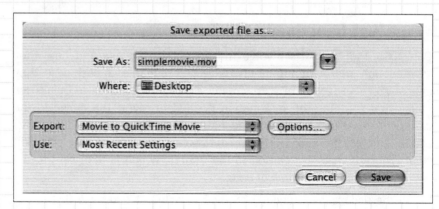

Figure 3-3. QuickTime Save As dialog

This dialog's Export selector gives the user four choices:

Movie
> Saves a QuickTime *reference movie*, a tiny (typically 4 or 8 KB) file that contains just references (pointers) to the media in their original locations

Movie, self-contained
> Copies all the media, in their original encodings, into a new Quick-Time movie file

Movie to Hinted Movie
> Creates a self-contained movie but lets the user adjust the hinting settings for use in a streaming server

Movie to QuickTime Movie
> Creates a self-contained movie, but lets the user choose different compressors and settings to re-encode the audio and video

Some of these options give the user additional choices. Saving a "self-contained" movie presents an Options... button that lets the user specify the audio and video codecs to be used in the saved movie, their quality and bitrate settings, etc. A "Use" pop up contains canned settings with appropriate choices for distributing the movie on CD-ROM, over dial-up, etc.

Once the user clicks Save, the program saves the movie to disk. This is a very fast operation for the reference movie option and a potentially slow operation for the other options because the media might be re-encoded into a new format as part of the save.

What just happened?

The key is the `Movie.convertToFile()` method. The version shown here takes five parameters:

- The `QTFile` to save to.
- An `int` to represent the old Mac OS file "type." Use the constant `kQTFileTypeMovie`, which gives it the QuickTime movie type `moov`.
- An `int` to represent the old Mac OS file "creator." The boilerplate option is `kMoviePlayer`, which associates it with the default Quick-Time Player application.
- An `int` to represent the old Mac OS "scriptTag," which indicates what kind of "script system" (character encoding, writing direction, etc.) is to be used. Common practice is to use the constant `smSystemScript` to use whatever the operating system's current script is.

- Behavior flags to affect the save operation, logically ORed together. The most important flag for this example is the showUserSettingsDialog; without it, the program would silently save the file with Apple's ancient "Video" codec and uncompressed sound. This example also uses the flag createMovieFileDeleteCurFile to delete any file already at the target location and createMovieFileDontCreateResFile to force the file to exist in a single data "fork," instead of using the old Mac OS' "resource" fork. This is required for making QuickTime movies that run on multiple platforms.

Most of the time, it's appropriate to use boilerplate code for things like type, creator, and system script, and not to have to read some Inside Macintosh book from 10 years ago.

What about...

...other interesting behavior flags? The docs for the native ConvertMovieToFile function offer two that aren't shown here because they seem to indicate behavior that is already the default:

- movieFileSpecValid indicates that the file passed in actually exists and should be shown as the default save location.
- movieToFileOnlyExport restricts the dialog to showing only the data export components that are actually present.

Can anything be done about the interminable wait when saving "Movie to QuickTime Movie"? One thing that helps is to provide a "progress function," which provides a visual representation of the progress being made on the long save operation. You can set up the default progress function with a one-line call right before convertToFile( ):

```
movie.setProgressProc()
```

This will bring up a progress dialog like the one shown in Figure 3-4.

Figure 3-4. Default QuickTime progress dialog

The Movie class also has a setProgressProc( ) method that takes a MovieProgress object as a parameter. The idea here is that of a typical callback arrangement—during a long save, MovieProgress.execute( ) is called repeatedly with four parameters: the movie being monitored, a "message" int, a "what operation" int, and a float that represents the percentage done on a scale from 0.0 to 1.0. Unfortunately, this interface has a couple of problems. First, the constants for the "message" aren't defined in QTJ (a few `println`s here and there show that the values are 0 for start, 1 for update, and 2 for done). More importantly, using this callback seems extremely unstable in QTJ 6.1—I find I often get an exception with an "Unknown Error Code," and the movie doesn't save. So, maybe the default behavior is the safe choice for now.

Flattening a Movie

Saving a movie can mean different things in QuickTime: saving a reference movie, saving a self-contained movie, or exporting to a different format. Typically, though, the idea of creating a self-contained movie is what users think of as "saving"—they want a single file that doesn't depend on any others, so they can put it on a server, email it to mom, etc. This process is called "flattening."

"Flattening" is also an old Mac OS term for turning a file with both a resource fork and a data fork into a single-fork file, suitable for use on non-Mac disk formats. In this book, we use "flatten" only in its QuickTime sense.

How do I do that?

The `FlattenableQTEditor` is similar to the `SaveableQTEditor`, adding the menu item and its typical GUI and action-handling support. The flattening is done in a `doFlatten( )` method:

```
public void doFlatten( ) throws QTException {
    // always attempts to save to a new location,
    // so prompt for filename
    FileDialog fd = new FileDialog (this,
                            "Flatten...",
                            FileDialog.SAVE);
    fd.setVisible(true); // blocks
    if ((fd.getDirectory( ) == null) ||
        (fd.getFile( ) == null))
        return;
    QTFile flatFile =
        new QTFile (new File (fd.getDirectory( ),
                            fd.getFile( )));
    if (flatFile.exists( )) {
        // JOptionPane is a bit of cheat-for-clarity here,
        // building a working AWT dialog would be punitive
        int choice =
            JOptionPane.showConfirmDialog (this,
                            "Overwrite " +
                            flatFile.getName( ) + "?",
                            "Flatten",
                            JOptionPane.OK_CANCEL_OPTION);
        if (choice != JOptionPane.OK_OPTION)
            return;
    }
    movie.flatten(StdQTConstants.flattenAddMovieToDataFork |
                StdQTConstants.flattenForceMovieResourceBeforeMovieData,
                flatFile, // fileOut
```

```
                              StdQTConstants.kMoviePlayer, // creator
                              IOConstants.smSystemScript, // scriptTag
                              StdQTConstants.createMovieFileDeleteCurFile,
                              StdQTConstants.movieInDataForkResID, // resID
                              null); // resName
        }
```

Compile and run this example with ant run-ch03-flattenablegt-editor.

When run, this creates a self-contained QuickTime movie file at the specified location, using whatever video and audio encoding was used in the original sources. This can result in some playback jitters if the user has mixed in different kinds of codecs—for example, pasting in some MPEG-4 video with some Sorenson 3 video. Flattening doesn't change encoding; it just resolves references and puts all the media into one file.

What just happened?

Many of these are the same parameters used by Movie.convertToFile(), covered in the previous lab.

The Movie.flatten() call creates the self-contained movie file, taking seven parameters to control its behavior:

- Behavior flags for the flatten operation, logically ORed together. This example uses flattenAddMovieToDataFork to create a single-fork movie that is more suitable for non-Mac operating systems. Using flattenForceMovieResourceBeforeMovieData creates a "quick start" movie, so named because all its metadata comes before its media samples, which allows QuickTime to start playing the movie from a stream, even an http://-style URL, before all the data is loaded, because all the information QuickTime needs (what tracks are present, what size the video is, how loud the audio is, etc.) is loaded first.

- The file to flatten to.

- The Mac OS "creator," typically kMoviePlayer.

- The Mac OS script tag, typically smSystemScript.

- The behavior flags that are used for the create file operation. createMovieFileDeleteCurFile is used here to delete any file already at the target file location.

- Resource ID. For cross-platform reasons, it's usually best to use movieInDataForkResID instead of old Mac OS-style resources.

- Resource name. Irrelevant here, so null will do.

What about...

...behavior flags for the flatten operation? The native docs for FlattenMovie define a bunch, but the ones not used here are largely esoteric.

flattenDontInterleaveFlatten
> Turns off "interleaving," an optimization that mixes audio and video samples together so that they're easier to read at playback time (if a movie had a couple of megabytes' worth of video samples, followed by a couple of megabytes' worth of audio samples, the hard drive would have a difficult time zipping back and forth between the two; interleaving puts the samples for the same time period in the same place so that they can be read together). The default behavior is *a good thing*, so this constant isn't used often.

flattenActiveTracksOnly
> Doesn't include disabled tracks from the movie in the flattened file.

flattenCompressMovieResource
> Compresses the movie's resource, and its organizational and metadata structure, if stored in the data fork. Like you care.

flattenFSSpecPtrIsDataRefRecordPtr
> This is meaningless in QTJ.

Saving a Movie with Dependencies

The opposite of flattening is saving a movie with dependencies. In this type of a save, the resulting file just contains pointers to the sources of the media in each track. The file typically is tiny, usually just 8 KB or less.

How do I do that?

The RefSaveableQTEditor example extends the FlattenableQTEditor with a "Save w/Refs" menu item that calls doRefSave( ):

```
public void doRefSave( ) throws QTException {
    // if no home file, then prompt for one
    if (file == null) {
        FileDialog fd = new FileDialog (this,
                                        "Save...",
                                        FileDialog.SAVE);
        fd.setVisible(true); // blocks
        if ((fd.getDirectory( ) == null) ||
```

```
                    (fd.getFile( ) == null))
                    return;
                file = new QTFile (new File (fd.getDirectory( ),
                                             fd.getFile( )));
            }
            // save ref movie to file
            if (! file.exists( )) {
                file.createMovieFile(StdQTConstants.kMoviePlayer,
                                     StdQTConstants.
        createMovieFileDontCreateResFile);
            }
            OpenMovieFile outFile =
                OpenMovieFile.asWrite(file);
            movie.updateResource (outFile,
                                  StdQTConstants.movieInDataForkResID,
                                  null);

    }
```

Compile and run this example with `ant run-ch03-refsaveablegt-editor`.

When run, this creates a movie file that, despite its tiny size, behaves exactly like any other movie file. Double-click it and it will open in QuickTime Player, just like a self-contained movie. QuickTime completely isolates the user from the fact that the file contains nothing more than metadata and pointers to the source media files.

Of course, there are limits to what QuickTime can do if those pointers cease to be valid. A user can move the source files and the movie still will play, but if the source movies are deleted, or if the reference movie is transferred to another system, QuickTime won't be able to resolve the references. This typically will result in a "searching..." dialog, followed by a dialog asking the user to locate the missing media, as shown in Figure 3-5.

Figure 3-5. Unresolvable media reference dialog

What just happened?

First, a call to `QTFile.createMovieFile( )` creates the file on disk, if it doesn't exist already. This method takes two parameters:

- A Mac OS "creator," for which StdQTConstants.kMoviePlayer is the typical boilerplate value.
- Behavior flags. The constant createMovieFileDontCreateResFile commonly is used to create cross-platform, single-fork files.

With the file created, the reference movie data can be put into the file with the updateResource() method. This method takes three parameters:

- An OpenMovieFile, opened for writing.
- A resource ID, for which the appropriately cross-platform, no-resource-fork value is movieInDataForkResId.
- An updated name for the resource; null is appropriate here.

The name updateResource() seems to be another Classic Mac OS legacy that doesn't make much sense today.

What about...

...the fragility of reference movies? Because a reference movie is fragile, why would anyone ever create one? This technique is very handy for the saving state in editing applications because it allows the user to quickly save his edited movie without the I/O grinding of flattening. Editing, after all, can be seen as a process of arranging pointers to source materials; in the professional realm, a document called an *Edit Decision List* (EDL) is a simple list of "in" and "out" points from source media that you can use to produce the edited media. The reference movie is equivalent to the EDL: it's just a collection of pointers, with the nice advantage that it continues to behave as a normal QuickTime movie. So, the reference movie can be used to save the progress of the user's editing work, and when finished, a final self-contained movie can be generated via flattening or exporting (see Chapter 4).

Editing Tracks

Often, it makes sense to perform edits on all tracks of a movie. But for serious editing applications, sometimes you need to work at the track level, to add and remove tracks, or to work on just one track in isolation from the others. This task will provide a taste of that by adding a second audio track to a movie.

How do I do that?

The `AddAudioTrackQTEditor` builds on `FlattenableQTEditor` by adding another Add Audio Track... menu item, calling the doAddAudioTrack( ) method:

```
public void doAddAudioTrack( ) throws QTException {
    // ask for an audio file
    QTFile audioFile =
        QTFile.standardGetFilePreview (QTFile.kStandardQTFileTypes);
    OpenMovieFile omf = OpenMovieFile.asRead (audioFile);
    Movie audioMovie = Movie.fromFile (omf);
    // find the audio track, if any
    Track audioTrack =
        audioMovie.getIndTrackType (1,
                                    StdQTConstants.audioMediaCharacteristic,
                                    StdQTConstants.movieTrackCharacteristic);
    if (audioTrack == null) {
        JOptionPane.showMessageDialog (this,
                        "Didn't find audio track",
                        "Error",
                        JOptionPane.ERROR_MESSAGE);
        return;
    }
    // now make new audio track and insert segment
    // from the loaded track
    Track newTrack =
        movie.newTrack (0.0f, // width
                        0.0f, // height
                        audioTrack.getVolume());
    // ick, need a dataref for our "new" media
    // http://developer.apple.com/qa/qtmtb/qtmtb58.html
    SoundMedia newMedia =
        new SoundMedia (newTrack,
                        audioTrack.getMedia().getTimeScale(),
                        new DataRef (new QTHandle()));
    newTrack.getMedia().beginEdits();
    audioTrack.insertSegment (newTrack,
                        0,
                        audioTrack.getDuration(),
                        0);
    controller.movieChanged();
}
```

Compile and run this example with *ant run-ch03-addaudiotrack-qteditor.*

This method is admittedly contrived—it prompts the user to open another file, and if an audio track can be found in the file, the program adds that track to the movie, starting at time 0. If the user has done only a few short pastes and then adds an audio track from a typical iTunes MP3 or AAC, the result probably will be a movie in which the new soundtrack is much longer than the pasted contents.

Also, QuickTime will eat more CPU cycles playing this movie, because it has to decode two compressed soundtracks at once. Like I said, it's a contrived example, but it covers some interesting ground.

What just happened?

The program tries to find an audio track with `Movie.getIndTrackType()`, passing `audioMediaCharacteristic` as the search criterion. Assuming an audio track is found in this movie, the program needs to create a new track in the movie being edited. `Movie.newTrack()` creates the new track, taking as parameters the width, height, and volume of the new track.

This new track is useless without a `Media` object to hold the actual sound data, so the next step is to construct a new `SoundMedia` object. The constructor takes the track that the media is to be associated with, a time scale, and a `DataRef` to indicate where media samples can be stored.

Interestingly, although the edit methods this program uses are in the `Track` class, first I have to call `Media.beginEdits()` to inform the track's underlying media that it's about to get edited. Having done this, the program then can call `Track.insertSegment()`, which is identical to its low-level-editing `Movie` equivalent, taking a target track, source in and out times, and a destination-in time. Following this, the program calls `movieChanged()` on the movie controller to let it know that a change was made to the movie behind the controller's back.

The result is an additional audio track in the movie. If the user then flattens the movie and opens it up with QuickTime Player, a "Get Info" shows the extra audio track, as seen in Figure 3-6. In this case, I imported clips from an MPEG-4 file and added an MP3 soundtrack.

What about...

...that crazy-looking `new DataRef (new QTHandle())` parameter in the `SoundMedia` constructor? OK, scary edge case—here's the story. Zoom out for a second: movies have tracks, tracks have media, media have samples. Those samples need to live *somewhere*. It's not a problem when you open a movie from disk, but when you create new media in a new movie, QuickTime has no idea where it's supposed to put any samples that you add, whether by way of inserting segments from other tracks or by adding individual samples one by one (which will be covered in Chapters 7, 8, and 9). So, this example uses the `SoundMedia` constructor that takes a `DataRef`, which represents a location to store the samples.

No, I'm not swearing in this filename. I combined a video of my son in an inflatable boat with an MP3 of a song called "Dam Dariram" from the video game "Dance Dance Revolution"; thus, "dam-boat.mov".

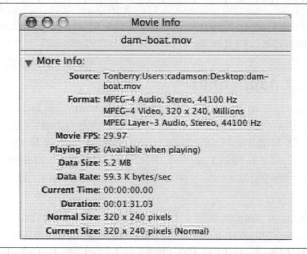

Figure 3-6. QuickTime Player "Get Info" for movie with multiple audio tracks

This DataRef can be practically anything, even a zero-length buffer in memory, which is pretty much what this example passes in by constructing a new DataRef out of a new, empty QTHandle.

TIP

For more on this icky little gotcha, and if you don't mind a C-oriented technote, see "BeginMediaEdits -2050 badDataRefIndex error after calling NewMovie" at *http://developer.apple.com/qa/qtmtb/qtmtb58.html*.

Also, what about the control bar? It tells the user nothing about the tracks in the movie. You're absolutely right. Being playback-oriented, the provided GUI is weak for editing movies, and utterly useless for editing tracks. It gives the user no idea how many tracks a movie has, where there's video without sound or vice versa, etc. Moreover, there's no default widget in QTJ to replace it. If you want to provide track-oriented editing, you'll need to develop your own GUI components to display tracks and their contents. I haven't provided one here, because the appearance and behavior of such a component would vary wildly with the kind of application it was needed for (a home movie editor, an MP3 playlist builder, etc.) and because it easily could contain more than 1,000 lines of AWT code with maybe a dozen lines of QuickTime...not exactly ideal for the format of this book.

What about other track-editing methods? Fortunately, many of the concepts from the low-level Movie editing lab from earlier in the chapter apply to tracks. Along with `Track.insertSegment()` are a `deleteSegment()` and a `scaleSegment()` that work like their `Movie` equivalents. The `insertEmptySegment()` does what its name implies, and could be useful for building a track in nonconsecutive segments. There's also a `Track.insertMedia()` that will be used in later chapters to build up a `Media` object from raw samples.

As for how the tracks relate to their parent movies, this example uses `Movie.newTrack()`, though it also is possible to use `addEmptyTrack()`, which takes a prototype track and a `DataRef`. Tracks can be removed with `Movie.removeTrack()` and temporarily turned on and off with `Track.setEnabled()`.

Working with Components

When QuickTime came out in 1990, it could play movies the size of a postage stamp—barely—on $7,000 hardware. It used audio and video codecs that, although still supported today, have long since been abandoned by users. Yet it's been a smooth transition from Apple Video to Cinepak to MPEG-4. This is thanks to an extraordinarily modular design—most of the heavy lifting in QuickTime is performed by *components*, or shared code fragments that can be discovered and used dynamically. Components provide support for importing and exporting image and movie formats, performing image and sound compression and decompression, accessing system resources, and much more. The QuickTime installer provides components for many features, and components added later by the end user, from either Apple or third parties, can provide more functionality, like support for more media formats.

Components aren't always front-and-center in the API—after all, the first few chapters have managed to avoid mentioning them entirely. Quick-Time has been assumed to just "do the right thing" when it comes to opening files and turning them into movies, decompressing and rendering the data, saving it to disk, etc. When needed, QuickTime looks through its catalog of components for required functionality and gets what it needs.

But sometimes it's desirable or necessary for the developer to work with components more directly, to figure out what's available or to specify behavior. Figuring out what tools are available at runtime can be a powerful asset.

Specifying a Component's Type

In QuickTime, components are identified by a *type* and a *subtype*. The type specifies a broad area of functionality, while the subtype is a specific implementation of that functionality. For example, there's a "movie exporter" type, which identifies components that can write a movie into a non-QuickTime format, with subtypes identifying the exporters for AVI, MPEG-4, etc.

"moov" shows up a lot in QuickTime: as an identifier for a movie's copy-and-paste type, as its Carbon file type, as the top-level "atom" in the file format, etc. Say it out loud if you don't get the joke: moo-vee.

These identifiers are 32-bit int values, but typically they're not enumerated constants like you might expect from Java. Usually, the 32 bits are read as four 8-bit ASCII characters, making a short, human-readable name. These are defined in the native API as OSTypes, but when populated with meaningful values, they're called "four character codes," from the native FOUR_CHAR_CODE function that returns an OSType for a string. This often is abbreviated as FCC, or 4CC.

The scheme makes a lot of sense from the C programmer's point of view. For example, defining the 4CC for a movie requires a nice, simple one-liner, as seen in the native Movies.h header file:

```
MovieResourceType = 'moov'
```

It turns out that dealing with 4CCs is harder in Java, thanks to Java's more modern approach to text. Specifically, the use of Unicode means Java characters are 2 bytes each, which means help is needed to turn a Java string into a 4CC.

How do I do that?

Fortunately, the QTUtils class provides two methods for converting to and from 4CCs: toOSType( ) and fromOSType( ). Example 4-1 exercises these methods by converting a Java string to and from its 4CC representation.

Example 4-1. Converting to and from FOUR_CHAR_CODEs

```java
package com.oreilly.qtjnotebook.ch04;

import quicktime.util.QTUtils;

public class FourCharCodeTest extends Object {

    public static void main (String[] args) {
        if (args.length < 1) {
            System.out.println ("Usage: FourCharCodeTest <fcc>");
            return;
        }
        System.out.println (args[0]);
```

Example 4-1. *Converting to and from FOUR_CHAR_CODEs (continued)*

```
        int fcc = QTUtils.toOSType (args[0]);
        System.out.println (fcc);
        System.out.println (Integer.toHexString (fcc));
        String fccString = QTUtils.fromOSType(fcc);
        System.out.println (fccString);
    }

}
```

Compile and run this example from the downloaded book code with ant run-ch04-fourcharcodetest.

The main( ) method takes a String from the command line, converts it to a 4CC, prints that value in decimal and hex, then converts it back to a String. When it's run with moov as an argument, the output looks like this:

```
cadamson% java -classpath classes
        com.oreilly.qtjnotebook.ch04.FourCharCodeTest moov
moov
1836019574
6d6f6f76
moov
```

What just happened?

These utility methods provide some good, old-fashioned bit-munging to do their conversions. toOSType( ) takes a String as its argument, grabbing the low 8 bits of each character and putting them in the proper place in the returned int. In other words, the bottom 8 bits of the first character take up the first 8 bits of the int, then the next character is used for the next 8 bits, and so on. Figure 4-1 shows where the bits end up in the bit-shifted "moov".

Really hard-core QuickTime developers can read 4CCs in hex without thinking about it. Drop a movie file on a hex editor and you'll probably see 6d6f6f76 *(moov) as bytes 4-8.*

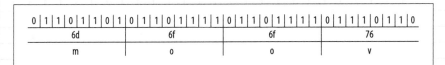

Figure 4-1. *Bit-wise, hex, and character representation of a FOUR_CHAR_CODE*

fromOSType( ) does the opposite conversion, masking off the bits of an int and returning a four-character Java string.

Exporting Movies

One of the most obviously useful components is the MovieExporter, which you can use to convert a QuickTime movie into a non-QuickTime format, such as AVI or MPEG-4.

How do I do that?

The `quicktime.std.qtcomponents.MovieExporter` class provides a convenient Java wrapper around movie exporter components. It requires that you pass it a subtype indicating which exporter you want—i.e., which format you want to export to. Example 4-2 shows how a `MovieExporter` can be created and used from a canned list of subtypes.

Example 4-2. Simple MovieExporter creation and use

```java
package com.oreilly.qtjnotebook.ch04;

import quicktime.*;
import quicktime.std.*;
import quicktime.std.movies.*;
import quicktime.io.*;
import quicktime.std.qtcomponents.*;
import quicktime.utils.QTUtils;

import java.awt.*;
import javax.swing.*;

import com.oreilly.qtjnotebook.ch01.QTSessionCheck;

public class SimpleMovieExport extends Object {

    public static final void main (String[] args) {
        new SimpleMovieExport();
    }

    public SimpleMovieExport() {
        // build choices
        ExportChoice[] choices = new ExportChoice[3];
        choices[0] =
            new ExportChoice ("QuickTime Movie",
                              StdQTConstants.kQTFileTypeMovie);
        choices[1] =
            new ExportChoice ("AVI file",
                              StdQTConstants.kQTFileTypeAVI);
        choices[2] =
            new ExportChoice ("MPEG-4 file",
                              QTUtils.toOSType("mpg4"));

        try {
            // query user for a movie to open
            QTSessionCheck.check();
            QTFile file =
                QTFile.standardGetFilePreview (QTFile.kStandardQTFileTypes);
            OpenMovieFile omFile = OpenMovieFile.asRead (file);
            Movie movie = Movie.fromFile (omFile);

            // offer a choice of movie exporters
```

Example 4-2. Simple MovieExporter creation and use (continued)

```
            JComboBox exportCombo = new JComboBox (choices);
            JOptionPane.showMessageDialog (null,
                                exportCombo,
                                "Choose exporter",
                                JOptionPane.PLAIN_MESSAGE);
            ExportChoice choice =
                (ExportChoice) exportCombo.getSelectedItem( );

            // create an exporter
            MovieExporter exporter =
                new MovieExporter (choice.subtype);

            QTFile saveFile =
                new QTFile (new java.io.File("Untitled"));

            // do the export
            movie.setProgressProc( );
            movie.convertToFile (null,
                                saveFile,
                                StdQTConstants.kQTFileTypeMovie,
                                StdQTConstants.kMoviePlayer,
                                IOConstants.smSystemScript,
                                StdQTConstants.showUserSettingsDialog |
                                StdQTConstants.movieToFileOnlyExport |
                                StdQTConstants.movieFileSpecValid,
                                exporter);

            // need to explicitly quit (since awt is running)
            System.exit(0);
        } catch (QTException qte) {
            qte.printStackTrace( );
        }

    }

    public class ExportChoice {
        String name;
        int subtype;
        public ExportChoice (String n, int st) {
            name = n;
            subtype = st;
        }
        public String toString( ) {
            return name;
        }
    }
}
```

Compile and run this example with ant run-ch04-simplemovieexport.

When run, this program prompts the user to open a movie file. Once the movie loads, the program offers a dialog with a choice of formats to export to, as shown in Figure 4-2.

Figure 4-2. Choice dialog with canned MovieExporter types

Next, it shows the user a save dialog detailing the proposed export (e.g., "Movie to MPEG-4") and an Options button. The button brings up a dialog specific to the export format. For example, the AVI export dialog is fairly simple, offering only a few settings to choose from. On the other hand, the MPEG-4 export dialog, seen in Figure 4-3, is extraordinarily busy, packed with descriptions of the many options to help end users understand their choices and potentially keep their exported file compliant with MPEG-4 standards.

MPEG-4 Settings

General | Video | Audio | Streaming | Compatibility

Video Track: Improved

Size: 320 x 240

Audio Track: Music

Video will make use of improved MPEG-4 features (known as ISMA Profile 1). This produces files of higher quality, while potentially being incompatible with some MPEG-4 devices. The video will have a data rate of 900 kbits/second and a frame rate of 30.0 frames per second. The resulting movie will be 320 by 240 pixels.

Audio will be optimized for music (known as Low Complexity AAC). The audio will have the current sample rate in stereo. The data rate of the audio will be 128 kbits/second. The audio encoding will be done in better quality mode.

This MPEG-4 file will support ISMA (Internet Streaming Media Alliance) specifications.

Cancel   OK

Figure 4-3. MPEG-4 export dialog

After the user makes his choices and clicks OK, the long export process begins. Because movie export is very computationally intensive—potentially every frame of video and every audio sample must be re-encoded—a progress dialog appears, so the user can see how much of the export has completed and how much longer it will take.

Chapter 4: Working with Components

What just happened?

This program uses an inner class called ExportType to wrap a subtype, int, and a String, largely for the purpose of simplifying the JComboBox used in the format-choice dialog. These subtypes come from constants defined in the StdQTConstants class.

Once a choice is made, the program instantiates a MovieExporter by passing the subtype to its constructor. Next, it requests a progress dialog by calling setProgressProc() on the movie.

Finally, the export is performed by calling convertToFile() and passing in the exporter. This method takes several parameters:

- A Track to indicate that only this track should be exported, or null for all tracks.
- A QTFile to export to.
- A file type, such as StdQTConstants.kQTFileTypeMovie.
- A creator, such as StdQTConstants.kMoviePlayer.
- A script tag, typically IOConstants.smSystemScript.
- Behavior flags. This example uses all three of the valid values: showUserSettingsDialog makes the export bring up the Save As dialog that includes the filename and the options button; movieToFileOnlyExport limits the export choices to formats supported by the exporter component; and movieFileSpecValid asserts that the QTFile is valid and should be used as the default name in the dialog.
- The MovieExporter to use for the export.

Including showUserSettingsDialog allows you to pick up the settings and the save-as GUIs in one call, instead of having to show separate dialogs for each. Too bad flags like this aren't described in Javadoc.

What about...

...using the MovieExporter itself to do the export? That's an alternative. The exporter's toFile() exports the movie to a file, and its toHandle() exports to memory. This also has the advantage of being able to export just part of a movie, as specified by the startTime and duration arguments. Note that doing this requires a different program flow, because first you'd need to get a valid QTFile (perhaps with an AWT file dialog) and then you'd need to call the exporter's doUserDialog() to configure the export. Also the Movie class's convertToFile() method can be more convenient, because, as seen here, it allows use of the default progress dialog. When using the MovieExporter methods, there's no access to the default dialog. In that case, the only alternative is to provide a custom progress dialog and handle progress callbacks with setProgressProc().

Also, a complaint: I tried exporting to MPEG-4 on Windows and didn't get any audio options. When I click the Audio Track menu in the Exporter dialog, I get the useless panel as shown in Figure 4-4.

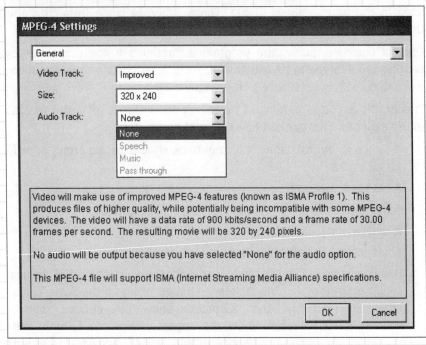

Figure 4-4. Audio non-options for MPEG-4 export on Windows

This is not a technical issue but a legal one. Apple has licensed MPEG-4 audio encoding for its Mac-based QuickTime users, but not for Windows users. The codecs exist, but apparently you have to contact Dolby about license terms to enable them for Windows.

Exporting Movies to Any Installed Format

Exporting to a list of known formats is limiting—if the end user has installed new movie exporters, either from third parties or via an update to QuickTime itself, a program that uses a canned list of exporters won't be able to pick them up. Fortunately, QuickTime provides a means of querying for installed components of a given type. You can use this strategy to offer a list of all available exporters.

How do I do that?

The AdvancedMovieExport eliminates the three canned entries in the choices array that were used by SimpleMovieExport (shown in Example 4-2) and instead builds the array through a process of discovery; this code would replace the short "build choices" block in the constructor for SimpleMovieExport but needs to go inside the try-catch, because it makes calls that can throw QTException:

```
Vector choices = new Vector();
ComponentIdentifier ci = null;
ComponentDescription cd =
    new ComponentDescription(StdQTConstants.movieExportType);
while ( (ci = ComponentIdentifier.find(ci, cd)) != null) {
    // check to see that the movie can be exported
    // with this component (this throws some obnoxious
    // exceptions, maybe a bit expensive?)
    try {
        MovieExporter exporter = new MovieExporter (ci);
        if (exporter.validate (movie, null)) {
            ExportChoice choice =
                new ExportChoice (ci.getInfo().getName(),
                                  ci);
            choices.addElement(choice);
        }
    } catch (StdQTException expE) {
        System.out.println ("** can't validate " +
                            ci.getInfo().getName() + " **");
        // expE.printStackTrace();
    } // ow!
}
```

Run this example with ant run-ch04-advanced movieexport.

When run, the list of supported exporters is surprisingly large, as seen in Figure 4-5. In this case, a "normal" movie, consisting of a video track and an audio track, is being exported, meaning that any audio-only format (Wave, AIFF, etc.) or audio/video format (QuickTime, AVI, MPEG-4, etc.) will work.

Hinted Movie, the format selected in Figure 4-5, is a QuickTime movie with "hints" to optimize streaming.

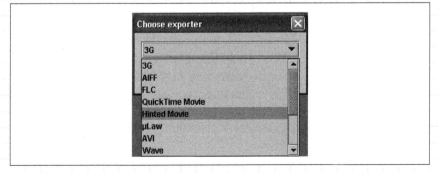

Figure 4-5. Discovered Movie Exporters

You also should take note of the discovered exporters that cannot export the movie. These are logged to standard out:

```
run-ch04-advancedmovieexport:
     [java] ** can't validate BMP **
     [java] ** can't validate Standard MIDI **
     [java] ** can't validate Picture **
     [java] ** can't validate Text **
     [java] ** can't validate QuickTime TeXML **
     [java] ** can't validate QuickTime Media Link **
```

These fail because the source movie doesn't contain tracks that can be exported to these formats. With a source movie with different kinds of tracks, some of these would succeed and others would fail.

What just happened?

The process of discovering components by subtype is rather peculiar. It hinges on making repeated calls to a "find" method, passing in the last matching component. Doing this requires a ComponentDescription, used as a template to match against, and a ComponentIdentifier, which refers to a specific component (though not a specific instance of that component). To find movie exporters, initialize a ComponentDescription template with the constant movieExporterType.

The static ComponentIdentifier.find() method finds matching components, but instead of offering an array or other collection of matches, it requires you to repeatedly pass in the ComponentDescription template, along with the previous ComponentIdentifier found by the method. For the first iteration, this will be null. The find() call returns a ComponentIdentifier, which you pass to the MovieExporter constructor to create a new exporter. When find() returns null, there are no more matches.

Yes, this is totally weird, at least from a Java perspective.

The matched ComponentIdentifier provides information about itself via the getInfo() method. This returns another ComponentDescription object, different from the one used as a template. You can use this to get type and subtype information (as FOUR_CHAR_CODE ints, of course), a name, an information String, a manufacturer code, etc.

Finding a MovieExporter is no guarantee that it actually will work. You can call validate(), as this example does, to check that the instantiated exporter can do an export from the given movie. In this example, if validate throws an exception, it's logged to standard out and the exporter is not added to the JComboBox.

What about...

...setting the export parameters programmatically, instead of using the export dialog every time? This is possible, although it will require using the export dialog at least once in development. A configured MovieExporter can return its configured state in the form of an AtomContainer object, by way of the getExportSettingsFromAtomContainer( ) method. This object can be passed to an exporter via the setExportSettingsFromAtomContainer( ) method.

"Atoms" are a low-level data structure that do almost all of QuickTime's heavy lifting. Application-level code uses them only for really advanced stuff (see Chapter 9).

Within a single running application, this is pretty straightforward. To persist between sessions, you must save off the native structure by calling getBytes( ) on the AtomContainer and then persist it to disk, database, etc. To recreate the settings in the future, read the bytes into a byte array, create a QTHandle from the array, and then pass that to AtomContainer.fromQTHandle( ) to create the AtomContainer.

QuickTime 6.3 introduced a new API for setting exporters programmatically, but as of this writing, it has not been exposed via QTJ method calls.

Also, if I specify type and subtype, will I always get one match? No, in some cases, you'll get multiple matching components, and you might need to use other criteria to pick which one to use. In a rather infamous case pointed out by one of my tech reviewers:

> Sometimes you get more than one exporter with the same subtype and need to use the "manufacturer" code to distinguish them. This applies particularly to AIFF exporters—the first exporter you find of that type only exports MIDI. To export an arbitrary QT audio file to AIFF you need to explicitly iterate and pick the second one!

Importing and Exporting Graphics

QuickTime offers many components whose job is to import from and export to different graphics formats. As you might expect, these components are wrapped by classes called GraphicsImporter and GraphicsExporter.

The GraphicImportExport example application (shown in Example 4-3) uses both of these classes to illustrate the dynamic lookup of importers and exporters.

Example 4-3. Graphics import and export

```
package com.oreilly.qtjnotebook.ch04;

import quicktime.*;
import quicktime.io.*;
```

Example 4-3. Graphics import and export (continued)

```java
import quicktime.std.*;
import quicktime.std.comp.*;
import quicktime.std.image.*;
import quicktime.app.view.*;
import java.awt.*;
import java.awt.event.*;
import javax.swing.*;
import java.util.Vector;
import java.io.*;

import com.oreilly.qtjnotebook.ch01.QTSessionCheck;

public class GraphicImportExport extends Object {

    Button exportButton;
    Frame frame;
    GraphicsImporter importer;

    static final int[] imagetypes =
        { StdQTConstants.kQTFileTypeQuickTimeImage};
    /* other interesting values:
        StdQTConstants.kQTFileTypeGIF,
        StdQTConstants.kQTFileTypeJPEG,
        StdQTConstants4.kQTFileTypePNG,
        StdQTConstants4.kQTFileTypeTIFF
        StdQTConstants.kQTFileTypeMacPaint,
        StdQTConstants.kQTFileTypePhotoShop,
        StdQTConstants.kQTFileTypePICS,
        StdQTConstants.kQTFileTypePicture,
    */

    public static void main (String[] args) {
        new GraphicImportExport();
    }

    public GraphicImportExport() {
        try {
            QTSessionCheck.check();
            QTFile inFile = QTFile.standardGetFilePreview (imagetypes);
            importer = new GraphicsImporter (inFile);
            // put image onscreen
            QTComponent qtc = QTFactory.makeQTComponent (importer);
            java.awt.Component c = qtc.asComponent();
            frame = new Frame ("Imported image");
            frame.setLayout (new BorderLayout());
            frame.add (c, BorderLayout.CENTER);
            exportButton = new Button ("Export");
            exportButton.addActionListener (new ActionListener() {
                public void actionPerformed (ActionEvent ae) {
                    try {
                        doExport();
                    } catch (QTException qte) {
```

Example 4-3. Graphics import and export (continued)

```
                    qte.printStackTrace( );
                }
            }
        });
        frame.add (exportButton, BorderLayout.SOUTH);
        frame.pack( );
        frame.setVisible(true);
    } catch (QTException qte) {
        qte.printStackTrace( );
    }
}

public void doExport( ) throws QTException {
    // build list of GraphicExporters
    Vector choices = new Vector( );
    ComponentDescription cd =
        new ComponentDescription (
            StdQTConstants.graphicsExporterComponentType);
    ComponentIdentifier ci = null;
    while ( (ci = ComponentIdentifier.find(ci, cd)) != null) {
        choices.add (new ExportChoice (ci.getInfo( ).getName( ),
                                        ci.getInfo( ).getSubType( )));
    }

    // offer a choice of movie exporters
    JComboBox exportCombo = new JComboBox (choices);
    JOptionPane.showMessageDialog (frame,
                                    exportCombo,
                                    "Choose exporter",
                                    JOptionPane.PLAIN_MESSAGE);
    ExportChoice choice =
        (ExportChoice) exportCombo.getSelectedItem( );
    System.out.println ("chose " + choice.name);

    // build a GE, wire up to the GraphicsImporter
    GraphicsExporter exporter =
        new GraphicsExporter (choice.subtype);
    exporter.setInputGraphicsImporter (importer);

    // ask for destination, settings
    FileDialog fd =
        new FileDialog (frame, "Save As",
                        FileDialog.SAVE);
    fd.setVisible(true);
    String filename = fd.getFile( );
    if (filename.indexOf('.') == -1)
        filename = filename + "." +
            exporter.getDefaultFileNameExtension( );
    File file = new File (fd.getDirectory( ), filename);
    exporter.setOutputFile (new QTFile(file));
    exporter.requestSettings( );

    // export
```

Compile and run this example with ant run-ch04- graphicimport- export. This note should be aligned with "import quicktime.std. comp.*" in the above code.

Example 4-3. Graphics import and export (continued)

```
        exporter.doExport( );

        // need to explicitly quit (since awt is running)
        System.exit(0);
    }

public class ExportChoice {
    String name;
    int subtype;
    public ExportChoice (String n, int st) {
        name = n;
        subtype = st;
    }
    public String toString( ) {
        return name;
    }
}

}
```

When run, the program shows a dialog to select a graphic to be imported. On Windows, the "file type" in this dialog is QuickTime Image. Once an image is selected, it appears in a window with an "export" button. When the user clicks the button, she is asked for an export type, as shown in Figure 4-6.

GraphicsIm- porter and GraphicsExporter are in quicktime. std.image, not quicktime.std. gtcomponents like most other components.

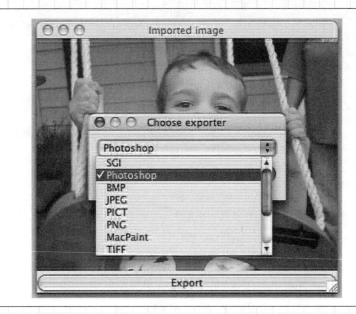

Figure 4-6. Selecting a GraphicsExporter

After this, the program displays a configuration dialog specific to the type of exporter selected—at a minimum, this dialog usually offers a choice of color depths (256 colors, 256 grays, millions of colors, etc.). Next, a save dialog requests the location of the exported file. Once approved, the program converts the image to the specified format and saves it to the supplied location.

What just happened?

Notice the QTFile.standardGetFilePreview( ). This shows a file-open dialog and takes an array of up to four ints, representing FOUR_CHAR_CODEs of various file format constants, which are used as a filter of what file types to make selectable. You can use kQTFileTypeQuickTimeImage as a convenient wildcard that matches any kind of image QuickTime can open, though it seems to work only on Windows (on the Mac, any file can be selected).

TIP

If you want to specify formats, interesting constants in StdQTConstants include kQTFileTypeGIF, kQTFileTypeJPEG, and kQTFileTypePhotoShop. The StdQTConstants4 class adds similarly named constants for PNG and TIFF. Unfortunately, you can send only four.

Given a file, you can construct a GraphicsImporter object to load it into QuickTime. To put the imported image on-screen, pass the importer to QTFactory.makeQTComponent( ), which returns a QTComponent that you can either cast to an AWT Component or, to be type-safe, convert with the asComponent( ) method.

WARNING

java.awt and quicktime.std.comp both define a class called Component. If you're casually importing every class from these packages, you're probably headed for a compile-time error. You'll have to make your imports more selective or use a fully qualified class name for one of the Components, like this example does.

To export an image to another format, you can search for graphics exporter subtypes by creating a ComponentDescription template to match components of the graphicsExporterComponentType. In the example, the names of matching components are shown in a JComboBox. With a subtype selected, create the GraphicsExporter by passing the subtype to its constructor.

This method of looking up exporter components was shown in the previous lab.

A GraphicsExporter needs to be wired up to some kind of source image. With a GraphicsImporter, you wire the two together with setInputGraphicsImporter( ). The exporter also needs a destination. If writing to a file (as opposed to, say, memory), you set this with setOutputFile( )—just to be safe, it's wise to sanity-check the user-provided filename extension against the value returned by the exporter's getDefaultFileNameExtension( ).

The user probably wants some say in the color depth, image quality, and other settings for the export, a dialog for which is provided with a requestSettings( ).

After all that, you finally can do the export with...doExport( ).

What about...

...other sources for the export? The Javadoc for GraphicsExporter shows a bunch of setInputXXX( ) methods. True enough, and in the next chapter, we'll explore some of these, including Picts, QDGraphics, and PixMaps.

And what about setting export parameters programmatically? QTJ exposes some methods that could be used instead of the user dialog, such as setDepth( ) and setCompressionMethod( ). One interesting method, setTargetDataSize( ), lets exporters with a "quality" option (like JPEG) find a value that will result in a file of the given size in bytes.

GraphicsExporters have an AtomContainer-based settings scheme that's just as painful as the MovieExporter equivalent from the last lab.

Discovering All Installed Components

I hope that by this point you're at least a little interested in what other kinds of components are available in QuickTime. It's easy to discover them all, in much the same way we discovered the various MovieExporters and GraphicExporters: by providing a ComponentDescription template and using ComponentIdentifier.find( ). With a "blank" template, all components can be revealed.

How do I do that?

Example 4-4 discovers all installed components and logs their type, sub-type, and description to standard out.

Example 4-4. Discovering all installed components

```
package com.oreilly.qtjnotebook.ch04;

import quicktime.*;
```

Example 4-4. *Discovering all installed components (continued)*

```java
import quicktime.std.*;
import quicktime.std.comp.*;
import quicktime.util.QTUtils;

import com.oreilly.qtjnotebook.ch01.QTSessionCheck;

public class ComponentTour {

    public static void main (String[] args) {
        try {
            QTSessionCheck.check();
            /* use this wildcard to show all components in QT
             */
            ComponentDescription wildcard =
                new ComponentDescription();
            ComponentIdentifier ci = null;
            while ( (ci = ComponentIdentifier.find(ci, wildcard)) != null) {
                ComponentDescription cd = ci.getInfo();
                System.out.println (cd.getName() +
                                " (" +
                                QTUtils.fromOSType (cd.getType()) +
                                "/" +
                                QTUtils.fromOSType (cd.getSubType()) +
                                ") " +
                                cd.getInformationString());
            }

        } catch (QTException qte) {
            qte.printStackTrace();
        }
    }

}
```

The resulting output is hundreds of lines long, looking something like this:

```
run-ch04-componenttour:
     [java] Apple MP3 Decoder (adec/.mp3) An AudioCodec that decodes MPEG-1,
MPEG-2, MPEG-2.5 Layer III into linear PCM data
     [java] MPEG-4 AAC Decoder (adec/aac ) An AudioCodec that decodes MPEG-4
AAC into linear PCM data
     [java] Apple Lossless Decoder (adec/alac) An AudioCodec that decodes
Apple Lossless into linear PCM data
     [java] Apple IMA4 Decoder (adec/ima4) An AudioCodec that decodes IMA4
into linear PCM data
     [java] MPEG-4 AAC Encoder (aenc/aac ) An AudioCodec that encodes linear
PCM data into MPEG-4 AAC
     [java] Apple Lossless Encoder (aenc/alac) An AudioCodec that encodes
linear PCM data into Apple Lossless
     [java] Apple IMA4 Encoder (aenc/ima4) An AudioCodec that encodes linear
PCM data into IMA4
```

```
[java] Applet (aplt/scpt) The component that runs script applications
[java] Apple: AUConverter (aufc/conv) AudioConverter unit
[java] Apple: AUVarispeed (aufc/vari) Apple's varispeed playback
[...]
```

What just happened?

The key is the line that gets a ComponentDescriptor via a no-arg constructor. This creates a completely blank template for ComponentIdentifier.
find() to run against. Of course, if you just wanted to tour components of a
specific type, you could pass in a type constant such as StdQTConstants.
movieImportType, which would limit the search to MovieImporters, and
thus indicate what kinds of formats QuickTime can import.

Documenting and explaining every kind of component is beyond the
scope of this book—in fact, it filled up a whole volume of the old *Inside
Macintosh* series. Still, a few of the important ones are listed in
Table 4-1. Note that not all components have (or need) a Java wrapper
class.

Yep, "eat" and
"spit" for movie
importers and
exporters. Hardy
har har.

Table 4-1. Some important QuickTime for Java components

Type	Java wrapper class	Sample subtypes
"eat "	MovieImporter	"AVI", "AIFF", "MP3", "SWF"
"spit "	MovieExporter	"VfW", "MooV", "mpg4"
"grip"	GraphicsImporter	"BMP", "GIF", "JPEG"
"grex"	GraphicsExporter	"BMP", "JPEG"
"clok"	Clock (provides timing and callback services)	"tick", "micr"
"mhlr"	MediaHandler	"vide", "soun", "text"
"imco"	None; image compres-sor (used for still images and video)	"jpeg", "mp4v", "h263"
"imdc"	None; image decom-pressor (used for still images and video)	"jpeg", "mp4v", "h263"
"rtpm"	None; real-time pack-etizer (used for streaming)	"263+", "mpeg", "mp4a", "mp4v"

It's important to remember that all types and subtypes are FOUR_CHAR_
CODEs—any type or subtype seemingly shorter than that is padded with
space characters.

Working with QuickDraw

And now, on to the oldest, cruftiest, yet can't-live-without-it-iest part of QTJ: QuickDraw. QuickDraw is a graphics API that can be traced all the way back to that first Mac Steve Jobs pulled out of a bag and showed the press more than 20 years ago. You know—back when Mac supported all of two colors: black and white.

Don't worry; it's gotten a lot better since then.

To be fair, a native Mac OS X application being written today from scratch probably would use the shiny new "Quartz 2D" API. And as a Java developer, the included Java 2D API is at least as capable as QuickDraw, with extension packages like Java Advanced Imaging (JAI) only making things better.

The real advantage to understanding QuickDraw is that it's what's used to work with captured images (see Chapter 6) and individual video samples (see Chapter 8). It is also a reasonably capable graphics API in its own right, supporting import from and export to many formats (most of which J2SE lacked until 1.4), affine transformations, compositing, and more.

Getting and Saving Picts

If you had a Mac before Mac OS X, you probably are very familiar with *picts*, because they were the native graphics file format on the old Mac OS. Taking screenshots would create pict files, as would saving your work in graphics applications. Developers used pict resources in their applications to provide graphics, splash screens, etc.

Actually, a number of tightly coupled concepts relate to picts. The native structure for working with a series of drawing commands is called a Picture actually. This struct, along with the functions that use it, are wrapped by the QTJ class `quicktime.qd.Pict`. There's also a file format for storing picts, which can contain either drawing commands or bit-mapped images—files in this format usually have a *.pct* or *.pict* extension. QTJ's `Pict` class has methods to read and write these files, and because it's easy to create `Pict`s from `Movies`, `Tracks`, `GraphicsImporters`, `SequenceGrabbers` (capture devices), etc., it's a very useful class.

How do I do that?

The `PictTour.java` application, shown in Example 5-1, exercises the basics of getting, saving, and loading `Pict`s.

Example 5-1. Opening and saving Picts

```java
package com.oreilly.qtjnotebook.ch05;

import quicktime.*;
import quicktime.app.view.*;
import quicktime.std.*;
import quicktime.std.image.*;
import quicktime.io.*;
import quicktime.qd.*;

import java.awt.*;
import java.io.*;
import com.oreilly.qtjnotebook.ch01.QTSessionCheck;

public class PictTour extends Object {

    static final int[] imagetypes =
        { StdQTConstants.kQTFileTypeQuickTimeImage};

    static int frameX = -1;
    static int frameY = -1;

    public static void main (String[] args) {
        try {
            QTSessionCheck.check();

            // import a graphic
            QTSessionCheck.check();
            QTFile inFile = QTFile.standardGetFilePreview (imagetypes);
            GraphicsImporter importer =
                new GraphicsImporter (inFile);
            showFrameForImporter (importer,
                                  "Original Import");
            // get a pict object and then save it
            // then load again and show
            Pict pict = importer.getAsPicture();
            String absPictPath = (new File ("pict.pict")).getAbsolutePath();
            File pictFile = new File (absPictPath);
```

Example 5-1. Opening and saving Picts (continued)

```
            if (pictFile.exists())
                pictFile.delete();
            try { Thread.sleep (1000); } catch (InterruptedException ie) {}
            pict.writeToFile (pictFile);
            QTFile pictQTFile = new QTFile (pictFile);
            GraphicsImporter pictImporter =
                new GraphicsImporter (pictQTFile);
            showFrameForImporter (pictImporter,
                                  "pict.pict");
            // write to a pict file from importer
            // then load and show it
            String absGIPictPath = (new File ("gipict.pict")).getAbsolutePath();
            QTFile giPictQTFile = new QTFile (absGIPictPath);
            if (giPictQTFile.exists())
                giPictQTFile.delete();
            try { Thread.sleep (1000); } catch (InterruptedException ie) {}
            importer.saveAsPicture (giPictQTFile,
                                    IOConstants.smSystemScript);
            GraphicsImporter giPictImporter =
                new GraphicsImporter (giPictQTFile);
            showFrameForImporter (giPictImporter,
                                  "gipict.pict");
        } catch (Exception e) {
            e.printStackTrace();
        }
    }

    public static void showFrameForImporter (GraphicsImporter gi,
                                             String frameTitle)
        throws QTException {
        QTComponent qtc = QTFactory.makeQTComponent (gi);
        Component c = qtc.asComponent();
        Frame f = new Frame (frameTitle);
        f.add (c);
        f.pack();
        if (frameX == -1) {
            frameX = f.getLocation().x;
            frameY = f.getLocation().y;
        } else {
            Point location = new Point (frameX += 20,
                                        frameY += 20);
            f.setLocation (location);
        }

        f.setVisible (true);
    }
}
```

Compile and run this example with ant run-ch05-picttour from the downloadable book code.

When run, this example prompts the user for a graphics file, which then is displayed in three windows, as shown in Figure 5-1. These represent three different means of loading the pict.

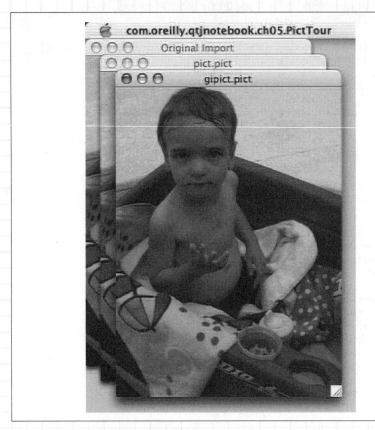

Figure 5-1. Writing and reading PICT files

What just happened?

You can get picts in a number of ways in QTJ. The first example here is to use a GraphicsImporter to load an image file in some arbitrary format, and then call getAsPicture( ) to get a Pict object. This is the easiest way to get a Pict from an arbitrary file—if you knew for sure that a given file was in the pict file format, you could use Pict.fromFile( ) instead, but that does not check to ensure the file really is a pict. So, the safe thing to do is to use a GraphicsImporter, let it figure out the format of the source file, and then convert to pict if necessary with getAsPicture( ).

Writing a pict file to disk is easy: just call writeToFile( ).

TIP

Curiously, this takes a java.io.File, not a QTFile, like so many other I/O routines in QTJ.

You also can write a Pict to disk by using the GraphicsImporter's saveAsPicture( ) method.

The example uses both of these methods to write pict files to disk—Pict. writeToFile( ) creates *pict.pict* and GraphicsImporter.saveAsPicture( ) creates *gipict.pict*. Each file is then reloaded with GraphicsImporters. Conveniently, a GraphicsImporter can be used with a QTFactory to create a QTComponent (see "Importing and Exporting Graphics" in Chapter 4), which is how the imported picts are shown on-screen.

Yes, it is kind of weird to use the "importer" for what is effectively an "export."

What about...

...other ways to get pictures? Look at the Pict class and you'll see several static fromXXX( ) methods that provide Picts from GraphicsImporters, GraphicsExporters, Movies, Tracks, and other QTJ classes.

Also, why does this example go through the hassle of creating absolute path strings and passing those to the QTFile constructor? It's a workaround to an apparent bug in QTJ for Windows: when you use a relative path (like Pict.writeToFile (new File("MyPict.pict"))), QTJ sometimes writes the file not to the current directory, but rather to the last directory it accessed. In this case, that means the directory it read the source image from. Specifying absolute paths works around this problem.

Getting a Pict from a Movie

If you're working with movies, you'll probably want to be able to get a pict from some arbitrary time in the movie. You could use this for identifying movies via thumbnail icons, identifying segments on a timeline GUI, etc. This action is so common, and it's really easy.

To grab a movie at a certain time, you just need a one-line call to Movie.getPict( ), as exercised by the dumpToPict( ) method shown here:

Notice I don't say
"grab the current
movie frame"
because the movie
could have other
on-screen
elements like text,
sprites, other
movies, etc., not
just one frame of
one video track.

```
public void dumpToPict () {
    try {
        float oldRate = movie.getRate( );
        movie.stop( );
        Pict pict = movie.getPict(movie.getTime( ));
        String absPictPath =
            (new File ("movie.pict")).getAbsolutePath( );
        pict.writeToFile (new File (absPictPath));
        movie.setRate (oldRate);
    } catch (Exception e) {
        e.printStackTrace( );
    }
}
```

This method stops the movie if it's playing and stores the previous play rate. Then it creates a Pict on the movie's current time and saves it to a file called *movie.pict*. Then it restarts the movie.

The download-
able book code
exercises this in a
demo called
PictFromMovie.
Run it with ant
run-ch05-
pictfrommovie.

What about...

...not stopping the movie? I haven't had good results with this call unless the movie is stopped. At best, it makes the playback choppy for a few seconds; at worst, it crashes.

Converting a Movie Image to a Java Image

It's possible you'll want to grab the current display of the movie and get it into a java.awt.Image. A convenient method call has been provided for just this task; unfortunately, it doesn't work very well, so a Pict-based workaround is needed.

How do I do that?

Makes sense,
doesn't it? The
MoviePlayer needs
to generate AWT
images for the
lightweight
QTJComponent,
so that's what you
get an ImagePro-
ducer from.

QTJ provides QTImageProducer, an implementation of the AWT ImageProducer interface. ImageProducer dates back to Java 1.0, and was designed to handle latency and unreliability when loading images over the network—issues that are irrelevant in typical desktop cases.

The most straightforward way to get an image from a movie is to get a QTImageProducer from a MoviePlayer, the object typically used to create a lightweight, Swing-ready QTJComponent. The ConvertToImageBad application in Example 5-2 demonstrates this approach.

Example 5-2. Using MoviePlayer's QTImageProducer

```
package com.oreilly.qtjnotebook.ch05;

import com.oreilly.qtjnotebook.ch01.QTSessionCheck;

import java.awt.*;
import java.awt.event.*;
import javax.swing.*;
import quicktime.*;
import quicktime.app.view.*;
import quicktime.io.*;
import quicktime.qd.*;
import quicktime.std.*;
import quicktime.std.clocks.*;
import quicktime.std.movies.*;

public class ConvertToJavaImageBad extends Frame
    implements ActionListener {

    Movie movie;
    MoviePlayer player;
    MovieController controller;
    QTComponent qtc;
    static int nextFrameX, nextFrameY;
    QTImageProducer ip;

    public static void main (String[] args) {
        ConvertToJavaImageBad ctji = new ConvertToJavaImageBad();
        ctji.pack();
        ctji.setVisible(true);
        Rectangle ctjiBounds = ctji.getBounds();
        nextFrameX = ctjiBounds.x + ctjiBounds.width;
        nextFrameY = ctjiBounds.y + ctjiBounds.height;
    }

    public ConvertToJavaImageBad() {
        super ("QuickTime Movie");
        try {
            // get movie
            QTSessionCheck.check();
            QTFile file =
                QTFile.standardGetFilePreview (QTFile.kStandardQTFileTypes);
            OpenMovieFile omFile = OpenMovieFile.asRead(file);
            movie = Movie.fromFile(omFile);
            player = new MoviePlayer (movie);
            controller = new MovieController (movie);
            // build gui
            qtc = QTFactory.makeQTComponent (controller);
            Component c = qtc.asComponent();
            setLayout (new BorderLayout());
            add (c, BorderLayout.CENTER);
            Button imageButton = new Button ("Make Java Image");
            add (imageButton, BorderLayout.SOUTH);
            imageButton.addActionListener (this);
```

Example 5-2. Using MoviePlayer's QTImageProducer (continued)

```
                        movie.start();
                        // set up close-to-quit
                        addWindowListener (new WindowAdapter() {
                                public void windowClosing (WindowEvent we) {
                                    System.exit(0);
                                }
                        });
                } catch (QTException qte) {
                    qte.printStackTrace();
                }
        }


        public void actionPerformed (ActionEvent e) {
            grabMovieImage();
        }

        public void grabMovieImage() {
            try {
                // lazy instantiation of ImageProducer
                if (ip == null) {
                    QDRect bounds = movie.getBounds();
                    Dimension dimBounds =
                        new Dimension (bounds.getWidth(), bounds.getHeight());
                    ip = new QTImageProducer (player, dimBounds);
                }

                // stop movie to take picture
                boolean wasPlaying = false;
                if (movie.getRate() > 0) {
                    movie.stop();
                    wasPlaying = true;
                }

                // convert from MoviePlayer to java.awt.Image
                Image image = Toolkit.getDefaultToolkit().createImage (ip);
                // make a swing icon out of it and show it in a frame
                ImageIcon icon = new ImageIcon (image);
                JLabel label = new JLabel (icon);
                JFrame frame = new JFrame ("Java image");
                frame.getContentPane().add(label);
                frame.pack();
                frame.setLocation (nextFrameX += 10,
                                   nextFrameY += 10);
                frame.setVisible(true);
                // restart movie
                if (wasPlaying)
                    movie.start();
            } catch (QTException qte) {
                qte.printStackTrace();
            }
        }
}
```

Run this example, if you dare, with ant run-ch05-converttojava-imagebad.

This application is shown in Figure 5-2. When you click the Make Java Image button, the movie is stopped, an AWT Image of the current display is made, and that Image is opened in another window.

Figure 5-2. Converting movie to Java AWT Image

WARNING

This is a *negative* example. Keep reading for why you don't want to use this code, and for a superior alternative.

What just happened?

The grabMovieImage( ) method creates a QTImageProducer from the MoviePlayer and hands it to the AWT Toolkit method createImage( ). This call returns an AWT Image that (because it's a nice, clean, one-line call) is stuffed into a Swing ImageIcon and put on-screen.

This is more of a "what the heck" than a "what just happened." If your results are anything like mine, you're probably wondering why the movie stopped the first time you snapped a picture, even though the sound continued. Or why, for that matter, subsequent pictures seem to be later in the movie, meaning the decompression and decoding of the video is still working, but that it's just not getting to the screen.

A Better Movie-to-Java Image Converter

The code shown in "Converting a Movie Image to a Java Image" is error-prone and nasty. On the other hand, a QTImageProducer is available from the GraphicsImporterDrawer. It does not have to work with a moving target like the MoviePlayer does. If only you could use that one instead....

How do I do that?

The example program ConvertToJavaImageBetter has a different implementation of the grabMovieImage( ) method, as shown in Example 5-3.

Example 5-3. In-memory pict import to use GraphicsImporterDrawer's QTImageProducer

```
public void grabMovieImage( ) {
    try {
        // stop movie to take picture
        boolean wasPlaying = false;
        if (movie.getRate( ) > 0) {
            movie.stop( );
            wasPlaying = true;
        }

        // take a pict
        Pict pict = movie.getPict (movie.getTime( ));

        // add 512-byte header that pict would have as file
        byte[ ] newPictBytes =
            new byte [pict.getSize( ) + 512];
        pict.copyToArray (0,
                          newPictBytes,
                          512,
                          newPictBytes.length - 512);
        pict = new Pict (newPictBytes);

        // export it
        DataRef ref = new DataRef (pict,
                          StdQTConstants.kDataRefQTFileTypeTag,
                          "PICT");
        gi.setDataReference (ref);
```

Example 5-3. In-memory pict import to use GraphicsImporterDrawer's
QTImageProducer (continued)

```
            QDRect rect = gi.getSourceRect ();
            Dimension dim = new Dimension (rect.getWidth(),
                                           rect.getHeight());
            QTImageProducer ip = new QTImageProducer (gid, dim);

            // convert from MoviePlayer to java.awt.Image
            Image image = Toolkit.getDefaultToolkit().createImage (ip);
            // make a swing icon out of it and show it in a frame
            ImageIcon icon = new ImageIcon (image);
            JLabel label = new JLabel (icon);
            JFrame frame = new JFrame ("Java image");
            frame.getContentPane().add(label);
            frame.pack();
            frame.setLocation (nextFrameX += 10,
                               nextFrameY += 10);
            frame.setVisible(true);

            // restart movie
            if (wasPlaying)
                movie.start();
        } catch (QTException qte) {
            qte.printStackTrace();
        }
    }
```

*Run this example
with ant run-
ch05-convert-
tojava-
imagebetter.*

Try out this example and you should be able to create multiple AWT
Images without harming playback of the movie, as exhibited in
Figure 5-3.

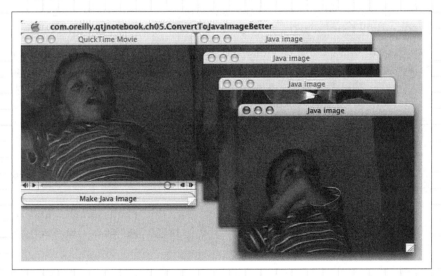

Figure 5-3. Converting movie to Java AWT image (a better way)

What just happened?

Note to self: pitch QuickTime for Java Hacks to O'Reilly!

This isn't a hack. It's close, though.

Once the movie is paused, the key is to get the movie's display into a GraphicsImporter. Once that's done, it's easy to get a QTImageProducer from a GraphicsImporterDrawer and an image from the AWT Toolkit.

The problem is getting the image into a GraphicsImporter. If you look at the Javadoc, you might see one way to connect the dots: get a Pict from the Movie, save that to disk, then turn around and import. It would look something like this:

```
Pict pict = movie.getPict (movie.getTime());
QTFile tempFile = new QTFile (new java.io.File ("temppict.pict"));
pict.writeToFile (tempFile);
GraphicsImporter importer = new GraphicsImporter (tempFile);
```

With the pict imported into a GraphicsImporter, you would get a QTImageProducer from the GraphicsImporterDrawer and generate AWT Images from the image producer, without messing up the movie playback.

The drawback of this approach is that you must read and write data to the hard drive, which is obviously much slower than an operation that takes place purely in memory.

In fact, an in-memory equivalent is possible. Look back at the GraphicsImporter Javadoc. Several setData() methods allow you to use sources other than just flat files for input to a GraphicsImporter. Two of them allow you to pass in more or less opaque pointers: setDataReference() and setDataHandle(). With these calls, the importer will read from memory the same way it would read from disk.

And they say Java doesn't have pointers!

The trick in this case is to make the GraphicsImporter think it's reading a *pict* file from disk, but actually it's reading from memory. One gotcha in this case is that pict files have a 512-byte header before their data—the header doesn't have to contain anything meaningful, it just has to be present. So, allocate a byte array 512 bytes longer than the size of the Pict data (getSize() and getBytes(), inherited from QTHandleRef, respectively, return the size and contents of the native structure pointed to by the Pict object, not the Java object itself), and copy those bytes over with an offset of 512.

Next, you need a GraphicsImporter for the Pict format, and a GraphicsImporterDrawer to provide the QTImageProducer. The example code creates these in its constructor:

```
// set up graphicsimporter
gi = new GraphicsImporter (StdQTConstants.kQTFileTypePicture);
gid = new GraphicsImporterDrawer (gi);
```

Build a `DataRef` to point to the byte array and pass it to the `GraphicsImporter` with `setDataReference( )`. You've now replaced the file write and file read with equivalent in-memory operations. Now it's a simple matter of getting a `GraphicsImporterDrawer` and, from that, a `QTImageProducer` to create Java images.

TIP

This technique is adapted from "Technical Q&A QTMTB56: Importing Image Data from Memory," at *http://developer.apple.com/qa/ qtmtb/qtmtb56.html*. Check it out for a comparison of QTJ versus straight-C QuickTime coding styles.

Drawing with Graphics Primitives

In AWT, a `Graphics` object represents a drawing surface—either on-screen or off-screen—and supplies various methods for drawing on it. QuickTime has a `GWorld` object that's so similar, the QT developers renamed it `QDGraphics` just to make Java developers feel at home. As with the AWT class, painting is driven by a callback mentality.

How do I do that?

Example 5-4 shows the `GWorldToPict` example, which creates a `QDGraphics` object and performs some simple drawing operations.

Example 5-4. Drawing on a QDGraphics object

```
package com.oreilly.qtjnotebook.ch05;

import quicktime.*;
import quicktime.std.*;
import quicktime.std.image.*;
import quicktime.qd.*;

import com.oreilly.qtjnotebook.ch01.QTSessionCheck;

public class GWorldToPict extends Object implements QDDrawer {

    public static void main (String[ ] args) {
        new GWorldToPict( );
    }

    public GWorldToPict( ) {
        try {
```

Example 5-4. Drawing on a QDGraphics object (continued)

```
            QTSessionCheck.check( );
            QDRect bounds = new QDRect (0, 0, 200, 250);
            ImageDescription imgDesc =
                new ImageDescription(QDConstants.k32RGBAPixelFormat);
            imgDesc.setHeight (bounds.getHeight( ));
            imgDesc.setWidth (bounds.getWidth( ));
            QDGraphics gw = new QDGraphics (imgDesc, 0);
            System.out.println ("GWorld created: " + gw);

            OpenCPicParams params = new OpenCPicParams(bounds);

            Pict pict = Pict.open (gw, params);
            gw.beginDraw (this);

            pict.close( );

            try {
                pict.writeToFile (new java.io.File ("gworld.pict"));
            } catch (java.io.IOException ioe) {
                ioe.printStackTrace( );
            }
        } catch (QTException qte) {
            qte.printStackTrace( );
        }
        System.exit(0);
    }

    public void draw (QDGraphics gw) throws QTException {
        System.out.println ("draw( ) called with GWorld " + gw);
        QDRect bounds = gw.getBounds( );
        System.out.println ("bounds: " + bounds);
        // clear drawing surface, set up colors
        gw.setBackColor (QDColor.lightGray);
        gw.eraseRect (bounds);
        // draw some shapes
        gw.penSize (2, 2);
        gw.moveTo (20,20);
        gw.setForeColor (QDColor.green);
        gw.line (30, 100);
        gw.moveTo (20,20);
        gw.setForeColor (QDColor.blue);
        gw.lineTo (30, 100);

        // draw some text
        gw.setForeColor (QDColor.red);
        gw.textSize (24);
        gw.moveTo (10, 150);
        gw.drawText ("QDGraphics", 0, 10);

        // draw some shapes
        gw.setForeColor (QDColor.magenta);
        QDRect rect = new QDRect (0, 170, 40, 30);
```

Example 5-4. Drawing on a QDGraphics object (continued)

```
        gw.paintRoundRect (rect, 0, 0);
        QDRect roundRect = new QDRect (50, 170, 40, 30);
        gw.paintRoundRect (roundRect, 10, 10);
        QDRect ovalRect = new QDRect (100, 170, 40, 30);
        gw.paintOval (ovalRect);
        QDRect arcRect = new QDRect (150, 170, 40, 30);
        gw.paintArc (arcRect, 15, 215);
    }
}
```

This is a headless application. When run, it does its imaging off-screen and writes the file to *gworld.pict*. Open this file in a pict-aware editor or viewer to see the output, as shown in Figure 5-4.

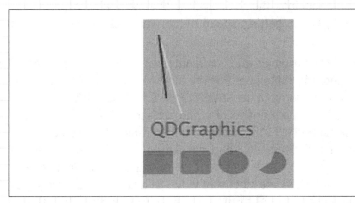

Figure 5-4. Graphics primitives drawn with QDGraphics

What just happened?

The program sets up an ImageDescription, specifying a color model and size information, and creates a QDGraphics drawing surface according to its specs. Next, a new Pict is created from the QDGraphics and an object called OpenCPicParams, which provides size and resolution information. For on-screen work, the default 72dpi is fine.

Next, it issues a Pict.beginDraw( ) command, passing in a QDDrawer object. QDDrawer is an interface for setting up callbacks to a draw( ) method that specifies the QDGraphics to be drawn on. This redraw-oriented API is kind of overkill for this headless, off-screen example, but it does get the job done. The Pict records the drawing commands made in the draw( ) call and saves the result to disk as *gworld.pict*.

So, what can you do with QDGraphics primitives? Some basics of geometry are shown in this example. QDGraphics work with a system of foreground and background colors, a pen of some number of horizontal and vertical pixels, and a concept of a current position. This example begins with two variants of line drawing: the first drawing a line specified by an offset in horizontal and vertical pixels, and the second drawing a line to a specific point. Next, it draws some text in the default font—note that as with AWT, the text will go above the current point. Finally, the example iterates through some of the simpler shapes available as graphics primitives: ovals, optionally rounded rectangles, and arcs.

What about...

...drawing an image into the QDGraphics, like with AWT's Graphics.drawImage( )? Ah, you're getting ahead of me. That will be covered later in the chapter.

Also, why are all the variables and comments here GWorld and gw instead of QDGraphics and qdg? Like I said at the start of this lab, QDGraphics is something of an analogy to an AWT Graphics. Unfortunately, it's a flawed analogy. It wraps a native drawing surface called a GWorld, and all the calls throughout QTJ that take or return it use the "GWorld" verbiage, such as the setGWorld( ) and getGWorld( ) calls that you'll see throughout the Javadoc. Once you start getting into QTJ, the desire to understand it from QuickTime's point of view, as a GWorld, outweighs the benefits of making an appeal to the AWT Graphics analogy. So, to me, it's a GWorld.

Getting a Screen Capture

One frequently useful source of image data is, unsurprisingly, the screen—or screens, if you're so fortunate. Each screen is represented by an object that can give you its current contents, though it takes a little work to do anything with it.

I use PNG for screenshots because it's lossless, widely supported, compressed, and patent-unencumbered.

How do I do that?

ScreenToPNG, shown in Example 5-5, is a headless application that starts up, grabs the screen, and writes out the image to a PNG file called *screen.png*.

Example 5-5. Grabbing screen pixels

```
package com.oreilly.qtjnotebook.ch05;

import quicktime.*;
import quicktime.std.*;
import quicktime.std.image.*;
import quicktime.qd.*;
import quicktime.io.*;
import quicktime.util.*;

import com.oreilly.qtjnotebook.ch01.QTSessionCheck;

public class ScreenToPNG extends Object  {

    public static void main (String[ ] args) {
        new ScreenToPNG( );
    }

    public ScreenToPNG( ) {
        try {
            QTSessionCheck.check( );

            GDevice gd = GDevice.getMain( );
            System.out.println ("Got GDevice: " + gd);
            PixMap pm = gd.getPixMap( );
            System.out.println ("Got PixMap: " + pm);
            ImageDescription id = new ImageDescription (pm);
            System.out.println ("Got ImageDescription: " + id);
            QDRect bounds = pm.getBounds( );
            RawEncodedImage rei = pm.getPixelData( );

            QDGraphics decompGW = new QDGraphics (id, 0);
            QTImage.decompress (rei,
                                id,
                                decompGW,
                                bounds,
                                0);

            GraphicsExporter exporter =
                new GraphicsExporter (StdQTConstants4.kQTFileTypePNG);
            exporter.setInputPixmap (decompGW);
            QTFile outFile = new QTFile (new java.io.File ("screen.png"));
            exporter.setOutputFile (outFile);
            System.out.println ("Exported " +
                                exporter.doExport( ) +
                                " bytes");

        } catch (QTException qte) {
            qte.printStackTrace( );
        }
        System.exit(0);
    }
}
```

Run this example with ant run-ch05-screentopng.

When finished, open the *screen.png* file with your favorite image editor or browser. A shot of my iBook's screen while writing the demo is shown in Figure 5-5.

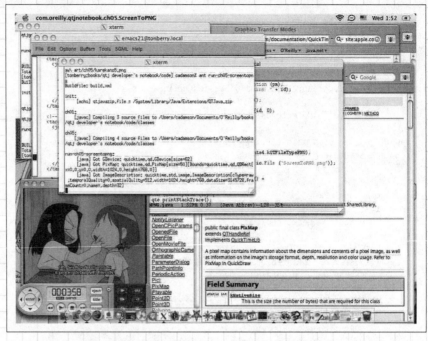

Figure 5-5. Screen capture

Notice at the bottom left that I have the DVD Player application running. Apple's tools for doing screen grabs—the Grab application and the Cmd-Shift-3 and Cmd-Shift-4 key combinations—won't work if you have the DVD Player running. However, this proves that those pixels are available to QuickDraw. That said, if you grab the screen while a DVD is playing, you might get *tearing* (if the capture grabs between frames) or even a blank panel (if the capture catches the repaint at a bad time). If you're going to use this to grab images from DVDs, hit Pause first.

Also, don't do anything with a DVD that will get you or me sued.

What just happened?

The program asks for the main screen by means of the static GDevice. getMain( ) method. From this, you can get a PixMap, which is an object that represents metadata about a stored image, such as its color table, pixel format, packing scheme, etc. This metadata also can be stored as an ImageDescription, which is a structure that many graphics methods take as a parameter. The PixMap also has a pointer to the byte array that holds the image data, which you can retrieve as the wrapper object RawEncodedImage.

So now you have an image of what's on the screen—what can you do with it? The goal is to get that image into a format suitable for a GraphicsExporter. One means of doing this is to render into a QDGraphics and send that to the exporter. To do this, look to the QTImage class, which has methods to compress (from a QDGraphics drawing surface to an EncodedImage) and decompress (from a possibly compressed EncodedImage to a QDGraphics). In this case, use decompress() to make a QDGraphics, then pass that to the exporter's setInputPixMap() method (yes, despite the name, it takes a QDGraphics, not a PixMap) and do the export.

Java 2D analogy: a PixMap is like a Raster, an ImageDescription is like a Sample-Model, and an EncodedImage is like a DataBuffer. Not exactly the same, but the same ideas throughout.

TIP

It's odd that EncodedImage is an interface, yet its relevant methods, like decompress(), are static in QTImage (which is in another package!). Maybe EncodedImage should have been an abstract class?

Why, oh why, are these methods named like this?

What about...

...getting other screens? If you do have multiple monitors, GDevice has a scheme for iterating through the screens. Call the static GDevice.getList() to get—wait for it—not a list of GDevices, but just the first one. You then call its instance method getNext() to return another GDevice, and so on, until getNext() returns null.

And why is the PNG file-type constant defined in StdQTConstants4? PNG came late to the QuickTime party and wasn't supported until QuickTime 4. The later constants classes (StdQTContants4, StdQTContants5, and StdQTContants6) define constants that were added in later versions of QuickTime. kQTFileTypeTIFF is also in StdQTConstants4, but most other values you'd want to use are in the original StdQTConstants.

Also, it's getting difficult to remember the various means of converting between EncodedImages, Picts, QDGraphics, etc. To keep track of all this for myself, I created the diagram in Figure 5-6 while writing this chapter and have found myself consulting it frequently since then.

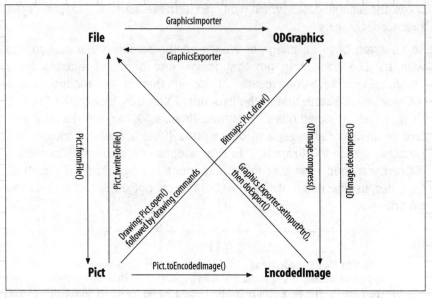

Figure 5-6. Converting between QuickDraw objects

Matrix-Based Drawing

Primitives and copying blocks of pixels are nice, but they're kind of limiting. Oftentimes, you must take pixels and scale them, rotate them, and move them around. Of course, if you've worked with Java 2D, you know this as the concept of *affine transformations*, which maps one set of pixels to another set of pixels, keeping straight lines straight and parallel lines parallel.

If you've really worked with Java 2D's affine transformations, you probably know that they're represented as a linear algebra matrix, with coordinates mapped from source to destination by multiplying and/or adding pixel values against coefficients of the matrix. By changing the coefficients in the matrix to interesting values (or trigonometric functions), you can define different kinds of transformations.

QuickTime does exactly the same thing, with the minor exception that rather than hiding the matrix in a wrapper (like J2D's `AffineTransformation` class), it puts the matrix front-and-center throughout the API. One reason for this is that it's also a major part of the file format—tracks in a movie all have a matrix in their metadata to determine how they're rendered at runtime.

QuickTime matrix manipulation can basically do three things for you:

Translation
Move a block of pixels from one location to another

Rotation
Rotate pixels around a given point

Scaling
Make block bigger or smaller, or change its shape

TIP

This is a lab, not a lecture, so you don't get the all-singing, all-dancing, all-algebra introduction to matrix theory here. If you must have this, Apple provides a pretty straightforward intro in "The Transformation Matrix," part of the "Introductions to QuickTime" documentation anthology on its web site.

How do I do that?

The example `GraphicImportMatrix` shows the effect of setting up a Matrix and then using it for drawing operations. A full listing is in Example 5-6.

Example 5-6. Drawing with matrix-based transformations

```
package com.oreilly.qtjnotebook.ch05;

import quicktime.*;
import quicktime.std.*;
import quicktime.std.image.*;
import quicktime.qd.*;
import quicktime.io.*;
import quicktime.util.*;
import quicktime.app.view.*;
import java.io.*;
import java.awt.*;

import com.oreilly.qtjnotebook.ch01.QTSessionCheck;

public class GraphicImportMatrix extends Object {

    public static void main (String[] args) {
        try {
            QTSessionCheck.check();

            File graphicsDir = new File ("graphics");
            QTFile pngFile1 = new QTFile (new File (graphicsDir, "1.png"));
            QTFile pngFile2 = new QTFile (new File (graphicsDir, "2.png"));
            GraphicsImporter gi1 = new GraphicsImporter (pngFile1);
```

Example 5-6. Drawing with matrix-based transformations (continued)

```
GraphicsImporter gi2 = new GraphicsImporter (pngFile2);

// define some matrix transforms on importer 1
QDRect bounds = gi1.getBoundsRect();
// combine translation (movement) and scaling into
// one call to rect
QDRect newBounds =
    new QDRect (bounds.getWidth()/4,
                bounds.getHeight()/4,
                bounds.getWidth()/2,
                bounds.getHeight()/2);
Matrix matrix = new Matrix();
matrix.rect(bounds, newBounds);
// rotate about its center
matrix.rotate (30,
               (bounds.getWidth() - bounds.getX())/2,
               (bounds.getHeight() - bounds.getY())/2);
gi1.setMatrix (matrix);

// draw somewhere
QDGraphics scratchWorld = new QDGraphics (gi2.getBoundsRect());
System.out.println ("Scratch world: " + scratchWorld);
// draw background
gi2.setGWorld (scratchWorld, null);
gi2.draw();
// draw foreground
gi1.setGWorld (scratchWorld, null);
gi1.draw();

int bufSize =
    QTImage.getMaxCompressionSize (scratchWorld,
                                   scratchWorld.getBounds(),
                                   0,
                                   StdQTConstants.codecNormalQuality,
                                   StdQTConstants4.kPNGCodecType,
                                   CodecComponent.anyCodec);
byte[] compBytes = new byte[bufSize];
RawEncodedImage compImg = new RawEncodedImage (compBytes);
ImageDescription id =
    QTImage.compress(scratchWorld,
                     scratchWorld.getBounds(),
                     StdQTConstants.codecNormalQuality,
                     StdQTConstants4.kPNGCodecType,
                     compImg);
System.out.println ("rei compressed from gw is " +
                     compImg.getSize());

System.out.println ("exporting");
GraphicsExporter exporter =
    new GraphicsExporter (StdQTConstants4.kQTFileTypePNG);
exporter.setInputPtr (compImg, id);
QTFile outFile = new QTFile (new File ("matrix.png"));
```

Example 5-6. Drawing with matrix-based transformations (continued)

Run this example with ant run-ch05-graphic-importmatrix.

```
        exporter.setOutputFile (outFile);
        exporter.doExport();
        System.out.println ("did export");

    } catch (QTException qte) {
        qte.printStackTrace();
    }
    System.exit(0);
  }
}
```

This headless app begins by importing two PNG files, the number *1* on a green background and the number *2* on cyan. Then it creates a GWorld (oops, I mean a QDGraphics—sorry!) big enough to hold the *2* image, which will serve as the background. Both GraphicsImporters call setGWorld() with the scratchWorld, which allows them to draw() into it. A Matrix defines a scale, translate, and rotate transformation for the *1*, which is drawn atop the *2*. The result is compressed as a PNG and saved as *matrix.png*, which is shown in Figure 5-7.

Figure 5-7. Drawing with a Matrix

What just happened?

Using setMatrix() with a GraphicsImporter allows you to tell the importer to use the transformation specified by the Matrix when you call the importer's draw() method. Of the three typical transformations, two can be combined into one call—scaling and translating can be expressed with a single call, Matrix.rect(), which defines a mapping from one source rectangle to a target rectangle. In the example, rect() maps from the full size of the image to a quarter-size image, centered horizontally and vertically.

TIP

The same thing can be done with separate calls to Matrix.
translate( ) and Matrix.scale( ), if you prefer.

The example also calls Matrix.rotate( ) to rotate the scaled and moved
box by 30 degrees clockwise.

TIP

You also can define matrix transformations by calling the various
setXXX( ) methods that set individual coordinates in the Matrix, if
you've read Apple's Matrix docs and understand each coefficient.
But why bother when you've got the convenience calls?

Having set this Matrix on *1*'s GraphicsImporter, the example draws *2*
into scratchWorld as a background, and then draws *1* on top of it,
scaled, translated, and rotated.

But what to do with the pixels that have been drawn into the
QDGraphics? It's not like the "Drawing with Graphics Primitives" lab, in
which a QDGraphics was wrapped by a Pict that could be saved off to
disk. Instead, use QTImage to create an EncodedImage from the drawing
surface. In the "Getting a Screen Capture" lab, QTImage.decompress( )
converted an image to a QDGraphics. In this case, QTImage.compress( )
can return the favor by compressing the possibly huge pixel map into a
compressed format.

Compressing is harder than decompressing. You need to know up front
how big of a byte array will be needed to hold the compressed bytes, so
first you call getMaxCompressionSize( ). This takes six parameters:

- A QDGraphics to compress from.

- A QDRect defining the region to be compressed.

- Color depth, as an int. Set this to 0 to let QuickTime decide.

- Codec quality. These are in StdQTConstants. From the worst to best,
  they are: codecMinQuality, codecLowQuality, codecNormalQuality,
  codecHighQuality, codecMaxQuality, codecLosslessQuality. Note
  that not all codecs support all these values.

- Codec type. These constants are identified as XXXCodecType constants in the StdQTConstants classes.
- Codec identifier. If you have a CodecComponent object you want to use for the compression, pass it here. Typically, you pass null to let QuickTime decide.

Most of these parameters are used in the subsequent compress() call. It goes without saying that you need to use the same values for each call, or else getMaxCompressionSize() will lead you to create a byte array that is the wrong size.

Passing pointers again! This is one of those cases where QTJ is very un-Java-like.

Along with many of the preceding parameters, the compress() call takes a RawEncodedImage created from a suitably large byte array. compress() puts the compressed and encoded image data into the RawEncodedImage and returns an ImageDescription. Taken together, these are enough to provide an input to a GraphicsExporter, in the form of a call to setInputPtr().

Compositing Graphics

Matrix transformations are nice, but you can do more with image drawing. QuickDraw supports a number of *graphics modes* so that instead of just copying pixels from a source to a destination, you can combine them to create interesting visual effects. The graphics mode defines the combination: blending, translucency, etc.

How do I do that?

Specifying a graphics mode for drawing is trivial. Create a GraphicsMode object and call setGraphicsMode() on the GraphicsImporter. In the included example, *GraphicImportCompositing.java*, the mode is set with the following code:

```
// draw foreground
GraphicsMode alphaMode =
    new GraphicsMode (QDConstants.blend,
                      QDColor.green);
gi1.setGraphicsMode (alphaMode);
```

Run this with ant-ch05-graphic-importcompositing.

This is another headless app, producing the *composite.png* file as shown in Figure 5-8. Notice that where the images overlap, the *2* can now show through the *1*.

Figure 5-8. Drawing with blend graphics mode

What just happened?

The "blend" GraphicsMode instructs QuickDraw to average out colors where they overlap. In this case, *1*'s black pixels are lightened up by averaging when averaged with cyan, and the green is slightly tinted where it overlaps with cyan or black.

The QDColor.green is irrelevant in this case, but change the first argument to QDConstants.transparent and suddenly the result is very different, as shown in Figure 5-9.

Figure 5-9. Drawing with transparent graphics mode

A GraphicsMode takes a constant to specify behavior, and a color that is used by *some* of the available modes. In the case of transparent, any pixels of the specified color (green in this case) become invisible, allowing the background picture to show through.

Chapter 5: Working with QuickDraw

There are too many supported graphics mode values to list here, but some of the most useful are as follows:

srcCopy

Copies source to destination. This is the normal behavior.

transparent

Punches out specified color and lets background show through.

blend

Mixes foreground and background colors.

addPin

Adds foreground and background colors, up to a maximum value.

subPin

Calculates the difference between sum and destination colors, to a minimum value.

ditherCopy

Replaces destination with a dither mix of source and destination.

A complete list of values is provided in "Graphic Transfer Modes" on Apple's developer web site at *http://developer.apple.com/*.

CHAPTER 6

Capture

Much of this book has assumed you already had media of some kind to play and edit—but where does this media come from in the first place? Digital media has to come from one of two places: either it's completely synthetic or it's *captured* from a real-world source. Capture, via devices like microphones and video cameras, is far more common.

The problem is that capture doesn't officially work in QuickTime for Java. The problem dates back to Apple's Java 1.4.1 rearchitecture, which broke QTJ and forced massive changes to the API in QTJ 6.1. One of the things that was not updated for QTJ was the ability to get an on-screen component from a `SequenceGrabber`, which is the QuickTime capture component. Instead, Apple just put a statement in the QTJ 6.1 documentation:

> Although sequence grabbing is currently not supported in QuickTime for Java 1.4.1, it may be provided in future releases.

But if you think back to how the QTJ 6.1 situation was described in Chapter 1, you might recall that QTJ classes that didn't require working with AWT—such as the `quicktime.std` classes that simply wrapped straight-C calls—were unaffected by the Java 1.4.1 changes and still worked. Given that, notice in the Javadoc the package called `quicktime.std.sg`, which contains the `SequenceGrabber` class among several others. Besides, capture, per se, doesn't necessarily imply using the screen, so shouldn't it still work?

The good news is that it *does*. In this chapter, I'll introduce the parts of the capture API that still work in QTJ, even without official support: capturing audio, capturing to disk, and even getting captured video on screen with a little QuickDraw voodoo. QTJ still needs proper support for on-screen, video-capture preview, but there's plenty to do in the meantime.

Capturing and Previewing Audio

Audio capture is a good place to start because that sidesteps the problem of the broken video preview. There's plenty to be learned in just opening up the default microphone and looking at the incoming *level data*—that is, how loud or soft the incoming sound data is.

How do I do that?

Don't scoff—there really are text-capture devices. For example, you could capture the closed captions off regular TV (also called "line 21" data).

Setting up audio capture requires a number of steps. You start by constructing a SequenceGrabber. This object coordinates all the capture channels (audio, video...even text capture), and allows you to set capture parameters like whether to save the captured data to disk, set a maximum amount of time to let the capture run, etc.

Once you have the SequenceGrabber, you use an optional prepare( ) call to indicate whether you intend to preview the captured media, record it to disk, or both.

To work with sound, you need to create a sound channel, by calling the SGSoundChannel constructor and passing in the SequenceGrabber. This object allows you to configure the audio capture, choose among audio capture devices (see the next lab), and get the device's driver. The driver, exposed by the SPBDevice class, provides methods for checking the input line level.

As an example, compile and run the AudioCapturePreview application as shown in Example 6-1. Note that you need to have at least one audio capture device hooked up to your computer. Most Macs come with a built-in microphone. If you don't have one, you can use a USB capture device (like a headset or external microphone) or a FireWire device (like an iSight).

Example 6-1. Previewing captured audio

```
package com.oreilly.qtjnotebook.ch06;

import quicktime.*;
import quicktime.io.*;
import quicktime.std.*;
import quicktime.std.sg.*;
import quicktime.std.movies.*;
import quicktime.std.image.*;
import quicktime.qd.*;
import quicktime.sound.*;
import java.awt.*;
import java.awt.event.*;
import javax.swing.Timer;
import com.oreilly.qtjnotebook.ch01.QTSessionCheck;
```

Example 6-1. Previewing captured audio (continued)

```java
public class AudioCapturePreview extends Frame
    implements ItemListener {
    static final Dimension meterDim = new Dimension (200, 25);
    Checkbox previewCheck;
    AudioLevelMeter audioLevelMeter;
    SequenceGrabber grabber;
    SGSoundChannel soundChannel;
    SPBDevice inputDriver;
    boolean grabbing = true;
    public AudioCapturePreview( ) throws QTException {
        super ("Audio Preview");
        QTSessionCheck.check( );
        setLayout (new GridLayout (3, 1));
        add (new Panel( )); // reserved for next lab
        previewCheck = new Checkbox ("Preview", false);
        previewCheck.addItemListener (this);
        add (previewCheck);
        audioLevelMeter = new AudioLevelMeter( );
        add (audioLevelMeter);
        // 4th row is reserved for later lab
        setUpAudioGrab( );
        grabbing = true;
    }
    public void itemStateChanged (ItemEvent e) {
        try {
            if (e.getSource( ) == previewCheck) {
                if (previewCheck.getState( ))
                    soundChannel.setVolume (1.0f);
                else
                    soundChannel.setVolume (0.0f);
            }
        } catch (QTException qte) {
            qte.printStackTrace( );
        }
    }
    protected void setUpAudioGrab( ) throws QTException {
        grabber = new SequenceGrabber( );
        soundChannel = new SGSoundChannel (grabber);
        System.out.println ("Got SGAudioChannel");
        System.out.println ("SGChannelInfo = " +
                        soundChannel.getSoundInputParameters( ));
        System.out.println ("SoundDescription = " +
                        soundChannel.getSoundDescription( ));
        // prepare and start previewing
        grabber.prepare(true,false);
        soundChannel.setUsage (StdQTConstants.seqGrabPreview);
        soundChannel.setVolume (0.0f);
        grabber.startPreview( );
        inputDriver = soundChannel.getInputDriver( );
        inputDriver.setLevelMeterOnOff (true);
        int[ ] levelTest = inputDriver.getActiveLevels( );
        System.out.println (levelTest.length + " active levels");
```

Example 6-1. *Previewing captured audio (continued)*

```java
            // set up thread to update level meter
            ActionListener timerCallback =
                new ActionListener( ) {
                    public void actionPerformed(ActionEvent e) {
                        if (grabbing) {
                            try {
                                grabber.idle( );
                                audioLevelMeter.repaint( );
                            } catch (QTException qte) {
                                qte.printStackTrace( );
                            }
                        }
                    }
                };
            Timer timer = new Timer (50, timerCallback);
            timer.start( );
        }
        public static void main (String[ ] args) {
            try {
                Frame f = new AudioCapturePreview( );
                f.pack( );
                f.setVisible(true);
            } catch (QTException qte) {
                qte.printStackTrace( );
            }
        }
        public class AudioLevelMeter extends Canvas {
            public void paint (Graphics g) {
                // get current level if available
                int level = 0;
                if (inputDriver != null) {
                    try {
                        int[ ] levels = inputDriver.getActiveLevels( );
                        if (levels.length > 0)
                            level = levels[0];
                    } catch (QTException qte) {
                        qte.printStackTrace( );
                    }
                }
                float levelPercent = level / 256f;
                System.out.println (level + ", " + levelPercent);
                // draw box
                g.setColor (Color.green);
                g.fillRect (0, 0,
                            (int) (levelPercent * getWidth( )),
                            getHeight( ));
            }
            public Dimension getPreferredSize( ) { return meterDim; }
        }
    }
}
```

Compile and run this example from the book's downloadable code with ant run-ch06-audiocapture-preview.

When run, the application brings up a small window with a green bar that indicates the current level on the line, as seen in Figure 6-1. At maximum input volume—if you're speaking loudly and directly into the microphone—it will stretch all the way to the right of the window.

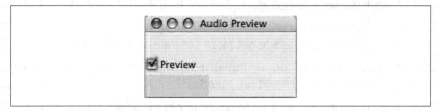

Figure 6-1. Audio capture preview window

There is also a Preview checkbox that is off initially. Clicking this will play the captured audio over the headset or speakers.

What just happened?

The constructor does some simple AWT business, adding the Preview checkbox and an AudioLevelMeter, which is an inner class that will be explained shortly. Then it calls setUpAudioGrab( ).

setUpAudioGrab( ) is responsible for initializing the audio capture. As described earlier, the first step is to create a new SequenceGrabber object. Next, tell the grabber what you intend to do with it, via the prepare( ) method, which takes two self-explanatory booleans: prepareForPreview and prepareForRecord.

TIP

You don't *have* to call prepare( ). If you don't, SequenceGrabber will take care of its setup when you start grabbing, possibly making the startup take longer.

You also need to tell the SGSoundChannel what you want to do via setUsage( ), inherited from SGChannel. As with all methods that take behavior flags, you logically OR together constants to describe your desired usage. In this case, seqGrabPreview indicates that the application is only previewing the captured sound, but you can use (and combine) four other usage constants:

seqGrabRecord
    Include this if you want to record the captured media to disk.

---

seqGrabPlayDuringRecord
    Add this to play while recording.

seqGrabLowLatencyCapture
    Used to get the freshest frame possible (used for video conferencing
    and live image processing).

seqGrabAlwaysUseTimeBase
    Used by video channels to get more accurate audio/video sync.

At this point, the capture is initialized. Begin capturing audio with
SequenceGrabber's startPreview( ) method.

*There may be
multiple levels in
the array, usually
two for stereo
input.*

To create the level meter, it's necessary to get an SPBDevice, which provides low-level access to the incoming data. This object provides level
meters as an array of ints by first enabling monitoring with
setLevelMeterOnOff(true) and then followed by getActiveLevels( ).
The returned ints range from 0 (silence), to 255 (maximum input volume). In the example, the AudioLevelMeter inner class gets the first level
on each repaint and draws a box whose width is proportional to the
audio level. A Swing Timer calls repaint( ) on the meter every 50 milliseconds to keep it up to date.

*SequenceGrabber.
idle( ) is a lot like
"tasking" back in
Chapter 2, except
there's no
convenience class
to do it for you.*

The repaint thread also calls idle( ) on the SequenceGrabber, which is
something you have to call as frequently as possible to give the
SequenceGrabber time to operate.

What about...

...defaulting the volume off with SoundChannel.setVolume( )? This is a
common practice because some users' speakers will be close enough to
their microphones to cause feedback when previewing the audio to the
speakers. On the other hand, users with headphones probably *do* want
to hear the preview. So, the best practice is "default off, but let the user
turn it on."

WARNING

One thing this demo lacks is a call to SequenceGrabber.stop( )
when the user quits. This is something you should usually do, but
I've left it out to make a point. On Mac OS X, if you don't stop the
SequenceGrabber and you leave the volume on, you will keep grabbing sound—feedback included—even after the application quits.
I've even seen this behavior survive a restart. So, try it out, don't
blow your speakers, and then remember to have your programs turn
off the volume and call SequenceGrabber.stop( ) when they quit.

Selecting Audio Inputs

It's not realistic to think the user has only one audio input device. The computer might be connected to a headset for audio conferencing, a webcam for video conferencing, and a camcorder for dumping pictures of the summer vacation into iMovie. Ideally, it should be possible to discover connected devices at runtime and specify which is to be used for capture.

How do I do that?

To provide a list of devices, you need to query the SGAudioChannel for what devices are available, and then present the choice to the user. So, take the code from the previous lab and add an AWT Choice called deviceChoice in the constructor (replacing a line with a comment that said "reserved for next lab"). Next, after the SGSoundChannel is created in setUpAudioGrab( ), insert this block of code to search for audio devices, adding the name of each to the deviceChoice:

```
// create list of input devices
SGDeviceList devices = soundChannel.getDeviceList(0);
int deviceCount = devices.getCount( );
for (int i=0; i<deviceCount; i++) {
    SGDeviceName deviceName = devices.getDeviceName(i);
    // is it available?
    if ((deviceName.getFlags( ) &
        StdQTConstants.sgDeviceNameFlagDeviceUnavailable) == 0)
    deviceChoice.add(deviceName.getName( ));
}
```

You need to update the itemStateChanged( ) callback to handle AWT events on the deviceChoice—in other words, when the user changes the selection. Fortunately, QuickTime allows you to change the input device by passing in a name, so switching devices is pretty easy. Add this to itemStateChanged( ), inside the try-catch block:

```
} else if (e.getSource( ) == deviceChoice) {
    System.out.println ("changed device to "+
                    deviceChoice.getSelectedItem( ));
    grabbing = false;
    // grabber.stop( );
    soundChannel.setDevice (deviceChoice.getSelectedItem( ));
    // also reset inputDriver
    inputDriver = soundChannel.getInputDriver( );
    inputDriver.setLevelMeterOnOff (true);

    grabbing = true;
}
```

Run this example with ant run-ch06-selectableaudio-capturepreview.

The boolean named grabbing is a simple gate to keep the repaint thread from trying to get levels while this device change is underway, because the old inputDriver will be invalid once the new device is set.

A demo of this technique, SelectableAudioCapturePreview, is shown in Figure 6-2.

Figure 6-2. Discovering and displaying audio capture devices

What just happened?

The key to switching capture devices is a single call, SGSoundChannel. setDevice( ), which lets you change device mid-grab, without pausing or doing other reinitializations. It takes a device by name, the same name that was retrieved by walking through the SGDeviceList.

What about...

...the "O" parameter on getDeviceList( )? This method takes flags, only one of which is even relevant to QTJ.

Actually, it's easier to explain by starting further down, with the test for whether to add a device to the Choice. The SGDeviceName used to iden-tify the capture devices wraps not just a name string, but also an int with some flag values. sgDeviceNameFlagDeviceUnavailable is the only publicly documented flag. As seen in this example, to test for whether such a flag is set, you AND the value with the flag you're interested in and check whether the result is nonzero. If so, it means that bit is set. So, in this case, if the value is 0, the device is available (literally, it's "not unavailable"), so it's OK to let the user select it.

If we were to return to the getDeviceList( ), the only flag available would be sgDeviceListDontCheckAvailability, which skips the device availability check, meaning that flag in SGDeviceName would never be set, and thus the device would never be reported as unavailable. That's clearly undesirable behavior here—you don't want to give the user an option that's only going to throw an exception when she chooses it.

Capturing Audio to Disk

Typically, you don't just capture media and immediately dispose of it—you want to save the media to disk as you capture so that you can use it later. Fortunately, the SequenceGrabber makes this pretty easy.

How do I do that?

Adding to the previous labs' code, the calls to set up the SequenceGrabber need to be changed to prepare for grabbing to disk. Specifically, the SGSoundChannel's setUsage() call gets a flag to indicate that it will be writing the captured audio to disk:

```
soundChannel.setUsage (StdQTConstants.seqGrabPreview |
                       StdQTConstants.seqGrabRecord);
```

Next, add a call to give the user an opportunity to configure the audio capture:

```
soundChannel.settingsDialog();
```

WARNING

The settingsDialog() call will crash Java 1.4.2 on Mac OS X if called from the AWT event-dispatch thread. Yes, it's a bug. To work around this until the bug is fixed, you can stash the call in another thread and block on it. For instance, in this example you could replace the settingsDialog() call with the following:

```
final SGSoundChannel sc = soundChannel;
Thread t = new Thread() {
public void run() {
try {
sc.settingsDialog();
} catch (QTException qte) {
qte.printStackTrace();
}
}
};
t.start();
while (t.isAlive())
Thread.yield();
```

After starting the preview, tell the SequenceGrabber where it should save the captured audio:

```
// create output file
grabFile = new QTFile (new java.io.File ("audiograb.mov"));
```

```
if (grabFile.exists())
    grabFile.delete();
grabber.setDataOutput(grabFile,
                    StdQTConstants.seqGrabToDisk
                    //seqGrabDontAddMovieResource);
                    );
```

Finally, start recording to this file with `startRecord()`:

```
grabber.startRecord();
```

The last step is to provide a Stop button because the data is written to disk only when the `SequenceGrabber.stop()` method is called. This Stop button is added near the bottom of the constructor, before the `SequenceGrabber` is set up:

```
stopButton = new Button ("Stop");
stopButton.addActionListener (this);
add (stopButton);
```

The button requires a new `ActionEventListener` to make the `SequenceGrabber.stop()` call and close down the sample program:

```
public void actionPerformed (ActionEvent e) {
    if (e.getSource() == stopButton) {
        System.out.println ("Stop grabbing");
        try {
            if (grabber != null) {
                grabber.stop();
            }
        } catch (QTException qte) {
            qte.printStackTrace();
        } finally {
            System.exit (0);
        }
    }
}
```

Run this example with ant run-ch06-audiocaptureto-disk.

When this `AudioCaptureToDisk` sample program runs, the user sees an audio settings dialog, as shown in Figure 6-3.

After OKing the settings dialog, the capture begins. When the user clicks Stop, the `SequenceGrabber` writes and closes the *audiograb.mov* file and the program exits.

What just happened?

Requesting that the `SequenceGrabber` save to disk requires just the few extra steps detailed earlier:

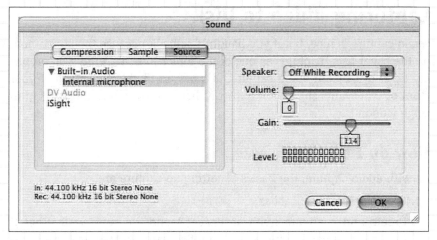

Figure 6-3. Audio channel settings dialog

1. Add seqGrabRecord to the channel's setUsage( ) call.

TIP

At this point, you optionally can call the channel's settingsDialog( ) to give the user a chance to configure the capture.

---

2. Call setOutput( ) on the SequenceGrabber.
3. Call SequenceGrabber.startRecord( ).

Also, the SequenceGrabber must be explicitly stop( )ped to write the captured data to disk.

What about...

...the SequenceGrabber.prepare( ) call? If the second argument is prepareForRecord, why isn't that set to true for this example? Well, inexplicably, when I did set it to true, I started getting erroneous "dskFulErr" exceptions every time I idle( )d, even though I had 9 GB free. No, I don't know why—it's totally insane. But given the choice of what *should* work and what *does* work, I'll go with the latter.

And what is the deal with the settings dialog? Could that have been used in the preview examples? Yes, absolutely. In fact, it's important to let the user adjust things like gain, or to specify a compressor before grabbing begins. But that's more important when you're actually grabbing to disk, so I held off introducing it until now.

Actually, it's usually best to capture uncompressed, so the CPU doesn't get bogged down with compression and possibly slow down the capture rate.

Capturing Video to Disk

Audio capture is nice, but if you bought this book because the sticky-note on the cover lists "capture" as one of the topics to be covered, you probably figured it meant video capture. Is there an iSight on the top of your monitor that wants some attention? OK, here's how to turn it on and grab some video.

How do I do that?

As with audio capture, the basics of setting up capture are:

1. Create a SequenceGrabber.
2. Create and configure (with setUsage( ) and the settingsDialog( )) the channels you're interested in—in this case, an SGVideoChannel.
3. Call SequenceGrabber.setOutput( ) to indicate the file to capture to.
4. Call SequenceGrabber.startRecord( ) to begin grabbing to disk.
5. Finish up with SequenceGrabber.stop( ).

There is, however, a *big* difference with video. With no on-screen preview component available in QTJ 6.1, you must indicate where the SequenceGrabber can draw to. The workaround is to create an off-screen QDGraphics and hand it to the SequenceGrabber via the setGWorld( ) call.

The VideoCaptureToDisk program, presented in Example 6-2, offers a bare-bones video capture to a file called *videograb.mov*.

Run this example with ant run-ch06-videocaptureto-disk.

Example 6-2. Recording captured video to disk

```
package com.oreilly.qtjnotebook.ch06;

import quicktime.*;
import quicktime.io.*;
import quicktime.std.*;
import quicktime.std.sg.*;
import quicktime.std.movies.*;
import quicktime.std.image.*;
import quicktime.qd.*;
import quicktime.sound.*;
import java.awt.*;
import java.awt.event.*;
import javax.swing.Timer;
import com.oreilly.qtjnotebook.ch01.QTSessionCheck;
public class VideoCaptureToDisk extends Frame
    implements ActionListener {
    SequenceGrabber grabber;
    SGVideoChannel videoChannel;
    QDGraphics gw;
```

Example 6-2. Recording captured video to disk (continued)

```java
QDRect grabBounds;
boolean grabbing;
Button stopButton;
QTFile grabFile;
public VideoCaptureToDisk( ) throws QTException {
    super ("Video Capture");
    QTSessionCheck.check( );
    setLayout (new GridLayout (2, 1));
    add (new Label ("Capturing video..."));
    stopButton = new Button ("Stop");
    stopButton.addActionListener (this);
    add (stopButton);
    setUpVideoGrab( );
}
public void actionPerformed (ActionEvent e) {
    if (e.getSource( ) == stopButton) {
        System.out.println ("Stop grabbing");
        try {
            grabbing = false;
            if (grabber != null) {
                grabber.stop( );
            }
        } catch (Exception ex) {
            ex.printStackTrace( );
        } finally {
            System.exit (0);
        }
    }
}

protected void setUpVideoGrab( ) throws QTException {
    grabber = new SequenceGrabber( );
    System.out.println ("got grabber");
    // force an offscreen gworld
    grabBounds = new QDRect (320, 240);
    gw = new QDGraphics (grabBounds);
    grabber.setGWorld (gw, null);
    // get videoChannel and set its bounds
    videoChannel = new SGVideoChannel (grabber);
    System.out.println ("Got SGVideoChannel");
    videoChannel.setBounds (grabBounds);
    // get settings
    // yikes! this crashes java 1.4.2 on mac os x!
    videoChannel.settingsDialog( );
    // prepare and start previewing
    // note - second prepare arg should seemingly be false,
    // but if it is, you get erroneous dskFulErr's
    videoChannel.setUsage (StdQTConstants.seqGrabRecord);
    grabber.prepare(false, true);
    grabber.startPreview( );
    // create output file
    grabFile = new QTFile (new java.io.File ("videograb.mov"));
```

Example 6-2. Recording captured video to disk (continued)

```
                grabber.setDataOutput(grabFile,
                                      StdQTConstants.seqGrabToDisk
                                      //seqGrabDontAddMovieResource);
                                     );
                grabber.startRecord();
                grabbing = true;
                // set up thread to idle
                ActionListener timerCallback =
                    new ActionListener() {
                        public void actionPerformed(ActionEvent e) {
                            if (grabbing) {
                                try {
                                    grabber.idle();
                                    grabber.update(null);
                                } catch (QTException qte) {
                                    qte.printStackTrace();
                                }
                            }
                        }
                    };
                Timer timer = new Timer (50, timerCallback);
                timer.start();
        }
        public static void main (String[] args) {
            try {
                Frame f = new VideoCaptureToDisk();
                f.pack();
                f.setVisible(true);
            } catch (QTException qte) {
                qte.printStackTrace();
            }
        }
    }
```

When it starts up, the program shows a settings dialog for your default camera, as seen in Figure 6-4. The video settings dialog is even more important for users than the audio settings dialog, as the video dialog gives them a chance to aim the camera, check the lighting, adjust brightness and color, etc.

WARNING

Just like its audio equivalent, calling SGVideoChannel. settingsDialog() will crash the virtual machine in Mac OS X Java 1.4.2 if called from the AWT event-dispatch thread. And just as before, you can work around this bug by firing off the settingsDialog() call in its own thread and blocking until the thread finishes. I've filed it as a bug, but feel free to file a duplicate to get Apple's attention.

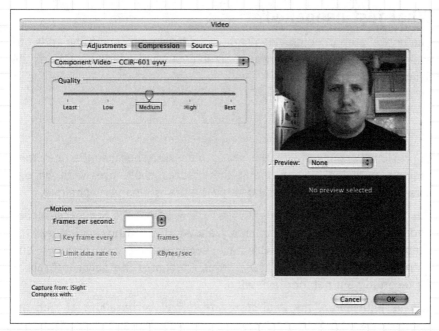

Figure 6-4. Video channel settings dialog

Once you click the Stop button, the video is written to *videograb.mov* and the application terminates. You can view the captured movie in any QuickTime application—Figure 6-5 shows it in the BasicQTController demo from Chapter 2.

Figure 6-5. Captured video playing in a window

What just happened?

The critical step in doing video capture, at least until QuickTime adds on-screen preview, is to create an off-screen QDGraphics and set that as the SequenceGrabber's GWorld:

```
// force an offscreen gworld
grabBounds = new QDRect (320, 240);
gw = new QDGraphics (grabBounds);
grabber.setGWorld (gw, null);
```

In previous versions of QTJ, this wasn't necessary because the on-screen preview provided a GWorld that the grabber could use. With no on-screen preview currently available in QTJ, this is a handy technique.

The next step is to create an SGVideoChannel from the SequenceGrabber and set its bounds. After optionally showing a settings dialog, set the usage (just seqGrabRecord this time because there's no preview) and then call prepare(false, true), which prepares the SequenceGrabber for recording but not for previewing.

This time, setting the second prepare() argument to true is the right thing to do.

Just as with audio, the final steps are to call setDataOutput( ) on the SequenceGrabber, followed by startRecord( ). When SequenceGrabber.stop( ) is called, the file is written out and closed up.

What about...

...using this on Windows...it doesn't find my webcam! This example pre-supposes that a *video digitizer component* for your camera will be found, and a lot of video cameras don't ship with a Windows QuickTime "vdig", supporting only Microsoft's media APIs instead. However, there's hope: you can use SoftVDIG from Abstract Plane (*http://www.abstractplane.com.au*), which acts as a proxy to bring captured video from the Microsoft Direct-Show world into QuickTime.

Capturing Audio and Video to the Same File

So, it's possible to capture audio and video in isolation. With QuickTime's editing API, it would be possible to put them in the same movie by add-ing each as a separate track (see Chapter 3). But wouldn't it be nice to just capture both audio and video into the same file at once, presumably keeping them in sync along the way? Fortunately, SequenceGrabber supports this, too.

How do I do that?

Starting with the previous lab's video-only example, you just need to add an SGSoundChannel in the setUpVideoGrab( ) method:

```
soundChannel = new SGSoundChannel (grabber);
```

The setUsage( ) and prepare( ) commands are identical to what was shown in the audio-only and video-only labs:

```
// prepare and start previewing
videoChannel.setUsage (StdQTConstants.seqGrabRecord);
soundChannel.setUsage (StdQTConstants.seqGrabPreview |
                       StdQTConstants.seqGrabRecord);
soundChannel.setVolume (0.0f);
grabber.prepare(false, true);
grabber.startPreview( );
```

Run this example with ant run-ch06-audiovideocapturetodisk.

Beyond that, everything is the same as in the video-only case. Because the setDataOutput( ) call is made on the SequenceGrabber—not just on an individual channel—the grabber writes data from all the channels it's capturing into the same file, called *audiovideograb.mov* in this case.

What just happened?

For once, the SequenceGrabber APIs behave pretty much as you might expect them to. With no obvious prohibition on creating both audio and video channels from the same SequenceGrabber, and assigning the grabber's output to a file, the captured data from both channels goes into a single movie file.

Making a Motion Detector

Capture isn't just about writing data to disk. You can grab images as they come in and analyze or manipulate them.

TIP

A great example of "grabbing different" is Lisa Lippincott's Scroll-Plate, a demo shown at ADHOC 2004. She used her iSight camera as a scroll wheel, by holding up a Styrofoam plate with either a large green arrow (for up) or a large red arrow (for down). Her code presumably grabbed from the camera, looked at the grabbed image for an abundance of green or red, and scrolled the top window in response.

This example offers a simple motion detector, which will display an alarm message if two subsequent grabs are markedly different. The idea is that if the camera is not moving, a significant difference between two subsequent grabs indicates that something in view of the camera has moved.

How do I do that?

In this case, what you want to do is to set up video-only capture, but instead of saving the data to disk, you do a little bit of image processing each time you idle( ). Specifically, there is a method in QTImage called getSimilarity( ), which compares two images (one as a QDGraphics and the other as an EncodedImage). Motion—objects entering, exiting, or significantly moving within the camera's field of vision—can be understood as a significant difference between two consecutive grabbed images.

See Chapter 5 for more on QTImage, QDGraphics, and EncodedImage.

Unfortunately, this requires jumping through quite a bit of QuickDraw hoops once an image is grabbed from the camera. Example 6-3 shows the SimpleMotionDetector code.

Example 6-3. Detecting motion by comparing grabbed images

```
package com.oreilly.qtjnotebook.ch06;

import quicktime.*;
import quicktime.io.*;
import quicktime.std.*;
import quicktime.std.sg.*;
import quicktime.std.movies.*;
import quicktime.std.movies.media.*;
import quicktime.std.image.*;
import quicktime.qd.*;
import quicktime.sound.*;
import quicktime.app.view.*;
import quicktime.util.*;
import java.awt.*;
import java.awt.event.*;
import javax.swing.Timer;
import java.text.*;
import com.oreilly.qtjnotebook.ch01.QTSessionCheck;
public class SimpleMotionDetector extends Frame
    implements ActionListener {
    SequenceGrabber grabber;
    SGVideoChannel videoChannel;
    QDGraphics gw;
    QDRect grabBounds;
    boolean grabbing;
    Button stopButton;
    Pict grabPict;
```

Example 6-3. Detecting motion by comparing grabbed images (continued)

```
byte[ ] importPictBytes;
Component importerComponent;
Label motionLabel;
GraphicsImporter importer;
RawEncodedImage lastImage;
ImageDescription lastImageDescription;
byte[ ] lastImageBytes;
QDGraphics newImageGW;
int thumbcount = 0;
// lesser numbers are more different (0 == totally different)
// public static float trigger = 0.0002f;
public static float trigger = 0.002f;

public SimpleMotionDetector( ) throws QTException {
    super ("Simple Motion Detector");
    QTSessionCheck.check( );
    setLayout (new BorderLayout( ));
    motionLabel = new Label ( );
    motionLabel.setForeground (Color.red);
    add (motionLabel, BorderLayout.NORTH);
    stopButton = new Button ("Stop");
    stopButton.addActionListener (this);
    add (stopButton, BorderLayout.SOUTH);
    importer = new GraphicsImporter (StdQTConstants.kQTFileTypePicture);
    importerComponent =
        QTFactory.makeQTComponent(importer).asComponent( );
    add (importerComponent, BorderLayout.CENTER);
    setUpVideoGrab( );
}
public void actionPerformed (ActionEvent e) {
    if (e.getSource( ) == stopButton) {
        System.out.println ("Stop grabbing");
        try {
            grabbing = false;
            if (grabber != null) {
                grabber.stop( );
            }
        } catch (Exception ex) {
            ex.printStackTrace( );
        } finally {
            System.exit (0);
        }
    }
}
protected void setUpVideoGrab( ) throws QTException {
    grabber = new SequenceGrabber( );
    System.out.println ("got grabber");
    // force an offscreen gworld
    grabBounds = new QDRect (320, 240);
    gw = new QDGraphics (grabBounds);
    grabber.setGWorld (gw, null);
    // get videoChannel and set its bounds
```

Example 6-3. Detecting motion by comparing grabbed images (continued)

```
            videoChannel = new SGVideoChannel (grabber);
            System.out.println ("Got SGVideoChannel");
            videoChannel.setBounds (grabBounds);
            // get settings
            // yikes! this crashes java 1.4.2 on mac os x!
            // videoChannel.settingsDialog();
            // prepare and start previewing
            videoChannel.setUsage (StdQTConstants.seqGrabPreview);
            grabber.prepare(true, false);
            grabber.startPreview();
            // get first grab, so we're ready
            // to calc diff's and draw component
            scanForDifference();
            updateImportedPict();
            grabbing = true;
            // set up thread to idle
            ActionListener timerCallback =
                new ActionListener() {
                    public void actionPerformed(ActionEvent e) {
                        if (grabbing) {
                            try {
                                grabber.idle();
                                grabber.update(null);
                                scanForDifference();
                                updateImportedPict();
                            } catch (QTException qte) {
                                qte.printStackTrace();
                            }
                        }
                    }
                };
            Timer timer = new Timer (2000, timerCallback);
            timer.start();
    }
    protected void scanForDifference() throws QTException {
        // this seems like overkill, but the GW we give
        // the grabber doesn't get updated.  Picts returned
        // from grabber are different each time, so use 'em
        if (newImageGW == null)
            newImageGW = new QDGraphics (grabBounds);
        grabPict = grabber.grabPict (grabBounds, 0, 0);
        grabPict.draw (newImageGW, grabBounds);
        if (lastImage != null) {
            // compare to last image
            float similarity = QTImage.getSimilarity (newImageGW,
                                              grabBounds,
                                              lastImageDescription,
                                              lastImage);
            System.out.println ("similarity == " +
                                formatter.format(similarity));
            if (similarity < trigger) {
                System.out.println ("*** Motion detect ***");
```

Example 6-3. Detecting motion by comparing grabbed images (continued)

```
                motionLabel.setText ("motion detect");
            } else {
                motionLabel.setText ("");
            }
        }
        // create a new lastImage from grabber GWorld
        int bufSize =
            QTImage.getMaxCompressionSize (newImageGW,
                                        newImageGW.getBounds( ),
                                        0,
                                        StdQTConstants.codecNormalQuality,
                                        StdQTConstants.kRawCodecType,
                                        CodecComponent.anyCodec);
        // make new lastImage
        lastImageBytes = new byte[bufSize];
        lastImage = new RawEncodedImage (lastImageBytes);
        lastImageDescription =
            QTImage.compress(newImageGW,
                            newImageGW.getBounds( ),
                            StdQTConstants.codecNormalQuality,
                            StdQTConstants.kRawCodecType,
                            lastImage);

    protected void updateImportedPict( ) throws QTException {
        importPictBytes = new byte [grabPict.getSize( ) + 512];
        grabPict.copyToArray (0,
                                importPictBytes,
                                512,
                                importPictBytes.length - 512);
        Pict wrapperPict = new Pict (importPictBytes);
        DataRef ref = new DataRef (wrapperPict,
                                StdQTConstants.kDataRefQTFileTypeTag,
                                "PICT");
        importer.setDataReference (ref);
        importer.draw( );
        if (importerComponent != null)
            importerComponent.repaint( );
        // wrapperPict.disposeQTObject( );
    }

    public static void main (String[ ] args) {
        try {
            Frame f = new SimpleMotionDetector( );
            f.pack( );
            f.setVisible(true);
        } catch (QTException qte) {
            qte.printStackTrace( );
        }
    }
}
```

Run this example with ant run-ch06-simple-motiondetector.

When running, if two frames differ by more than a specified amount, the label "motion detect" will appear at the top of the window. Figure 6-6 shows the running application.

Figure 6-6. Video motion detector window

What just happened?

This is a huge example, but much of it draws on the video-grabbing techniques of the previous two labs. setUpVideoGrab() sets up the SequenceGrabber for grabbing video, but in this case, it doesn't need to save to disk, so the setUsage() argument is seqGrabPreview, and the arguments to prepare() are true and false (for preview and record, respectively). A Swing Timer calls back every two seconds—the long delay is intentional, so the potential for change between grabbed frames is greater—and calls the SequenceGrabber idle() and update() methods, followed by calls to the brains of this example: scanForDifference() and updatePict().

It might be better to call scanFor-Difference() on another thread, so the image analysis doesn't block the repeated calls to SequenceGrabber. idle().

scanForDifference() evaluates the difference between the current frame and the last one. It does this by grabbing a Pict from the SequenceGrabber and drawing it into a QDGraphics (also known as a GWorld). It compares this GWorld to an EncodedImage of the last grab, via the QTImage.getSimilarity() method. This method returns a float that expresses the similarity of the two grabbed images, where 0 means the images are totally different and 1 means they're identical. At the end of this method, QTImage.compress() is used to compress the grabbed GWorld into a new EncodedImage for use on the next call to scanForDifference().

updatePict( ) updates a GraphicsImporter that is used to provide the preview image in the middle of the window. This uses a Pict-to-GraphicsImporter trick that was introduced in Chapter 5's "A Better Movie-to-Java Image Converter" lab. In this case, it's used not to get a Java AWT Image, but to get new pixels into a GraphicsImporter, which is wired up to a QTComponent for on-screen preview.

What about...

...the ideal value for triggering a difference? It probably depends on lighting, your camera, and other factors. In a professional application, you'd want to give the user a slider or some similar means of configuring the sensitivity of the detection.

Also, there seems to be a lot of inefficient code here, particularly with drawing into the newImageGW. Why is that necessary when the Grabber was initially set up with a brand-new off-screen QDGraphics/GWorld? This, admittedly, is weird. When I was debugging, I found that the GWorld used to set up the Grabber is drawn to *once* and never again. On the other hand, the Pict generated from SequenceGrabber.grabPict( ) is always fresh, so that's what's used for testing similarity. However, to apply the getSimilarity( ) method, you need to have a GWorld, so you Pict.draw( ) the pixels from the Pict into the GWorld.

Come to think of it, with this application updating the component with a new grab every couple of seconds, isn't that effectively an on-screen pre-view? Yes, it is, in an extraordinarily roundabout way. You could take out the motion-detecting stuff and make a preview component by just grabbing a Pict each time, making a new Pict with a 512-byte header, setting the GraphicsImporter to read that, and calling GraphicsImporter.draw( ) to draw into its on-screen component. I didn't split that out as its own lab because the performance is pathologically bad (one frame per second—at best), and because it's an awkward workaround in lieu of a better way of getting a component from a SequenceGrabber. Presumably, someday there will be a proper call to get a QTComponent from a SequenceGrabber—maybe another overload of QTFactory.makeQTComponent( )—and kludgery like this won't be necessary.

CHAPTER 7

Audio Media

This is the first of three chapters dealing with specific media types. Video will be covered in Chapter 8, and several other kinds of media—including things you might not have thought of as media, such as text and time codes—will be covered in Chapter 9.

It's possible that you've never thought of QuickTime as being the engine for audio-only applications—the ubiquity of QuickTime's *.mov* file format probably makes it more readily recognized as a video standard. But QuickTime's support for audio has been critical to many applications. For example, the fact that QuickTime was already ported to Windows made bringing iTunes and its music store over to Windows a lot easier.

In fact, iTunes is probably responsible for getting QuickTime onto a lot more Windows machines than it would have reached otherwise. So, I'll begin with a few labs that are particularly applicable to the MP3s and AACs collected by iTunes users.

Reading Information from MP3 Files

If you've ever listened to an MP3 music file—and at this point, who hasn't—you've surely appreciated the fact that useful information like artist, song title, album title, etc., is stored *inside* the file. Not only does this make it convenient to organize your music, but also, when you move a song from one device to another, this *metadata* travels with it.

The most widely accepted standard for doing this is the ID3 standard, which puts this metadata into parts of the file that are not interpreted as containing audio data—MP3s arrange data in *frames*, and ID3 puts metadata between these frames. ID3 tags typically are found at the beginning of

Visit *http://www. id3.org/* to learn more about *ID3*.

a file, which makes them stream-friendly, although some files tagged with earlier versions of the standard have the metadata at the end of the file.

When QuickTime imports an MP3 file, it reads ID3 tags and makes them available to your program through the movie's *user data*, allowing you to display the tags to the user, or use them in any other way you see fit.

How do I do that?

Once you open an MP3 as a movie, you need to get at the user data, which contains the imported ID3 tags. Fortunately, it's wrapped as an object called UserData:

```
UserData userData = movie.getUserData();
```

The user data is something of a grab bag of data that you can read from and write to freely. Items are keyed by FOUR_CHAR_CODEs, and the contents aren't required to adhere to any particular standard or format (after all, you're free to write whatever you like in user data). For example, QuickTime Player writes a "WLOC" entry that stores the window location last used for the movie.

Apple has a standard set of keys that you can use to retrieve the data parsed from an MP3's ID3 tags. Because these are text values, you use UserData's getTextAsString() method to pull them out. getTextAsString() takes three arguments: the type you're requesting; an index to indicate whether you want the first, second, etc., instance of that type; and a region tag that's irrelevant in the ID3 case.

Example 7-1 shows a basic exercise of this technique, getting the UserData object and asking for album, artist, creation date, and song title information.

Example 7-1. Retrieving ID3 metadata

```
package com.oreilly.qtjnotebook.ch07;

import quicktime.*;
import quicktime.std.*;
import quicktime.std.movies.*;
import quicktime.std.movies.media.*;
import quicktime.io.*;
import java.util.*;

import com.oreilly.qtjnotebook.ch01.QTSessionCheck;

public class ID3TagReader extends Object {

    /* these values are straight out of Movies.h
```

Example 7-1. Retrieving ID3 metadata (continued)

```
    */
    final static int  kUserDataTextAlbum          = 0xA9616C62; /*'@alb' */
    final static int  kUserDataTextArtist         = 0xA9415254;
    final static int  kUserDataTextCreationDate    = 0xA9646179; /*'@day' */
    final static int  kUserDataTextFullName        = 0xA96E616D; /*'@nam' */

    /* This array maps all the tag constants to human-readable strings
     */
    private static final Object[ ][ ] TAG_NAMES = {
        {new Integer (kUserDataTextAlbum), "Album"},
        {new Integer (kUserDataTextArtist),"Artist" },
        {new Integer (kUserDataTextCreationDate), "Created"},
        {new Integer (kUserDataTextFullName), "Full Name"}
    };

    private static final HashMap TAG_MAP =
        new HashMap(TAG_NAMES.length);
    static {
        for (int i=0; i<TAG_NAMES.length; i++) {
            TAG_MAP.put (TAG_NAMES[i][0],
                         TAG_NAMES[i][1]);
        }
    }

    public static void main (String[ ] args) {
        new ID3TagReader( );
        System.exit(0);
    }

    public ID3TagReader( ) {
        try {
            QTSessionCheck.check( );
            QTFile f = QTFile.standardGetFilePreview (null);
            OpenMovieFile omf = OpenMovieFile.asRead(f);
            Movie movie = Movie.fromFile (omf);
            // get user data
            UserData userData = movie.getUserData( );
            dumpTagsFromUserData(userData);
        } catch (Exception e) {
            e.printStackTrace( );
        }
    }

    protected static void dumpTagsFromUserData (UserData userData) {
        // try for each key in TAG_MAP
        Iterator it = TAG_MAP.keySet( ).iterator( );
        while (it.hasNext( )) {
            Integer key = (Integer) it.next( );
            int tag = key.intValue( );
            String tagName = (String) TAG_MAP.get(key);
            try {
                String value =
```

*Run this example
from the
downloadable
book code with
ant run-ch07-
id3tagreader.*

Example 7-1. Retrieving ID3 metadata (continued)

```
                    userData.getTextAsString (tag,
                                               1,
                                        IOConstants.langUnspecified);
            System.out.println (tagName + ": " + value);
        } catch (QTException qte) {} // no such tag
    }
}
}
```

When run, this dumps the found tags to standard out, as seen in the following console output:

```
cadamson% ant run-ch07-id3tagreader
Buildfile: build.xml

run-ch07-id3tagreader:
    [java] Album: Arthur Or The Decline And Fall Of The British Empire
    [java] Full Name: Victoria
    [java] Artist: The Kinks
```

What just happened?

The application sets up some static values for keys it is interested in and maps them to human-readable names. For example, the FOUR_CHAR_CODE "@alb" is mapped to "Album."

The program prompts the user to select an MP3 file and imports it as a movie, from which it gets a UserData object. In dumpTagsFromUserData( ), it calls getTextAsString( ) to attempt to get a value for each known tag. If successful, it writes the key and value to the console. If a given tag is absent from the user data, QuickTime throws an exception, which this program quietly ignores.

QuickTime has an important and disappointing limitation: it does not import tags written in non-Western scripts. For example, here's the output when I run the application against an MP3 whose "artist" tag is in Japanese *kana* (characters):

```
cadamson% ant run-ch07-id3tagreader
Buildfile: build.xml

run-ch07-id3tagreader:
    [java] Album: COWBOY BEBOP O.S.T.1
    [java] Created: 1998
    [java] Full Name: SPACE LION
```

Because the artist (菅野よう子, or "Yoko Kanno" in *romaji*) is written in non-Western characters, QuickTime doesn't attempt to import it, and thus there's no artist item to retrieve from the user data.

What about...

...other tags? A big list of metadata tags are defined in the native API's *Movies.h* file. Unfortunately, these aren't in the StdQTConstants classes, or anywhere else in QTJ, so you have to define your own constants for them. Table 7-1 is the list of supported values.

Table 7-1. Audio metadata tag constants

Constant name	Hex value	4CC
kUserDataTextAlbum	0xA9616C62	©alb
kUserDataTextArtist	0xA9415254	©ART
kUserDataTextAuthor	0xA9617574	©aut
kUserDataTextChapter	0xA9636870	©chp
kUserDataTextComment	0xA9636D74	©cmt
kUserDataTextComposer	0xA9636F6D	©com
kUserDataTextCopyright	0xA9637079	©cpy
kUserDataTextCreationDate	0xA9646179	©day
kUserDataTextDescription	0xA9646573	©des
kUserDataTextDirector	0xA9646972	©dir
kUserDataTextDisclaimer	0xA9646973	©dis
kUserDataTextEncodedBy	0xA9656E63	©enc
kUserDataTextFullName	0xA96E616D	©nam
kUserDataTextGenre	0xA967656E	©gen
kUserDataTextHostComputer	0xA9687374	©hst
kUserDataTextInformation	0xA9696E66	©inf
kUserDataTextKeywords	0xA96B6579	©key
kUserDataTextMake	0xA96D616B	©mak
kUserDataTextModel	0xA96D6F64	©mod
kUserDataTextOriginalArtist	0xA96F7065	©ope
kUserDataTextOriginalFormat	0xA9666D74	©fmt
kUserDataTextOriginalSource	0xA9737263	©src
kUserDataTextPerformers	0xA9707266	©prf
kUserDataTextProducer	0xA9707264	©prd
kUserDataTextProduct	0xA9505244	©PRT
kUserDataTextSoftware	0xA9737772	©swr
kUserDataTextSpecialPlayback Requirements	0xA9726571	©req
kUserDataTextTrack	0xA974726B	©trk
kUserDataTextWarning	0xA977726E	©wrn
kUserDataTextWriter	0xA9777274	©wrt
kUserDataTextURLLink	0xA975726C	©url
kUserDataTextEditDate1	0xA9656431	©ed1

This technique is a lot like the "Discovering All Installed Components" lab in Chapter 4.

Also, instead of requesting specific keys from the user data, can I just tour what's in there? Yes, you can use UserData.getNextType( ) to discover the types of items in the user data. This method takes an int of the last discovered type (use 0 on the first call), and returns the next type after that one. When it returns 0, there are no more types to discover. Given a type, you can get its data with getTextAsString( ), but because you can't know that a discovered piece of user data necessarily represents textual data, it might be safer to call getData( ), which returns a QTHandle, from which you can get a byte array with getBytes( ).

Reading Information from iTunes AAC Files

Buckle up, this one is rough.

If you read the last lab and thought about how ID3 metadata is imported into a QuickTime movie's UserData, you might well expect that the same thing would be true of AAC files created by iTunes: *.m4a* files for songs "ripped" by the user and *.m4p* files sold by the iTunes Music Store. In fact, because these files use an MPEG-4 file format that is itself based on QuickTime, you might think that using the same user data scheme would be a slam dunk.

But...you'd be wrong.

These AAC files do put the metadata in the user data, but they do so in a way that resists straightforward retrieval via QuickTime. Fortunately, it's not *too* hard to get the values out with some parsing.

How do I do that?

For once, theory needs to come before code—you need to see the format to understand how to parse it. Here's a /usr/bin/hexdump of an iTunes Music Store AAC file from my collection, *Toto Dies.m4p*:

```
0000b010  00 3d 5f 3c 00 3d 7d 5e  00 3d 9a fb 00 03 18 da  |.=_<.=}^.=......
          |
0000b020  75 64 74 61 00 03 18 d2  6d 65 74 61 00 00 00 00  |udta....meta....
          |
0000b030  00 00 00 22 68 64 6c 72  00 00 00 00 00 00 00 00  |..."hdlr........
          |
0000b040  6d 64 69 72 61 70 70 6c  00 00 00 00 00 00 00 00  |mdirappl........
          |
0000b050  00 00 00 03 11 9b 69 6c  73 74 00 00 00 21 a9 6e  |......ilst...!.
          n|
0000b060  61 6d 00 00 00 19 64 61  74 61 00 00 00 01 00 00  |am....data......
          |
0000b070  00 00 54 6f 74 6f 20 44  69 65 73 00 00 00 24 a9  |..Toto Dies...$.
          |
```

```
0000b080   41 52 54 00 00 00 1c 64   61 74 61 00 00 00 01 00   |ART....data.....
     |
0000b090   00 00 00 4e 65 6c 6c 69   65 20 4d 63 4b 61 79 00   |...Nellie McKay.
     |
0000b0a0   00 00 24 a9 77 72 74 00   00 00 1c 64 61 74 61 00   |..$.wrt....data.
     |
0000b0b0   00 00 01 00 00 00 00 4e   65 6c 6c 69 65 20 4d 63   |.......Nellie Mc
     Mc|
0000b0c0   4b 61 79 00 03 0e 76 63   6f 76 72 00 03 0e 6e 64   |Kay...vcovr...
     nd|
0000b0d0   61 74 61 00 00 00 0d 00   00 00 00 ff d8 ff e0 00   |ata............
     |
0000b0e0   10 4a 46 49 46 00 01 01   01 02 f9 02 f9 00 00 ff   |.JFIF..........
     |
```

Granted, this is *not* easy to read, but I'll bet you can pick out the artist (Nellie McKay) and the song title ("Toto Dies"), so you know this is the relevant section of the file. In fact, you also might notice the string "udta"...sounds a little like "user data," doesn't it?

At work here is the QuickTime file format and its concept of *atoms*, which are tree-structured pieces of data used to describe a movie, its contents, and its metadata. Without going too deeply into the details—there's a whole book on the format—each atom consists of 4 bytes of size, a 4-byte type, and then data. Atoms contain either data or other atoms, but not both. The 4 bytes before "udta", 0x000318da, indicate the size of all the user data. The first child is an atom called "meta". Because its size is 0x000318d2, just 8 less than the size of "udta", the "meta" atom is clearly the only child of "udta".

Unfortunately, because this is user data, the contents don't have to adhere to any published standard, and they don't. The first thing after "meta" should be the 4-byte size of its first child atom, but the value is 0x00000000—an illegal "no size" value—so, a normal QuickTime parser would ignore the contents of "meta".

Funny thing is, although these contents aren't real QuickTime atoms, they're *awfully* close. Start with the stuff that's obviously the metadata and work backward: "Toto Dies" is preceded by an 8-byte pad (0x00000001 and 0x00000000), and before that is "data" and a 4-byte number. That number, 0x00000019, is the size of itself, plus "data", plus the 8-byte pad, plus the string "Toto Dies." And just before that, you'll find the string "©nam", preceded by a 4-byte size. Better yet, "©nam" is one of the constants defined in *Movies.h* for metadata tagging.

See the previous lab for a list of QuickTime's metadata tags.

Dig further and you'll find that there's a run of these tag-name/data structures, each of which has the structure discovered earlier:

Full size
    4 bytes

Type
> 4 bytes

Contents size
> 4 bytes

"data"
> 4 bytes

Unknown
> 8 bytes

Value
> Variable number of bytes (size is implicit from earlier size data)

The run of metadata blocks exists within a single pseudo-atom parent called "ilst". So, this analysis provides a strategy for getting iTunes AAC metadata:

1. Get the user data.

2. Look for a user data item called "meta" and get it as a byte array.

3. Inside this array, find "ilst".

4. Start reading 8-byte blocks as possible size/type combinations. If the type is known as a metadata type, skip past the 24 bytes of junk (the 8-byte pad, the "data", etc.) and read the String.

The sample program in Example 7-2 implements this strategy.

Example 7-2. Retrieving iTunes AAC metadata

```
package com.oreilly.qtjnotebook.ch07;

import quicktime.*;
import quicktime.std.*;
import quicktime.std.movies.*;
import quicktime.std.movies.media.*;
import quicktime.io.*;
import quicktime.util.*;
import java.util.*;
import java.math.BigInteger;

import com.oreilly.qtjnotebook.ch01.QTSessionCheck;

public class AACTagReader extends Object {

    /* these values are straight out of Movies.h
     */
    final static int  kUserDataTextAlbum          = 0xA9616C62; /*'@alb' */
    final static int  kUserDataTextArtist         = 0xA9415254;
    final static int  kUserDataTextCreationDate   = 0xA9646179; /*'@day' */
    final static int  kUserDataTextFullName       = 0xA96E616D; /*'@nam' */
```

Example 7-2. Retrieving iTunes AAC metadata (continued)

```java
/* This array maps all the tag constants to human-readable strings
*/
private static final Object[ ][ ] TAG_NAMES = {
    {new Integer (kUserDataTextAlbum), "Album"},
    {new Integer (kUserDataTextArtist),"Artist" },
    {new Integer (kUserDataTextCreationDate), "Created"},
    {new Integer (kUserDataTextFullName), "Full Name"}
};

private static final HashMap TAG_MAP =
    new HashMap(TAG_NAMES.length);
static {
    for (int i=0; i<TAG_NAMES.length; i++) {
        TAG_MAP.put (TAG_NAMES[i][0],
                        TAG_NAMES[i][1]);
    }
}

public static void main (String[ ] args) {
    new AACTagReader( );
    System.exit(0);
}

public AACTagReader( ) {
    try {
        QTSessionCheck.check( );
        QTFile f = QTFile.standardGetFilePreview (null);
        OpenMovieFile omf = OpenMovieFile.asRead(f);
        Movie movie = Movie.fromFile (omf);
        // get user data
        UserData userData = movie.getUserData( );
        dumpTagsFromUserData(userData);
    } catch (Exception e) {
        e.printStackTrace( );
    }
}

protected void dumpTagsFromUserData (UserData userData)
    throws QTException {
    int metaFCC = QTUtils.toOSType("meta");
    QTHandle metaHandle = userData.getData (metaFCC, 1);
    System.out.println ("Found meta");
    byte[ ] metaBytes = metaHandle.getBytes( );

    // locate the "ilst" pseudo-atom, ignoring first 4 bytes
    int ilstFCC = QTUtils.toOSType("ilst");
    PseudoAtomPointer ilst = findPseudoAtom (metaBytes, 4, ilstFCC);

    // iterate over the pseudo-atoms inside the "ilst"
    // building lists of tags and values from which we'll
    // create arrays for the DefaultTableModel constructor
    int off = ilst.offset + 8;
```

Example 7-2. Retrieving iTunes AAC metadata (continued)

```java
        ArrayList foundTags = new ArrayList (TAG_NAMES.length);
        ArrayList foundValues = new ArrayList (TAG_NAMES.length);
        while (off < metaBytes.length) {
            PseudoAtomPointer atom = findPseudoAtom (metaBytes, off, -1);
            String tagName = (String) TAG_MAP.get (new Integer(atom.type));
            if (tagName != null) {
                // if we match a type, read everything after byte 24
                // which skips size, type, size, 'data', 8 junk bytes
                byte[] valueBytes = new byte [atom.atomSize - 24];
                System.arraycopy (metaBytes,
                                  atom.offset+24,
                                  valueBytes,
                                  0,
                                  valueBytes.length);
                String value = new String (valueBytes);
                System.out.println (tagName + ": " + value);
            } // if tagName != null
            off = atom.offset + atom.atomSize;
        }
    }

    /** find the given type in the byte array, starting at
        the start position.  Returns the offset within the
        byte array that begins this pseudo-atom.  a helper method
        to populateFromMetaAtom( ).
        @param bytes byte array to search
        @param start offset to start at
        @param type type to search for.  if -1, returns first
        atom with a plausible size
     */
    private PseudoAtomPointer findPseudoAtom (byte[] bytes,
                                              int start,
                                              int type) {
        // read size, then type
        // if size is bogus, forget it, increment offset, and try again
        int off = start;
        boolean found = false;
        while ((! found) &&
               (off < bytes.length-8)) {
            // read 32 bits of atom size
            // use BigInteger to convert bytes to long
            // (instead of signed int)
            byte sizeBytes[] = new byte[4];
            System.arraycopy (bytes, off, sizeBytes, 0, 4);
            BigInteger atomSizeBI = new BigInteger (sizeBytes);
            long atomSize = atomSizeBI.longValue( );

            // don't bother if the size would take us beyond end of
            // array, or is impossibly small
            if ((atomSize > 7) &&
                (off + atomSize <= bytes.length)) {
                byte[] typeBytes = new byte[4];
```

Example 7-2. Retrieving iTunes AAC metadata (continued)

```
            System.arraycopy (bytes, off+4, typeBytes, 0, 4);
            int aType = QTUtils.toOSType (new String (typeBytes));

            if ((type == aType) ||
                (type == -1))
                return new PseudoAtomPointer (off, (int) atomSize, aType);
            else
                off += atomSize;

        } else {
            System.out.println ("bogus atom size " + atomSize);
            // well, how did this happen?  increment off and try again
            off++;
        }
    } // while
    return null;
}

/** Inner class to represent atom-like structures inside
    the meta atom, designed to work with the byte array
    of the meta atom (i.e., just wraps pointers to the
    beginning of the atom and its computed size and type)
 */
class PseudoAtomPointer {
    int offset;
    int atomSize;
    int type;
    public PseudoAtomPointer (int o, int s, int t) {
        offset=o;
        atomSize=s;
        type=t;
    }

}

}
```

Run this example with ant run-ch07-aactagreader.

When run with *Toto Dies.m4p,* the output to the console looks like this:

```
cadamson% ant run-ch07-aactagreader
Buildfile: build.xml

run-ch07-aactagreader:
    [java] Found meta
    [java] Full Name: Toto Dies
    [java] Artist: Nellie McKay
    [java] Album: Get Away from Me
    [java] Created: 2004-02-10T08:00:00Z
```

The "album" and "created" data didn't appear in the earlier hexdump because in the file they occur after the cover art data, which is several kilobytes long.

What just happened?

The program gets the UserData, gets its "meta" atom as a byte array, and looks for the "ilst" pseudo-atom. If it finds one, it skips ahead 8 bytes (over "ilst" and its size) and goes into a loop of discovering and parsing potential pseudo-atoms.

To parse, you look at the first 4 bytes and consider whether it's a plausible size—in other words, whether it's big enough to contain data, but small enough to not run past the end of the byte array. If so, interpret the next 4 bytes as a FOUR_CHAR_CODE type and check against the list of known metadata types. If it matches one of the known types, you've got a valid piece of metadata, which this program simply writes to standard out.

What about...

...combining this with the MP3 approach of the previous lab so that there's just one codebase? A good strategy for that would be to get the UserData and look for a "meta" atom. If you get one, assume you have iTunes AAC and do the previous parsing. If not, assume you have an MP3, and start asking for the various metadata types with UserData. getTextAsString( ), as in the previous lab.

Providing Basic Audio Controls

Most audio applications provide some basic audio controls to allow the user to customize the sound output to suit his environment. The MovieController provides a volume control, but you can do better than that: you can control balance, bass, and treble with simple method calls.

How do I do that?

The AudioMediaHandler class provides the methods setBalance( ) and setSoundBassAndTreble( ), so it's just a matter of getting the handler object. The key is to remember that:

- Movies have tracks.
- Tracks have exactly one Media each.
- Each Media has a MediaHandler.

Iterate over the movie's tracks to get each track's media and handler. To figure out whether a given track is audio, you can use a simple instanceof to see if the handler is an AudioMediaHandler.

setBalance( ) takes a float, which ranges from -1.0 (all the way to the left) to 1.0 (all the way to the right), with 0 representing equal balance.

setSoundBassAndTreble( ) is interesting because it's officially undocumented. As it turns out, you pass in ints for bass and treble, where 0 is normal, -256 is minimum bass or treble, and 256 is maximum.

Well, the native version is undocumented. For once, the Javadocs have the useful info.

Example 7-3 provides a simple GUI to exercise these methods.

Example 7-3. Providing balance, bass, and treble controls

```
package com.oreilly.qtjnotebook.ch07;

import quicktime.*;
import quicktime.std.*;
import quicktime.std.movies.*;
import quicktime.std.movies.media.*;
import quicktime.app.view.*;
import quicktime.io.*;

import java.awt.*;
import javax.swing.*;
import javax.swing.event.*;

import com.oreilly.qtjnotebook.ch01.QTSessionCheck;

public class BasicAudioControlsPlayer extends Frame
    implements ChangeListener {

    JSlider balanceSlider, trebleSlider, bassSlider;

    AudioMediaHandler audioMediaHandler;

    public static void main (String[ ] args) {
        try {
            QTSessionCheck.check( );
            Frame f= new BasicAudioControlsPlayer( );
            f.pack( );
            f.setVisible(true);
        } catch (QTException qte) {
            qte.printStackTrace( );
        }
    }

    public BasicAudioControlsPlayer ( ) throws QTException {
        super ("Basic Audio Controls");
        // prompt for audio file
        QTFile file = QTFile.standardGetFilePreview(null);
        OpenMovieFile omf = OpenMovieFile.asRead (file);
        Movie movie = Movie.fromFile (omf);
        MovieController controller = new MovieController (movie);
        // get AudioMediaHandler for first audio track
        for (int i=1; i<=movie.getTrackCount( ); i++) {
```

Example 7-3. Providing balance, bass, and treble controls (continued)

```
                Track t = movie.getTrack(i);
                Media m = t.getMedia( );
                MediaHandler mh = m.getHandler( );
                if (mh instanceof AudioMediaHandler) {
                    audioMediaHandler = (AudioMediaHandler) mh;
                    break;
                }
            }
            if (audioMediaHandler == null) {
                System.out.println ("No audio track");
                System.exit(-1);
            }
            // add controller to GUI
            setLayout (new BorderLayout( ));
            Component comp =
                QTFactory.makeQTComponent(controller).asComponent( );
            add (comp, BorderLayout.NORTH);
            // build balance, treble, bass controls in a panel
            Panel controls = new Panel(new GridLayout (3,2));
            controls.add (new JLabel ("Balance"));
            balanceSlider = new JSlider (-1000, 1000, 0);
            balanceSlider.addChangeListener (this);
            controls.add (balanceSlider);
            controls.add (new JLabel ("Treble"));
            trebleSlider = new JSlider (-256, 256, 0);
            trebleSlider.addChangeListener (this);
            controls.add (trebleSlider);
            controls.add (new JLabel ("Bass"));
            bassSlider = new JSlider (-256, 256, 0);
            bassSlider.addChangeListener (this);
            controls.add (bassSlider);
            add (controls, BorderLayout.SOUTH);
        }

        public void stateChanged (ChangeEvent ev) {
            Object source = ev.getSource( );
            try {
                if (source == balanceSlider) {
                    // balance
                    float newBal =
                        (float) (balanceSlider.getValue( ) / 1000f);
                    audioMediaHandler.setBalance (newBal);
                } else {
                    // bass & treble
                    audioMediaHandler.setSoundBassAndTreble (
                                    bassSlider.getValue( ),
                                    trebleSlider.getValue( ));
                }


            } catch (QTException qte) {
                qte.printStackTrace( );
```

Example 7-3. Providing balance, bass, and treble controls (continued)

```
      }
    }
  }
}
```

Run this example with ant-ch07- basicaudiocontrol- splayer.

When run, the program asks the user to select a file to play, and then shows a GUI, as seen in Figure 7-1.

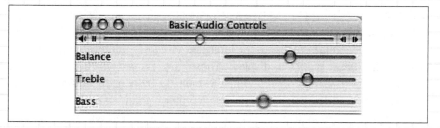

Figure 7-1. Balance, treble, and bass controls

What just happened?

The key to this example is the use of Swing JSliders, which can be configured with appropriate bounds for the features they represent. For example, the bass and treble sliders run in a -256 to 256 range, with 0 as a default:

```
trebleSlider = new JSlider (-256, 256, 0);
```

The balance slider needs to pass a float between -1 and 1, but JSliders work with ints, so it uses a range of -1000 to 1000, which is scaled to an appropriate float before calling setBalance():

```
balanceSlider = new JSlider (-1000, 1000, 0);
```

All the sliders share a ChangeListener implementation that reads the new value from the affected JSlider and make a corresponding call to the AudioMediaHandler.

Providing a Level Meter

Many audio applications also provide a graphical "level meter," which is an on-screen display of the loudness or softness of certain frequencies within the audio. In QuickTime Player, this is shown as a set of bars on the right side of the control bar, as seen in Figure 7-2.

The intensity of lower frequencies, like bass, is shown in the leftmost columns, while higher frequencies are to the right.

Figure 7-2. Audio level meter in QuickTime Player

How do I do that?

AudioMediaHandler provides two key methods: setSoundEqualizerBands( ) to set up monitoring and getSoundLevelMeterLevels( ) to actually get the data. setSoundEqualizerBands( ) indicates which frequencies you want to monitor for your graphics display. These are passed in the form of a MediaEqSpectrumBands object, which is built up by constructing it with the number of bands you intend to monitor, then repeatedly calling setFrequency( ) to indicate which frequency a given band will monitor.

As the audio plays, you can repeatedly call getSoundLevelMeterLevels( ), which returns an array of ints representing the measured levels.

Example 7-4 creates a basic audio level meter in an AWT Canvas.

Example 7-4. Providing an audio level meter

```
package com.oreilly.qtjnotebook.ch07;

import quicktime.*;
import quicktime.std.*;
import quicktime.std.movies.*;
import quicktime.std.movies.media.*;
import quicktime.app.view.*;
import quicktime.io.*;

import java.awt.*;
import java.awt.event.*;
import javax.swing.*;

import com.oreilly.qtjnotebook.ch01.QTSessionCheck;

public class LevelMeterPlayer extends Frame {

    // bands used by apple sndequalizer example; equivalent to qt player's
    // http://developer.apple.com/samplecode/sndequalizer/sndequalizer.html
    int[ ] EQ_LEVELS = {
        200,
        400,
        800,
        1600,
        3200,
        6400,
        12800,
        21000
    };
```

The margin note on the left reads:

Unfortunately, most of the level-metering methods are officially undocumented.

Example 7-4. Providing an audio level meter (continued)

```
    static final Dimension meterMinSize =
        new Dimension (300, 150);
    LevelMeter meter;
    AudioMediaHandler audioMediaHandler;

    public static void main (String[ ] args) {
        try {
            QTSessionCheck.check( );
            Frame f= new LevelMeterPlayer( );
            f.pack( );
            f.setVisible(true);
        } catch (QTException qte) {
            qte.printStackTrace( );
        }
    }

    public LevelMeterPlayer ( ) throws QTException {
        super ("Basic Audio Controls");
        // prompt for audio file
        QTFile file = QTFile.standardGetFilePreview(null);
        OpenMovieFile omf = OpenMovieFile.asRead (file);
        Movie movie = Movie.fromFile (omf);
        MovieController controller = new MovieController (movie);
        // get AudioMediaHandler for first audio track
        for (int i=1; i<=movie.getTrackCount( ); i++) {
            Track t = movie.getTrack(i);
            Media m = t.getMedia( );
            MediaHandler mh = m.getHandler( );
            if (mh instanceof AudioMediaHandler) {
                audioMediaHandler = (AudioMediaHandler) mh;
                break;
            }
        }
        if (audioMediaHandler == null) {
            System.out.println ("No audio track");
            System.exit(-1);
        }
        // add controller to GUI
        setLayout (new BorderLayout( ));
        Component comp =
            QTFactory.makeQTComponent(controller).asComponent( );
        add (comp, BorderLayout.NORTH);
        // add level meter to GUI
        meter = new LevelMeter( );
        add (meter, BorderLayout.SOUTH);
        // set up repainting timer
        Timer t = new Timer (50, new ActionListener() {
                public void actionPerformed (ActionEvent ae) {
                    meter.repaint( );
                }
            });
        t.start( );
```

Example 7-4. *Providing an audio level meter (continued)*

```java
}

class LevelMeter extends Canvas {
    public Dimension getPreferredSize() { return meterMinSize; }
    public Dimension getMinimumSize() { return meterMinSize; }
    public LevelMeter() throws QTException {
        MediaEQSpectrumBands bands =
            new MediaEQSpectrumBands (EQ_LEVELS.length);
        for (int i=0; i<EQ_LEVELS.length; i++) {
            bands.setFrequency (i, EQ_LEVELS[i]);
            audioMediaHandler.setSoundEqualizerBands (bands);
            audioMediaHandler.setSoundLevelMeteringEnabled (true);
        }
    }

    public void paint (Graphics g) {
        int gHeight = this.getHeight();
        int gWidth = this.getWidth();

        // draw baseline
        g.drawLine (0, gHeight, gWidth, gHeight);
        try {
            if (audioMediaHandler != null) {
                int[] levels =
                    audioMediaHandler.getSoundEqualizerBandLevels(
                                            EQ_LEVELS.length);
                int maxHeight = gHeight - 1;
                int barWidth = gWidth / levels.length;
                int segInterval = gHeight / 20;
                for (int i=0; i<levels.length; i++) {
                    // calculate height of each set of boxes,
                    // proportional to level
                    float levPct = ((float)levels[i]) / 255.0f;
                    // math is a little weird here; y axis has 0 at top,
                    // but we have 0 at bottom of this graph
                    int barHeight = (int) (levPct * maxHeight);
                    // draw the bar as set of 0-20 rectangles
                    int barCount = 0;
                    for (int j=maxHeight;
                         j > (maxHeight - barHeight);
                         j-=segInterval) {
                        switch (barCount) {
                        case 20:
                        case 19:
                        case 18:
                            g.setColor (Color.red);
                            break;
                        case 17:
                        case 16:
                        case 15:
                            g.setColor (Color.yellow);
                            break;
                        default:
```

Example 7-4. Providing an audio level meter (continued)

```
                          g.setColor (Color.green);
                    }
                    g.fillRect (i * barWidth,
                                j - segInterval,
                                barWidth - 1,
                                segInterval - 1);
                    barCount++;
              }
         }

      }
   } catch (QTException qte) {
      qte.printStackTrace( );
   }


}
}
```

Run this example with ant run-ch07-levelmeterplayer.

When run, this example provides the graphics-level display as shown in Figure 7-3.

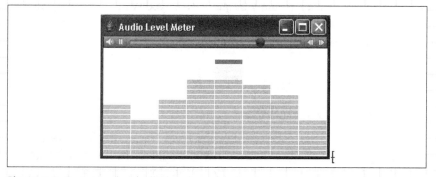

Figure 7-3. Frequency bands displayed as a level meter

What just happened?

This example sets up levels that, according to a demo in the native API, correspond to the same frequency bands metered by QuickTime Player:

```
int[ ] EQ_LEVELS = {
    200,
    400,
    800,
    1600,
    3200,
    6400,
    12800,
```

```
          21000
      };
```

When the user opens a movie, the program finds the AudioMediaHandler of the first audio track and calls setSoundEqualizerBands( ) with these bands. Then it creates an instance of the LevelMeter inner class, along with a Swing Timer to repaint the level meter every 50 milliseconds.

When the repaint calls the meter's paint( ) method, it divides its width by the number of bands to figure out how wide each bar should be. The height takes a little more work: the returned levels are in the range 0 to 255, so the program calculates a "level percent" float by dividing by 255, then multiplying this by the height of the component. With the height and width of each frequency band, the component can draw a set of boxes, up to that height, to represent the band's level.

What about...

...the values passed in for frequencies and the number that can be passed in? Unfortunately, with no documentation for this feature, there's only trial-and-error to fall back on. One thing I've found is that you can have only 10 bands—you can pass in as many frequencies as you want, and you'll get that many back in the int array returned by getSoundLevelMeterLevels( ), but only the first 10 will have nonzero values.

Building an Audio Track from Raw Samples

As I've said many times before: movies have tracks, tracks have media, media have samples. But what are these samples? In the case of sound, they indicate how much voltage should be applied to a speaker at an instant of time. By itself, a sample is meaningless, but as a speaker is repeatedly excited and relaxed, it creates waves of sound that move through the air and can be picked up by the ear.

So, why would you want to do this? One plausible scenario is that you have code that generates this uncompressed *pulse code modulation* (PCM) data, like a decoder for some format that QuickTime doesn't support. By writing the raw samples to an empty movie, you can expose it to QuickTime and then play it, export it to QT-supported formats, and use other QuickTime-related functions.

How do I do that?

SoundMedia inherits an addSample( ) method from the Media class. This can be used to pack samples into a Media, which in turn can be added to a Track, which then can be added to a Movie.

But what values do you provide to create an audible sound? The example shown in Example 7-5 creates a *square wave* at a constant frequency. A square wave is one in which the voltage is either fully on or completely off. To create a 1000-hertz (Hz) tone, you write samples to alternate between full voltage and zero voltage, 1,000 times per second. Figure 7-4 shows a graph of sample values for the square wave.

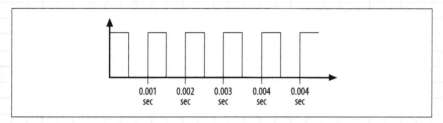

Figure 7-4. Square wave

Example 7-5. Building audio media by adding samples

Run this example with ant-ch07-audiosample-builder.

```
package com.oreilly.qtjnotebook.ch07;

import quicktime.*;
import quicktime.std.*;
import quicktime.std.movies.*;
import quicktime.std.movies.media.*;
import quicktime.io.*;
import quicktime.util.*;

import com.oreilly.qtjnotebook.ch01.QTSessionCheck;

public class AudioSampleBuilder extends Object {

    static final int SAMPLING = 44100;
    static final byte[ ] ONE_SECOND_SAMPLE = new byte [SAMPLING * 2];
    static final int FREQUENCY = 262;

    public static void main (String[ ] args) {
        try {
            QTSessionCheck.check( );

            QTFile movFile = new QTFile (new java.io.File("buildaudio.mov"));
            Movie movie =
                Movie.createMovieFile(movFile,
                        StdQTConstants.kMoviePlayer,
                        StdQTConstants.createMovieFileDeleteCurFile |
```

Example 7-5. Building audio media by adding samples (continued)

```
                         StdQTConstants.createMovieFileDontCreateResFile);

System.out.println ("Created Movie");

// create an empty audio track
int timeScale = SAMPLING; // 44100 units per second
Track soundTrack = movie.addTrack (0, 0, 1);

System.out.println ("Added empty Track");

// create media for this track
Media soundMedia = new SoundMedia (soundTrack,
                                        timeScale);
System.out.println ("Created Media");

// add samples
soundMedia.beginEdits();

// see native docs for other format consts
int format = QTUtils.toOSType ("NONE");

SoundDescription soundDesc = new SoundDescription(format);
System.out.println ("Created SoundDescription");

soundDesc.setNumberOfChannels(1);
soundDesc.setSampleSize(16);
soundDesc.setSampleRate(SAMPLING);

for (int i=0; i<5; i++) {
    // build the one-second sample
    QTHandle mediaHandle =  buildOneSecondSample (i);

    soundMedia.addSample(mediaHandle, // QTHandleRef data,
                         0, // int dataOffset,
                         mediaHandle.getSize(), // int dataSize,
                         1, // int durationPerSample,
                         soundDesc, // SampleDescription sampleDesc,
                         SAMPLING, // int numberOfSamples,
                         0 // int sampleFlags)
                         );
}

// finish editing and insert media into track
soundMedia.endEdits();
System.out.println ("Ended edits");
soundTrack.insertMedia (0, // trackStart
                        0, // mediaTime
                        soundMedia.getDuration(), // mediaDuration
                        1); // mediaRate
System.out.println ("inserted media");

// save up
```

Example 7-5. Building audio media by adding samples (continued)

```
        System.out.println ("Saving...");
        OpenMovieFile omf = OpenMovieFile.asWrite (movFile);
        movie.addResource (omf,
                            StdQTConstants.movieInDataForkResID,
                            movFile.getName( ));
        System.out.println ("Done");

        System.exit(0);

    } catch (QTException qte) {
        qte.printStackTrace( );
    }
} // main

/** Fill ONE_SECOND_SAMPLE with two-byte samples, according
    to some scheme (like square wave, sine wave, etc.)
    then wrap with QTHandle
 */
public static QTHandle buildOneSecondSample (int inTime)
    throws QTException {
    // convert inTime to sample count (i.e., how many samples
    // past 0 we are)
    int wavelengthInSamples = SAMPLING / FREQUENCY;
    int halfWavelength = wavelengthInSamples / 2;
    int sample = inTime * SAMPLING;
    for (int i=0; i<SAMPLING*2; i+=2) {
        int offset = sample % wavelengthInSamples;
        // square wave - bytes are either 7fff or 0000
        if (offset < halfWavelength) {
            ONE_SECOND_SAMPLE[i] = (byte) 0x7f;
            ONE_SECOND_SAMPLE[i+1] = (byte) 0xff;
        } else {
            ONE_SECOND_SAMPLE[i] = (byte) 0x00;
            ONE_SECOND_SAMPLE[i+1] = (byte) 0x00;
        }
        sample ++;
    }
    return new QTHandle (ONE_SECOND_SAMPLE);
    }
}
```

Square waves are not easy on the ears. Turn down your speakers or headphones before you play this file.

When run, this creates a five-second, audio-only movie file called *build-audio.mov*. Open it in QuickTime Player or an equivalent (like the level meter player from the previous lab) to listen to the file.

What just happened?

Two constants at the beginning define important values. SAMPLING is the number of samples to be played every second. This example uses 44,100, which is the same as on a compact disc.

TIP

An important consideration for choosing a sampling frequency is the *Nyquist-Shannon Sampling Theorem*, which states that you need to sample at a rate double the highest frequency you want to capture. So, a sampling rate of 44,100 will properly reproduce frequencies less than 22,050 Hz. Given that human hearing typically ranges from 20 to 20,000 Hz, this effectively covers any humanly audible sound.

The FREQUENCY constant is the frequency of the sound wave to be produced. This example uses 262, which is approximately middle C on a piano.

To be more precise, middle C is approximately 261.625565 Hz.

To start writing samples, you need a SoundMedia object and a place to put your data. The example does this by:

1. Creating a new Movie with createMovieFile( ). Using this approach—instead of the no-arg Movie constructor—has the benefit of indicating where the samples are to be stored.

2. Adding a new track to the movie, with no size, and a volume of 1 (full volume).

3. Creating a new SoundMedia object. This constructor takes the track the media is associated with and a time scale for the media. In this case, 44,100 is a good choice because then each sample will correspond to one unit of the media's time scale. You could use higher values, but not lower ones, because a sample can't be expressed as less than one unit of the time scale.

4. Calling beginEdits( ) on the media to indicate that the program will be making changes to the media.

See Chapter 2 for more on time scales.

Most of the rest of the code in the example has to do with setting up the call to addSample( ), which is somewhat tricky. The method takes seven arguments:

- A QTHandleRef that points to the data to be added
- An offset into the handle
- The size of the data to be inserted
- The durationPerSample—how much time the sample represents, in the media's time scale
- A SampleDescription to describe the data in the handle
- The number of samples being added with this call
- Behavior flags

The first thing to do is to create a SampleDescription that can be reused on every call to addSample(). To do this, create a SoundDescription object. The constructor takes a "format" FOUR_CHAR_CODE, which for uncompressed data is "NONE".

TIP

Other valid formats are defined in "QuickTime API Reference: SOund Formats" on Apple's developer site.

Next, you customize the SampleDescription object with some setter methods to indicate the number of channels, the size of each sample in bits, and the sampling frequency. For this example, I used one channel and 16 bits per sample. This means that when the byte array with the data is parsed, QuickTime will take the data 2 bytes at a time and assume it to be a 16-bit value. If there were two channels, there would be 4 bytes per sample: two 2-byte samples, one for each speaker.

You might expect that you'd then simply loop through, adding one sample at a time to the Media and creating one second of audio every 44,100 times through the loop. Although this is legal, the resulting file won't actually play. The problem is that QuickTime wants you to put audio data in larger and more manageable chunks. To quote from the native AddMediaSample docs:

> You should set the value of this parameter so that the resulting sample size represents a reasonable compromise between total data retrieval time and the overhead associated with input and output. [...] For a sound media, choose a number of samples that corresponds to between 0.5 and 1.0 seconds of sound. In general, you should not create groups of sound samples that are less than 2 KB in size or greater than 15 KB.

So, in this example, I've created a byte array to represent one second of samples, which is filled in a method called buildOneSecondSample(). This method figures out where the waveform is at each sample time and writes either 0x7fff or 0x0000 to each 2-byte pair. Because the "NONE" format assumes signed shorts, 0x7fff is the maximum, not 0xffff.

With the byte array filled, you can wrap it with a QTHandle, and you're ready to call addSample(). The call looks like this:

```
soundMedia.addSample(mediaHandle, // QTHandleRef data,
                0, // int dataOffset,
                mediaHandle.getSize(), // int dataSize,
                1, // int durationPerSample,
                soundDesc, // SampleDescription sampleDesc,
                SAMPLING, // int numberOfSamples,
                0 // int sampleFlags)
                );
```

Once you're done adding samples, it's cleanup time. You use endEdits() to tell the Media you're done editing, then actually put the media into the track with Track.insertMedia(), which tells the track what parts of the media object to use and where it goes relative to the track's time scale. Finally, the movie is written to disk with the curiously named Movie.addResource().

What about...

...some other kind of wave because hearing that square wave is really unpleasant? A sine wave offers a nicer alternative, because it is much more like a naturally occurring sound. Figure 7-5 shows what its waveform looks like.

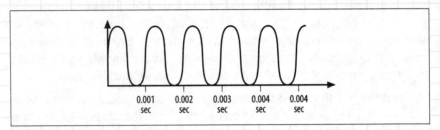

Figure 7-5. Sine wave

The following alternate implementation of buildOneSecondSample() produces a sine wave—I didn't want to put it in the preceding example, which is already complicated enough without having to use *trigonometry*, like this does:

```
public static QTHandle buildOneSecondSample (int inTime)
        throws QTException {
        // convert inTime to sample count (i.e., how many samples
        // past 0 we are)
        int wavelengthInSamples = SAMPLING / FREQUENCY;
        int sample = inTime * SAMPLING;
        double twoPi = 2 * Math.PI;
        double radiansPerSample = twoPi / wavelengthInSamples;
        // each sample should be one n/th of twoPi

        for (int i=0; i<SAMPLING*2; i+=2) {
            int offset = sample % wavelengthInSamples;
            // sine wave
            double angle = offset * radiansPerSample;
            double sine = Math.sin (angle);
            // sines are -1<x<1.  we want from 0 to 0x7fff
            double heightD = (sine + 1) * (0x7fff / 2);
            // cast to int and fix endianness if on little (x86, etc.)
            short height = (short) heightD;
            // pack this into array as two bytes
```

```
        ONE_SECOND_SAMPLE [i] = (byte) ((height & 0xff00) >> 8);
        ONE_SECOND_SAMPLE [i+1] = (byte) (height & 0xff);
        sample ++;
    }
    return new QTHandle (ONE_SECOND_SAMPLE);
}
```

This implementation calculates the width of a wavelength in samples, then divides that into equal segments of a 2π radius for its calls to `Math.sin( )`. The returned values are then translated so that instead of running from -1.0 to 1.0, they run from 0 to 0x7fff.

It's also worth noting that the middle C sine wave is pretty hard to hear over basic computer speakers. You might have better results with a frequency of 440, which is the A above middle C.

CHAPTER 8

Video Media

It probably seems like half of this book has already been about video—I've assumed you had video media for the chapters on playback, editing, and components (Chapters 2 and 4), even though the material there would be perfectly well suited for use on audio-only media like MP3 files. Well, this chapter is *only* about video, showing a handful of useful tricks for working with video.

Because video is simply a progression of images, alternated quickly enough to suggest movement, you probably won't be too surprised to know that the material covered in the QuickDraw graphics chapter (Chapter 5) pays off in this chapter. QuickDraw and QD-like APIs are the means by which you create and/or manipulate video media. If you skipped that chapter and have problems herein with QDGraphics (a.k.a. GWorlds), Matrixes, GraphicsImporters, or compression, you might need to check back there. But I'll try to keep things fairly self-explanatory.

Combining Video Tracks

It's not hard to understand how two audio tracks can coexist in a movie—the sounds are mixed and played together. But the idea of combining video tracks is less intuitive.

By default, if you have two video tracks of the same size in a movie, one will totally overlap the other. But you can change the default behavior by specifying 2D transformations with Matrix objects, and the Z-axis ordering by setting "layering" behavior.

One way to play with Matrix-based spatial arrangement is to set up a *picture-in-picture* movie. In such a movie, the foreground video is scaled and moved into a corner relative to the background video.

How do I do that?

To do a picture-in-picture effect, you must have a movie with two video tracks and you must do three things to the foreground video track:

- Scale it to a size smaller than the background track.
- Optionally move it to a location other than (0,0).
- Set layering to ensure it appears above the background track.

Fortunately, a few methods in the Track class provide all of this. The application in Example 8-1 brings up a window with a picture-in-picture effect achieved with matrix transformations and layering.

Run this example from the downloaded book code with ant run-ch08-matrixvideotracks.

Example 8-1. Matrix-based video picture-in-picture

```
package com.oreilly.qtjnotebook.ch08;

import quicktime.*;
import quicktime.std.*;
import quicktime.std.movies.*;
import quicktime.std.movies.media.*;
import quicktime.std.image.*;
import quicktime.io.*;
import quicktime.qd.*;
import quicktime.util.*;
import quicktime.app.view.*;

import com.oreilly.qtjnotebook.ch01.QTSessionCheck;

import java.awt.*;

public class MatrixVideoTracks extends Frame {

    static Movie foreMovie, backMovie;

    public static void main(String[] args) {
        try {
            QTSessionCheck.check();
            // get background movie
            QTFile file =
                QTFile.standardGetFilePreview (QTFile.kStandardQTFileTypes);
            OpenMovieFile omf = OpenMovieFile.asRead(file);
            backMovie = Movie.fromFile (omf);
            // get foreground movie
            file = QTFile.standardGetFilePreview (QTFile.kStandardQTFileTypes);
            omf = OpenMovieFile.asRead(file);
            foreMovie = Movie.fromFile (omf);
            // get frame
            Frame frame = new MatrixVideoTracks (backMovie, foreMovie);
            frame.pack();
            frame.setVisible (true);
        } catch (QTException qte) {
```

Example 8-1. Matrix-based video picture-in-picture (continued)

```
        qte.printStackTrace( );
    }
}

public MatrixVideoTracks (Movie backMovie, Movie foreMovie)
    throws QTException {
    super ("Matrix Video Tracks");
    Movie matrixMovie = new Movie( );
    // build tracks
    Track foreTrack = addVideoTrack (foreMovie, matrixMovie);
    Track backTrack = addVideoTrack (backMovie, matrixMovie);
    // set matrix transformation
    Matrix foreMatrix = new Matrix( );
    // set matrix to move fore to bottom right 1/4 or back
    QDRect foreFrom =
        new QDRect (0, 0,
                    foreTrack.getSize( ).getWidth( ),
                    foreTrack.getSize( ).getHeight( ));
    QDRect foreTo =
        new QDRect (backTrack.getSize( ).getWidth( ) / 2,
                    backTrack.getSize( ).getHeight( ) / 2,
                    backTrack.getSize( ).getWidth( ) / 2,
                    backTrack.getSize( ).getHeight( ) / 2);
    System.out.println ("foreTo is = " + foreTo);
    foreMatrix.rect (foreFrom, foreTo);
    foreTrack.setMatrix (foreMatrix);
    // set foreTrack's layer
    foreTrack.setLayer (-1);
    // now get component and add to frame
    MovieController controller = new MovieController(matrixMovie);
    Component c = QTFactory.makeQTComponent(controller).asComponent( );
    add (c);
}

public Track addVideoTrack (Movie sourceMovie, Movie targetMovie)
    throws QTException {
    // find first video track
    Track videoTrack =
        sourceMovie.getIndTrackType (1,
                                     StdQTConstants.videoMediaType,
                                     StdQTConstants.movieTrackMediaType);
    if (videoTrack == null)
        throw new QTException ("can't find a video track");
    // add videoTrack to targetMovie
    Track newTrack =
        targetMovie.newTrack (videoTrack.getSize( ).getWidthF( ),
                              videoTrack.getSize( ).getHeightF( ),
                              1.0f);
    VideoMedia newMedia =
        new VideoMedia (newTrack,
                        videoTrack.getMedia( ).getTimeScale( ),
                        new DataRef(new QTHandle( )));
```

Example 8-1. Matrix-based video picture-in-picture (continued)

```
        videoTrack.insertSegment (newTrack,
                                   0,
                                   videoTrack.getDuration( ),
                                   0);
        return newTrack;
    }
}
```

This example looks for a track with video media, so don't use audio-only files, or MPEG-1, which has a special "MPEG media" track instead of video.

When this is run, the user is shown two consecutive movie-opening dialogs, for the background and foreground movies, respectively. Assuming that both have video tracks, the result looks like Figure 8-1.

What just happened?

After the two movies are loaded, this demo creates a new empty target movie and, through a convenience method called addVideoTrack( ), finds the video tracks of the selected movies, creates new video tracks in the target movie, and inserts the VideoMedia from the source movies. This produces a movie with two concurrent video tracks.

Figure 8-1. Matrix-based transformation of foreground video track

Chapter 5 introduced Matrix. It's a mathematical object used in QuickTime to describe 2D transformations like scaling, rotation, etc.

To scale and move the foreground track, you use a Matrix transformation. In this case, the example takes the background movie's video track size and finds its center point, then sets up a destination rectangle with that point as its upper-left corner, with width and height equal to half the foreground's width and height, respectively. Finally, it tells the foreground track to use this matrix by calling Track.setMatrix( ):

```
QDRect foreFrom =
    new QDRect (0, 0,
                foreTrack.getSize().getWidth(),
                foreTrack.getSize().getHeight());
QDRect foreTo =
    new QDRect (backTrack.getSize().getWidth() / 2,
                backTrack.getSize().getHeight() / 2,
                backTrack.getSize().getWidth() / 2,
                backTrack.getSize().getHeight() / 2);
foreMatrix.rect (foreFrom, foreTo);
foreTrack.setMatrix (foreMatrix);
```

Next, to ensure that the foreground track draws above the background—if it doesn't, all this matrix work will be wasted—the demo calls Track.setLayer(-1). The layers are numbered from -32,767 to 32,767, with lower-numbered layers appearing above higher-numbered layers. The background track keeps its default layer, 0, so setting the foreground to -1 forces it to be on top.

What about...

...the point of this? Am I really ever going to want to overlay video tracks? It's more common than you might think. Consider Apple's iChat AV application—it uses a very similar picture-in-picture effect, so you can see yourself when you videoconference with a friend.

But there's one other interesting thing that iChat AV does: it shows the video of you as a *mirror image*. This, presumably, is more natural for users—if you raise your right hand, it somehow makes more sense to see your hand go up on the right side of the preview window, even if that's not what the camera is really seeing. Fortunately, a mirror image is really simple to do with a Matrix transformation.

In the preceding example, add the following two lines right after the Matrix is created:

```
foreMatrix.scale (-1, 1, 0, 0);
foreMatrix.translate ((float) foreTrack.getSize().getWidth(), 0f );
```

The scale() call makes the matrix multiply all pixels by -1, effectively "flipping" them around the x-axis. The y-coordinates are unchanged, so the scaling factor there is 1. The last two arguments define the "anchor point." By using 0, this says "flip around the x-axis" (the y-coordinate is similar but irrelevant here). Given an image width of w, this scaling operation makes the pixels run from $-w$ to 0. The translate() call moves the coordinates back into positive coordinate space. Figure 8-2 shows this transformation conceptually.

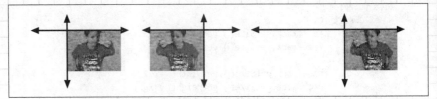

Figure 8-2. Matrix-based mirror image transformation steps: original, scaled by x-factor of -1, translated by adding width

For this to work you also need to change the `Matrix.rect()` call to `Matrix.map()`. `rect()` clears out any previous transformations, essentially defining a new matrix that represents only the translate-and-scale from one rectangle to another, while `map()` maintains the previous transformations and *then* applies the translate-and-scale.

Figure 8-3 shows the demo running with this mirror image added to the foreground transformation. For this figure, I've used the same video source for foreground and background, to make the mirror transformation more obvious.

Figure 8-3. Matrix-based mirror image of foreground video track

This mirror effect is pretty handy, and you might use it all by itself for doing something like a capture preview. Because the `Matrix` can be used on movie tracks, `GraphicsImporters`, and various other parts of the QuickTime API, mastering `Matrix` transformations will get you pretty far.

Did you notice the capture settings dialog in Chapter 6 showed a mirror image? You could use a Matrix to make the motion detector in that chapter render a mirror image, too.

Overlaying Video Tracks

When one video track is drawn on top of another, the top doesn't necessarily have to obscure the bottom. QuickTime gives you the option of specifying a GraphicsMode to combine pixels from multiple video layers to create interesting effects.

How do I do that?

Run this example with ant run-ch08-composit-evideotracks.

You can create a GraphicsMode object to describe the means of combining overlapping colors. To try it out, take the previous lab's code and replace all the matrix stuff (after the foreTrack and backTrack are created, but before the MovieController is created) with the following:

```
GraphicsMode gm = new GraphicsMode (QDConstants.addMax,
                                    QDColor.green);
VisualMediaHandler foreHandler =
    (VisualMediaHandler) foreTrack.getMedia().getHandler();
foreHandler.setGraphicsMode(gm);
foreTrack.setLayer(-1);
```

When run, this sample program asks you to open two movies, then creates a new movie with video tracks from the source movies' media, and combines the pixels of the foreground movie with the background, so the foreground appears atop the background. The result is shown in Figure 8-4.

Figure 8-4. Composited video tracks with addMax graphics mode

What just happened?

Setting a GraphicsMode instructs QuickTime to apply a specific behavior to combine overlapping pixels. The GraphicsMode has a "mode" int, which indicates which kind of behavior to use, and a QDColor that is used by some behaviors to indicate a color to operate on. For example, you might use mode QDConstants.transparent and QDColor.green to make all green pixels transparent. The default mode is srcCopy, which simply copies one set of pixels on top of another.

Chapter 5 showed how to set up GraphicsMode compositing of still images. Video works in pretty much the same way.

To apply this GraphicsMode to overlapping video tracks, you call setGraphicsMode( ), a method not defined by Track but, rather, by the VideoMediaHandler. As a reminder, movies have tracks, tracks have media, and media have handlers. Actually, the setGraphicsMode( ) is defined by the VisualMediaHandler interface, making it available for all visual media (MPEGMedia, TextMedia, etc.).

The addMax behavior combines background and foreground pixels, using the maximum red, green, and blue values of each. This has the effect of producing something of a washed-out combination of the two video tracks, because bright colors in either source will be copied over to the screen.

The available QDConstant modes offer several dozen behaviors—check them out in the QuickTime documentation by searching Apple's site for "Graphics Transfer Modes"—though some of them aren't suitable for color images, and many of them produce garish results with real-world video. For example, Figure 8-5 shows the rather psychedelic effect of using the srcBic mode.

Figure 8-5. Composited video tracks with srcBic graphics mode

What about...

...practical uses for this? Granted, compositing two full-frame natural images is atypical, but composited video is used all the time in TV production. Modern video often represents many layers of overlapping sources. Watch a football game and you might see a shot of the game, overlaid by a graphic of a player and his stats (and maybe a video "head shot" of him), overlaid with a scoreboard for the corner, overlaid with a moving "bug" of the network's logo in another corner. Each source contains some amount of "useful" video, and the rest is a solid color (often black for synthetic video, green or blue for real-world video). The solid color becomes transparent, so only the useful data is copied over to the target. In terms of GraphicsModes, this would be the transparent mode, with the specified color as the operand.

TIP

If you're serious about shooting bluescreen video, there are sites on the Internet that list the supplies you'll need. For example, *http://www.studiodepot.com/* sells chroma-key-friendly fabric and tape for making bluescreen and greenscreen backdrops.

Building a Video Track from Raw Samples

You can create a video track "from scratch" by adding video samples, one by one, to the video media. This is perhaps the ultimate in low-level access to QuickTime video, because it makes you responsible for every pixel in every frame. One way to demonstrate this is by making a movie from a still image and using slightly different parts of it in each frame to suggest a camera moving across the image.

TIP

This concept is called the "Ken Burns Effect" in Apple's iMovie, after the documentary filmmaker who used the technique extensively in documentaries like *The Civil War*, for which no film or video sources were available.

How do I do that?

To build a movie from samples taken from an image, use the following approach:

1. Import an image.
2. Pick source and destination rectangles.
3. Calculate a series of rectangles between the source and destination. These represent which part of the source image will be used for each frame.
4. Create an empty movie, new video track, and new video media.
5. Use a `Matrix` to convert each source rectangle to the size of the movie.
6. Compress each frame and add it to the `VideoMedia`.

You might already know how to do some of this; the new part is how to compress frames into a movie. Chapter 5 made use of the `QTImage.compress()` method to compress `QDGraphics` (a.k.a. `GWorlds`) into `EncodedImages`, but video is a little different in that you use a `CSequence`, short for *compression sequence*. The difference is that in many video compression formats, you may need information from previous or subsequent frames to render a specific frame. In other words, some frames are encoded as just the data that has changed from a previous frame. So, you can't compress a single image in isolation; you must work with a sequence of images. This is called *temporal compression* because it is time-based.

The `VideoSampleBuilder` demo, shown in Example 8-2, creates a movie called *videotrack.mov* from a source graphic.

TIP

This is the most involved example in the book and uses concepts from several chapters, such as enabling editing and adding a new Track (Chapter 3), using a GraphicsImporter (Chapter 4), setting up an off-screen GWorld (Chapter 5), using Matrix-based image manipulation (Chapter 5 and this chapter), and adding raw samples to a Media (a sound equivalent was shown in Chapter 7). So, don't be intimidated if it seems a little complicated the first time you read it.

Run this demo with ant run-ch08-videosample-builder.

Example 8-2. Building a video track from image samples

```
package com.oreilly.qtjnotebook.ch08;

import quicktime.*;
```

Example 8-2. Building a video track from image samples (continued)

```java
import quicktime.io.*;
import quicktime.util.QTPointer;
import quicktime.qd.*;
import quicktime.std.*;
import quicktime.std.movies.*;
import quicktime.std.movies.media.*;
import quicktime.std.image.*;
import quicktime.util.*;

import com.oreilly.qtjnotebook.ch01.QTSessionCheck;

import java.io.*;
import java.util.Random;
import java.util.Properties;

public class VideoSampleBuilder extends Object {

    public static final int VIDEO_TRACK_WIDTH = 320;
    public static final int VIDEO_TRACK_HEIGHT = 240;
    public static final int VIDEO_TRACK_VOLUME = 0;
    public static final int KEY_FRAME_RATE = 30;

    Properties userProps = new Properties();
    QDRect startRect = null;
    QDRect endRect = null;

    public VideoSampleBuilder() throws QTException, IOException {

        /* try to load "videoSampleBuilder.properties" from
           current directory.  this contains file.location and
           start.x/y/width/height and end.x/y/width/height params
         */
        try {
            userProps.load (new FileInputStream (
                new File ("videosamplebuilder.properties")));
            System.out.println ("Loaded properties");
        } catch (Exception e) {
            System.out.println ("Couldn't load properties");
        }

        int CODEC_TYPE = QTUtils.toOSType ("SVQ3");

        // create a new empty movie
        QTFile movFile = new QTFile (new java.io.File("videotrack.mov"));
        Movie movie =
            Movie.createMovieFile(movFile,
                    StdQTConstants.kMoviePlayer,
                    StdQTConstants.createMovieFileDeleteCurFile |
                    StdQTConstants.createMovieFileDontCreateResFile);
        System.out.println ("Created Movie");

        // now create an empty video track
```

Example 8-2. Building a video track from image samples (continued)

```java
int timeScale = 600; // 100 units per second
Track videoTrack = movie.addTrack (VIDEO_TRACK_WIDTH,
                                    VIDEO_TRACK_HEIGHT,
                                    VIDEO_TRACK_VOLUME);
System.out.println ("Added empty Track");

// now we need media for this track
VideoMedia videoMedia = new VideoMedia(videoTrack,
                                       timeScale);

// get image file from props or dialog
QTFile imgFile = getImageFile();
if (imgFile == null)
    return;

// get a GraphicsImporter
GraphicsImporter importer = new GraphicsImporter (imgFile);
System.out.println ("Got GraphicsImporter - Bounds are " +
                    importer.getNaturalBounds());

// Create an offscreen QDGraphics / GWorld that's the
// size of our frames.  Importer will draw into this,
// and we'll then hand it to the CSequence
QDGraphics gw =
    new QDGraphics (new QDRect (0, 0,
                               VIDEO_TRACK_WIDTH,
                               VIDEO_TRACK_HEIGHT));
System.out.println ("Created GWorld, - Bounds are " +
                    gw.getBounds());

// get start, end rects
getRects (importer);
System.out.println ("startRect = " + startRect);
System.out.println ("endRect = " + endRect);

// set importer's gworld
importer.setGWorld (gw, null);
System.out.println ("Reset importer's GWorld, now: " +
                    importer.getGWorld());

// get to work
videoMedia.beginEdits();

// figure out per-frame offsets
QDRect gRect = new QDRect (0, 0,
                          VIDEO_TRACK_WIDTH,
                          VIDEO_TRACK_HEIGHT);

int frames = 300;
int startX = startRect.getX();
int startY = startRect.getY();
int endX = endRect.getX();
int endY = endRect.getY();
```

Example 8-2. Building a video track from image samples (continued)

```
float xOffPerFrame = ((float)(endX - startX) / (float)frames);
float yOffPerFrame = ((float)(endY - startY) / (float)frames);
float widthOffPerFrame = ((float) (endRect.getWidth() -
                                    startRect.getWidth()) /
                          (float) frames);
float heightOffPerFrame = ((float) (endRect.getHeight() -
                                    startRect.getHeight()) /
                           (float) frames);

System.out.println ("xOffPerFrame=" + xOffPerFrame +
                    ", yOffPerFrame=" + yOffPerFrame +
                    ", widthOffPerFrame=" + widthOffPerFrame +
                    ", heightOffPerFrame=" + heightOffPerFrame);

// reserve an image with enough space to hold compressed image
// this is needed by the last arg of CSequence.compressFrame
int rawImageSize =
    QTImage.getMaxCompressionSize (gw,
                                   gRect,
                                   gw.getPixMap().getPixelSize(),
                                   StdQTConstants.codecNormalQuality,
                                   CODEC_TYPE,
                                   CodecComponent.bestFidelityCodec);
QTHandle imageHandle = new QTHandle (rawImageSize, true);
imageHandle.lock();
RawEncodedImage compressedImage =
    RawEncodedImage.fromQTHandle(imageHandle);

// create a CSequence
CSequence seq = new CSequence (gw,
                               gRect,
                               gw.getPixMap().getPixelSize(),
                               CODEC_TYPE,
                               CodecComponent.bestFidelityCodec,
                               StdQTConstants.codecNormalQuality,
                               StdQTConstants.codecNormalQuality,
                               KEY_FRAME_RATE,
                               null,
                               StdQTConstants.codecFlagUpdatePrevious);

// remember an ImageDescription from this sequence definition
ImageDescription imgDesc = seq.getDescription();

// loop through the specified number of frames, drawing
// scaled instances into our GWorld and compressing those
// to the CSequence
for (int i=1; i<frames; i++) {
    System.out.println ("i==" + i);

    // compute a rect for this frame
    int x = startX + (int) (xOffPerFrame * i);
    int y = startY + (int) (yOffPerFrame * i);
```

Example 8-2. Building a video track from image samples (continued)

```java
int width = startRect.getWidth() + (int) (widthOffPerFrame * i);
int height = startRect.getHeight() + (int) (heightOffPerFrame * i);
QDRect fromRect = new QDRect (x, y, width, height);

// create a Matrix to represent the move/scale from
// the fromRect to the GWorld and make importer use it
Matrix drawMatrix = new Matrix();
drawMatrix.rect (fromRect, gRect);
System.out.println ("fromRect = " + fromRect);
importer.setMatrix (drawMatrix);

// have importer draw (scaled) into our GWorld
importer.draw();
System.out.println ("Importer drew");

// compress a frame
CompressedFrameInfo cfInfo =
    seq.compressFrame (gw,
                       gRect,
                       StdQTConstants.codecFlagUpdatePrevious,
                       compressedImage);
System.out.println ("similarity = " + cfInfo.getSimilarity());

// is this a key frame?
boolean syncSample = (cfInfo.getSimilarity() == 0);
int flags = syncSample ? 0 : StdQTConstants.mediaSampleNotSync;

// add compressed frame to the video media
videoMedia.addSample (imageHandle,
                      0,
                      cfInfo.getDataSize(),
                      20, // time per frame, in timescale
                      imgDesc,
                      1, // one sample
                      flags
                      );
} // for

// done editing
videoMedia.endEdits();

// now insert this media into track
videoTrack.insertMedia (0, // trackStart
                        0, // mediaTime
                        videoMedia.getDuration(), // mediaDuration
                        1); // mediaRate
System.out.println ("inserted media into video track");

// save up
System.out.println ("Saving...");
OpenMovieFile omf = OpenMovieFile.asWrite (movFile);
movie.addResource (omf,
```

Example 8-2. Building a video track from image samples (continued)

```java
                        StdQTConstants.movieInDataForkResID,
                        movFile.getName());
    System.out.println ("Done");

}

/** Gets imageFile from props file, or file-preview if
    that doesn't work.
 */
protected QTFile getImageFile () throws QTException {
    // is it in the props?
    QTFile imageFile = null;
    if (userProps.containsKey ("file")) {
        imageFile = new QTFile (userProps.getProperty("file"));
        if (! imageFile.exists())
            imageFile = null;
    }

    // if not, or if that failed, then use a dialog
    if (imageFile == null) {
        int[] types = {};
        imageFile = QTFile.standardGetFilePreview (types);
    }
    return imageFile;
}

/** Gets startRect, endRect from userProps, or selects
    randomly if that doesn't work
 */
protected void getRects (GraphicsImporter importer) throws QTException {
    Random rand = new Random();
    int rightStop =
        importer.getNaturalBounds().getWidth() - VIDEO_TRACK_WIDTH;
    int bottomStop =
        importer.getNaturalBounds().getHeight() - VIDEO_TRACK_HEIGHT;

    // try to get startRect from userProps
    try {
        int startX = Integer.parseInt (userProps.getProperty("start.x"));
        int startY = Integer.parseInt (userProps.getProperty("start.y"));
        int startWidth =
            Integer.parseInt (userProps.getProperty("start.width"));
        int startHeight =
            Integer.parseInt (userProps.getProperty("start.height"));
        startRect = new QDRect (startX, startY, startWidth, startHeight);
    } catch (Exception e) {
        // make random start rect
        int startX = Math.abs (rand.nextInt() % rightStop);
        int startY = Math.abs (rand.nextInt() % bottomStop);
        startRect = new QDRect (startX, startY,
                                VIDEO_TRACK_WIDTH,
                                VIDEO_TRACK_HEIGHT);
```

Example 8-2. Building a video track from image samples (continued)

```
            }

            // try to get endRect from userProps
            try {
                int endX = Integer.parseInt (userProps.getProperty("end.x"));
                int endY = Integer.parseInt (userProps.getProperty("end.y"));
                int endWidth = Integer.parseInt (userProps.getProperty("end.width"));
                int endHeight = Integer.parseInt (userProps.getProperty("end.
height"));
                endRect = new QDRect (endX, endY, endWidth, endHeight);

            } catch (Exception e) {
                float zoom = (rand.nextFloat( ) - 0.5f); // -0.5 <= zoom <= 0.5
                System.out.println ("zoom = " + zoom);
                int endX = Math.abs (rand.nextInt( ) % rightStop);
                int endY = Math.abs (rand.nextInt( ) % bottomStop);
                endRect = new QDRect (endX, endY,
                                      VIDEO_TRACK_WIDTH * zoom,
                                      VIDEO_TRACK_HEIGHT * zoom);
            }
        }

    public static void main (String[ ] arrrImAPirate) {
        try {
            QTSessionCheck.check( );
            new VideoSampleBuilder( );
        } catch (Exception e) {
            e.printStackTrace( );
        }
        System.exit(0);
    }
}
```

When run, the demo looks for a file called *videosamplebuilder.properties*, in which you can define the source image and the start and end rectangles. The properties file should have entries like this:

```
file=/Users/cadamson/Pictures/keagy/DSC01763.jpg

start.x=545
start.y=370
start.width=1500
start.height=1125

end.x=400
end.y=390
end.width=800
end.height=600
```

If no properties file is found, the demo queries the user for an image and randomly selects the start and end rectangles.

As each frame is compressed, the program prints an update to the console indicating the frame count, the source frame, and how "similar" the CSequence decided the frame was to its predecessor. The console log looks something like this:

```
cadamson% ant run-ch08-videosamplebuilder
Buildfile: build.xml

run-ch08-videosamplebuilder:
    [java] Couldn't load properties
    [java] Created Movie
    [java] Added empty Track
    [java] Got GraphicsImporter - Bounds are quicktime.qd.QDRect[x=0.0,y=0.
0,width=800.0,height=600.0]
    [java] Created GWorld, - Bounds are quicktime.qd.QDRect[x=0.0,y=0.
0,width=320.0,height=240.0]
    [java] zoom = -0.45799363
    [java] startRect = quicktime.qd.QDRect[x=158.0,y=30.0,width=320.
0,height=240.0]
    [java] endRect = quicktime.qd.QDRect[x=282.0,y=158.0,width=146.
55795,height=109.91846]
    [java] Reset importer's GWorld, now: quicktime.qd.
QDGraphics@8f10820[size=108][PortRect=quicktime.qd.QDRect[x=0.0,y=0.
0,width=320.0,height=240.0],isOffscreen=true]
    [java] xOffPerFrame=0.41333333, yOffPerFrame=0.42666668,
widthOffPerFrame=-0.58, heightOffPerFrame=-0.43666667
    [java] i==1
    [java] fromRect = quicktime.qd.QDRect[x=158.0,y=30.0,width=320.
0,height=240.0]
    [java] Importer drew
    [java] similarity = 0
    [java] i==2
    [java] fromRect = quicktime.qd.QDRect[x=158.0,y=30.0,width=319.
0,height=240.0]
    [java] Importer drew
    [java] similarity = 128
```

When finished, you can play the *videotrack.mov* file in QuickTime Player, the player and editor examples in Chapters 2 and 3, or equivalent. Figure 8-6 shows two screenshots from different times in the movie to indicate the zoom effect that is created by using different parts of the picture.

What just happened?

One of the first things to notice is the constant CODEC_TYPE, which is used later on in setting up the CSequence. This indicates which of the supported QuickTime video codecs is to be used for the video track. The codec is indicated by a FOUR_CHAR_CODE int, in this case "SVQ3", which identifies the Sorenson Video 3 codec. Most of the usable codecs exist as constants in the

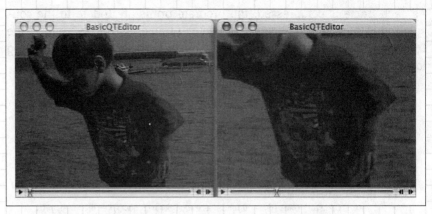

Figure 8-6. Movie built via addSample( ) from portions of a static image

See Chapter 4 for more info on FOUR_CHAR_CODEs. You can use the "component tour" demo there to find supported compressors on your system—just type "imco".

StdQTConstants classes—for example, I could have put this as StdQTConstants6.kSorenson3CodecType. The advantage of using the FOUR_CHAR_CODE directly is that you can use any supported codec, even those that don't have constants defined in QTJ yet. In fact, Sorenson Video 3 and MPEG-4 video (StdQTConstants6.kMPEG4VisualCodecType) didn't have constants in QTJ until I filed a bug report for them, and the Pixlet codec (whose 4CC is "pxlt") still doesn't, as of this writing.

TIP

"So, what's the best codec?" I hear someone asking. Don't go there. There's no such thing as a best codec. There are so many different codecs, because they're engineered to serve different purposes. For example, some codecs are difficult to compress (in terms of CPU power, encoder expertise, etc.) but easy to decompress, making them well suited for mass-distribution media like DVDs where the encoding is done only once. On the other hand, a codec used for video conferencing must be light enough to do on the fly, with minimal configuration. Others are tuned to specific bitrates and uses, losing their advantages outside their preferred realm. The new MPEG-4 codec, H.264 (AVC), claims to be able to scale from cell phone to HDTV bandwidths...we'll see if it delivers on this.

These steps are similar to those in Chapter 7's square-wave sample-building example.

To build the image movie, create an empty movie file, add a track, and create a VideoMedia for the track. You do this by creating a Movie with the constructor that takes a file reference (so that QuickTime knows where to put the samples you'll be adding), calling Movie.addTrack( ) to create the track, and constructing a VideoMedia. Then call Media.beginEdits( ) to signal that you're going to be altering the VideoMedia.

The next step is to get the image with a GraphicsImporter. This will be the source of every frame of the movie. However, it's not the right size. So create an off-screen QDGraphics (a.k.a. GWorld, the term used in the native API and all its getters and setters in QTJ) with the desired movie dimensions. By calling GraphicsImporter.setGWorld(), you tell the importer that subsequent calls to draw() will draw pixels from the imported graphic into the off-screen GWorld, which will be the source of the compressed frames later on.

Next, after calculating how far the source rectangle will move each frame, you set up the compression sequence. To do this, you need a buffer big enough to hold compressed images, which in turn requires a call to figure out how big that buffer needs to be. QTImage.getMaxCompression() size provides this size. You need to pass in the following data (in the order shown):

1. The QDGraphics/GWorld to compress from.
2. A QDRect indicating what part of the QDGraphics will be used.
3. The color depth of the pixels (i.e., how many bits are in each pixel).
4. A constant to indicate the compressed image quality level.
5. The codec's FOUR_CHAR_CODE.
6. A constant to indicate which codec component to pick if several can handle the codec. You can pass a specific component, or the behavior constants anyCodec, bestSpeedCodec, bestFidelityCodec, and bestCompressionCodec.

Given this, you can allocate memory for the image by constructing a new QTHandle, and then wrap it with a RawEncodedImage object. This is where the compressed frames will go.

Now you have enough information to create the CSequence. Its constructor takes a whopping 10 arguments:

- The QDGraphics/GWorld to compress from
- A QDRect indicating what part of the QDGraphics will be used
- The color depth of the pixels (i.e., how many bits are in each pixel)
- The codec's FOUR_CHAR_CODE
- A specific codec component or a selection strategy constant (anyCodec, bestSpeedCodec, etc.)
- Spatial quality (in other words, the quality of images after 2D compression, using one of the constants codecMinQuality, codecLowQuality, codecNormalQuality, codecHighQuality, codecMaxQuality, or codecLosslessQuality)

- Temporal quality (this uses the same constants as for spatial quality, but refers to quality maintained or lost when using data from adjacent frames; you also can set this to 0 to not use temporal compression)
- Key frame rate (the maximum number of frames allowed between "key frames" [those that have all image data for a frame and don't depend on other frames], or 0 to not use key frames)
- A custom color lookup table, or null to use the table from the source image
- Behavior flags (these can include the codecFlagWasCompressed flag, which indicates the source image was previously compressed and asks the codec to compensate, and codecFlagUpdatePrevious and codecFlagUpdatePreviousComp, both of which hold on to previously compressed frames for temporal-compression codecs, the latter of which may produce better results but consumes more CPU power)

Now you've got everything you need to build the frames: a GWorld for source images, a RawEncodedImage to compress into, a CSequence to compress frames, and a VideoMedia to put them into.

So, start looping. Each time through the loop, you draw a different part of the source image into the off-screen GWorld. This is done by resetting the GraphicImporter's Matrix, using rect() to scale-and-translate from a source rectangle to a new rectangle at (0,0) and with the dimensions of the off-screen GWorld. Use GraphicsImporter.draw() to draw from the source image into the GWorld.

With the frame's pixels in the GWorld, call CSequence.compressFrame() to compress the pixels into the RawEncodedImage. This returns a CompressedFrameInfo object that wraps the size of the compressed image and a "similarity" value that represents the similarity or difference between the current frame and the previous frame. The similarity is used to determine if this sample is a "key frame" (also called a "sync sample" in Apple's terminology), which in this context means an image so different from its predecessors that the compressor should encode all the data for this image in this frame instead of depending on any previous frames.

Finally, you call addSample() to add the frame to the VideoMedia. This call, inherited from Media, takes a pointer to the sample data, an offset into the data, the data size, the time represented by the sample (in the media's time scale), a description of the data (here an ImageDescription retrieved from the CSequence), the number of samples being added with the call, and a flag that indicates whether this sample is a key frame (if it's not, pass StdQTConstants.mediaSampleNotSync).

Notice addSample() has the same signature for any kind of media. That's why it needs a parameter like the ImageDescription to explain what's in the essentially untyped QTHandle.

When you're done adding frames, call Media.endEdits( ), then insert the media into the track with Track.insertMedia( ). Finally, save the movie with the Movie.addResource( ) call.

Again, this wrap-up is the same as Chapter 7's audio sample-building technique.

What about...

...appropriate codecs to use? I've pointed out Sorenson Video 3 and MPEG-4 Visual, because they have very nice compression ratios and still look pretty good with natural images. Other codecs of interest in a standard QuickTime installation are shown in Table 8-1.

Table 8-1. Some standard QuickTime codecs

Name	Constant	4CC	Description
Animation	kAnimationCodecType	"rle "	Good for long runs of solid colors, such as those found in simple synthetic 2D graphics.
Cinepak	kCinepakCodecType	"cvid"	This was the most popular codec of the early to mid-1990s, thanks to a good compression/quality tradeoff, wide support (even Sun's JMF handles it), and the fact that it could run on very modest CPUs. Today, there are better options.
H.263	kH263CodecType	"h263"	This standard originally was designed for video-conferencing, yet is surprisingly good in a wide range of bitrates.
Pixlet	N/A	"pxlt"	This wavelet-based codec, introduced in 2003, achieves high compression rates (20:1) without showing graphics artifacts like other codecs at similar compression levels. It requires powerful CPUs (PowerPC G4 or G5 at 1GHz and up) to decode.

As of this writing, Apple has demonstrated but not released an H.264 (aka AVC) codec for QuickTime. This is the newest and most powerful MPEG-4 codec, offering broadcast-quality video at 1.5 megabits per second (Mbps) and HDTV quality at 5-9Mbps, assuming your computer is powerful enough to decode it.

Considering Chapter 5 showed how to grab the screen (even with the DVD Player running) into a GWorld, and considering you can make video tracks from any GWorld...uh-oh.

Also, other than making these "Ken Burns Effects," what am I going to do with writing video samples? This technique is the key to creating *anything you want* in a video track. Want to make a movie of your screen? Use the screen-grab lab from Chapter 5 and compress its GWorld into a video track. Have some code to decode a format that QuickTime doesn't understand? Now you can transcode to any QuickTime-supported format. You even can take 3D images from an OpenGL or JOGL application and make them into movies.

Miscellaneous Media

Audio and video are the most obvious and prominent kinds of media that can be found in a QuickTime movie, but the story doesn't end there. Take a look at quicktime.std.movies.media, and you'll find more than a dozen subclasses of Media, each representing media types that can be referenced by tracks in QuickTime movies.

This chapter is going to show off four of these, as much to show the variety of QuickTime as to illuminate their practical uses. These four are:

- Text media
- HREF media (actually a special case of text)
- Timecode media
- Effects media (actually a special case of video)

Elsewhere in the book, I've also mentioned MPEG media, which isn't so much a new media type as it is a disappointing compromise—QuickTime can't present the audio and video of a multiplexed MPEG-1 or MPEG-2 file as separate tracks, so instead it uses a single track pointing to "MPEGMedia," which has both visual and audio characteristics (i.e., its media handler implements both VisualMediaHandler and AudioMediaHandler).

I'm not covering several media types for reasons of space and concision. Sprites (represented by SpriteMedia) and QuickTime VR (QTVRMedia) are plenty cool; however, each required an entire volume of the old *Inside Macintosh* series, making them too involved to handle in this format. ThreeDMedia is effectively deprecated and isn't even present in Mac OS X. A few other media types are present largely as implementations for higher-level features—for instance, MovieMedia came about as part of the implementation of SMIL (an XML markup that lets authors, among other things, make movies that contain movies).

Creating Captions with Text Media

Have you ever turned on captions on a DVD, perhaps for a foreign-language film? Have you ever wondered how that works, especially given that the DVD might have captions for several different languages? QuickTime can do the same thing, easily and efficiently.

The idea is that a movie can have zero-to-many text tracks (literally, tracks with text media), each of which has a collection of text samples. Each sample contains some text and a time to display it. In that sense, they're like any other media samples—they have some data to be presented and a time and duration indicating when to present it. So, to do a caption, you'd just have a single text sample that begins at a relevant time in the movie (like when someone on-screen starts speaking) and has an appropriate duration (how long the person speaks).

How do I do that?

To keep things simple, I'll focus on creating a movie with a single text track. Once you know how to do that, it's easy to add your own text track to existing movies.

These are the steps for adding any kind of media.

If you read the sample-building examples in Chapters 7 or 8, you probably already know what's coming. To build a text track, you:

1. Add a track to a movie.
2. Create new media for the track.
3. Call `Media.beginEdits( )`.
4. Add samples.
5. Call `Media.endEdits( )`.
6. Insert the media into the track.
7. Save the movie.

The biggest difference between adding different kinds of media is the setup you have to do for the `Media.addSample( )` call. In the case of text, use TextMedia.getTextHandler() to get a TextMediaHandler object, which offers a convenient addTextSample() call. This method lets you specify font, size, color, and various other options. In fact, it takes *14* parameters (amazingly, in this exact order):

- A QTPointerRef to the string to be added (typically, you call getBytes() on a Java string and wrap them with a QTPointer to provide this argument)
- A font number (you can look up the font number from a font family's name via the QDFont.getFNum() method, or just pass 0 for a sensible default font)
- Font size
- Text face, meaning style information like QDConstants.bold, QDConstants.italic, or QDConstants.underline, combined with the | operator
- Text color, as a QDColor value (this defaults to black if you pass null)
- Background color, as a QDColor value (this defaults to white if you pass null)
- Text justification, using one of the QDConstants values teFlushLeft, teFlushRight, teCenter, or teFlushDefault (the "teJust..." constants in this class seem to do the same thing, too)
- Text box, a QDRect defining the bounding rectangle of the text (don't worry about this matching the size of a movie you want to add it to—you can make a small text box at (0,0) and move it into position by adding a Matrix translation to the text track)
- Display flags (covered later)
- Scroll delay (covered later)
- Highlight start (this is the index of the first character to be highlighted)
- Highlight end (this is the index of the last character to be highlighted)
- Highlight color, as a QDColor value
- Duration, in the media's time scale

The display flags parameter takes any number of the df constants from StdQTConstants, combined with the | operator. The possible behaviors are shown in Table 9-1.

Table 9-1. Text sample display flags

Display flag	Behavior
dfDontDisplay	Don't show this sample.
dfDontAutoScale	Don't scale text if bounding rectangle is resized.
dfClipToTextBox	Clips to the size of the bounding rectangle; useful if overlaying video.
dfShrinkTextBoxToFit	Recalculates the size of the text box parameter to just fit the text.
dfScrollIn	Scrolls the text in. If set, the scroll delay argument determines how long the text lingers before being scrolled out.
dfScrollHoriz	Makes the text scroll in horizontally, instead of vertically (the default).
dfReverseScroll	Reverses the typical scroll direction, which is bottom-to-top for vertical scrolling and left-to-right for horizontal.
dfContinuousScroll	Causes new samples to force previous samples to scroll out. You must set dfScrollIn and/or dfScrollOut for this to do anything.
dfFlowHoriz	Allows text to flow within the bounding rectangle instead of going off to the right.
dfContinuousKaraoke	Ignores the highlight start argument and highlights from the beginning of the text to "highlight end." This allows you to progressively "grow" a highlight through a line of lyrics, presumably for a karaoke application.
dfDropShadow	Displays text with a drop shadow.
dfAntiAlias	Displays text with anti-aliasing.
dfKeyedText	Displays text without drawing a background color. This is ideal for putting captions on top of video.
dfInverseHilite	Highlights with inverse video instead of the highlight color.

Who knew QuickTime was optimized for karaoke? すごい

Example 9-1 shows a simple application that creates a movie with a single text track, containing four samples, each lasting 2.5 seconds.

If you downloaded the book code, run this example with ant run-ch09-texttrackbuilder.

Example 9-1. Creating a text track

```
package com.oreilly.qtjnotebook.ch09;

import quicktime.*;
import quicktime.std.*;
import quicktime.std.movies.*;
import quicktime.std.movies.media.*;
import quicktime.io.*;
import quicktime.util.*;
import quicktime.qd.*;
```

Example 9-1. Creating a text track (continued)

```java
import com.oreilly.qtjnotebook.ch01.QTSessionCheck;

public class TextTrackBuilder extends Object {

    public static int TEXT_TRACK_WIDTH = 320;
    public static int TEXT_TRACK_HEIGHT = 24;

    static String[] MESSAGES = {
        "QuickTime for Java",
        "A Developer's Notebook",
        "from O'Reilly Media",
        "Coming Fall 2004"
    };
    static QDRect textBox = new QDRect(0, 0,
                                      TEXT_TRACK_WIDTH,
                                      TEXT_TRACK_HEIGHT);

    public static void main (String[] args) {
        try {
            QTSessionCheck.check();

            QTFile movFile = new QTFile (new java.io.File("buildtext.mov"));
            Movie movie =
                Movie.createMovieFile(movFile,
                            StdQTConstants.kMoviePlayer,
                            StdQTConstants.createMovieFileDeleteCurFile |
                            StdQTConstants.createMovieFileDontCreateResFile);

            System.out.println ("Created Movie");

            // create an empty text track
            int timeScale = 10; // time measured in 1/10ths of a sec
            Track textTrack = movie.addTrack (TEXT_TRACK_WIDTH,
                                        TEXT_TRACK_HEIGHT, 0);
            System.out.println ("Added empty Track");

            // create media for this track
            Media textMedia = new TextMedia (textTrack,
                                       timeScale);
            TextMediaHandler handler =
                (TextMediaHandler) textMedia.getHandler();
            System.out.println ("Created Media");

            textMedia.beginEdits();
            for (int i=0; i<MESSAGES.length; i++) {
                byte[] msgBytes = MESSAGES[i].getBytes();
                QTPointer msgPoint = new QTPointer (msgBytes);
                // add sample
                handler.addTextSample (msgPoint, // text
                                    0, // font number
                                    14, // font size,
                                    QDConstants.bold, // style,
```

Example 9-1. *Creating a text track (continued)*

```
                                QDColor.yellow, // fg color,
                                QDColor.black, // bg color,
                                QDConstants.teCenter,// justification
                                textBox, // box
                                0, // displayFlags
                                0, // scrollDelay
                                0, // hiliteStart
                                0, // hiliteEnd
                                QDColor.white, // rgbHiliteColor
                                25 // duration
                                );
        } // for

        // done editing
        textMedia.endEdits();

        // now insert this media into track
        textTrack.insertMedia (0, // trackStart
                            0, // mediaTime
                            textMedia.getDuration(), // mediaDuration
                            1); // mediaRate


        // save up at this point
        System.out.println ("Saving...");
        OpenMovieFile omf = OpenMovieFile.asWrite (movFile);
        movie.addResource (omf,
                        StdQTConstants.movieInDataForkResID,
                        movFile.getName());

        System.out.println ("Done");


    } catch (QTException qte) {
        qte.printStackTrace();
    }
    System.exit(0);
} // main

}
```

Running this example creates a file called *buildtext.mov* in the current directory. It's a normal QuickTime movie, so you can open it with Quick-Time Player, or the various players and editors from Chapters 2 and 3. Figure 9-1 shows what it looks like when played.

Figure 9-1. Text track movie

What just happened?

The application walks through the basic steps of creating a text track as described earlier. First, it creates an empty movie on disk (giving the movie a place to store the samples), and then adds an empty track and creates a `TextMedia` object for this track.

From there, it's a pretty simple matter of getting a `TextMediaHandler` and using it to make calls to `addTextSample( )`, looping through the array of `Strings` that are used as samples. For each `String`, get its bytes and wrap them with a `QTPointer`, creating a `QTPointerRef` that can be used for `addTextSample( )`. When this is done, add the media to the track, then save the movie to disk with `Movie.addResource( )`.

What about...

...adding this text track on top of an existing movie I've opened, to make actual captions? To do this, you'd want to do a few extra things. First, you'd add your samples with the `dfKeyedText` display flag, to remove the background color and thus have only the text appear above the video. You might also consider using `dfAntiAlias` to make the text easier to read, though this is a little more CPU-intensive at playback time.

Next, you'd want to move the captions to the bottom of the movie's box because this example uses a box anchored at (0,0). You do this by setting a `Matrix` on the text track, defining it as a translation to a box along the bottom of the movie's box (e.g., where the y-coordinate is the movie's height minus the height of the text track).

See Chapter 8 for coverage of transforming tracks with Matrix objects. The timecode example later in this chapter does this, too.

Creating Links with HREF Tracks

One peculiar trick you can do with text tracks is to use them to turn your movie into a set of time-based hyperlinks. The idea is that by adding a so-called "HREF track," you can make portions of your movie act like an anchor tag in HTML—clicking the movie takes you to a specified web page.

How do I do that?

Creating an HREF track is virtually identical to creating a text track—it is a real text track, after all—with URLs as the text samples. To actually activate its special features, though, you have to rename the track to HREFTrack. Also, because the URLs are not meant to be seen, you typically want to hide them by calling `setEnabled(false)` on the track.

Assuming there is an array of URL Strings called URLS, you can make the previous lab's movie linkable by adding the following code after the first text media has been inserted into its track:

```
// add HREF track
Track hrefTrack = movie.addTrack (TEXT_TRACK_WIDTH,
                                   TEXT_TRACK_HEIGHT, 0);
// create media for this track
Media hrefMedia = new TextMedia (hrefTrack,
                                 timeScale);
handler = (TextMediaHandler) hrefMedia.getHandler();
System.out.println ("Created HREF Media");

hrefMedia.beginEdits();
for (int i=0; i<URLS.length; i++) {
    byte[] msgBytes = URLS[i].getBytes();
    QTPointer msgPoint = new QTPointer (msgBytes);
    // add sample
    handler.addTextSample (msgPoint, // text
                           0, // font number
                           14, // font size,
                           QDConstants.bold, // style,
                           QDColor.yellow, // fg color,
                           QDColor.black, // bg color,
                           QDConstants.teJustCenter,// justification
                           textBox, // box
                           0, // displayFlags
                           0, // scrollDelay
                           0, // hiliteStart
                           0, // hiliteEnd
                           QDColor.white, // rgbHiliteColor
                           25 // duration
                           );
} // for

// done editing
hrefMedia.endEdits();

// now insert this media into track
hrefTrack.insertMedia (0, // trackStart
                       0, // mediaTime
                       hrefMedia.getDuration(), // mediaDuration
                       1); // mediaRate

// disable href track because we don't want it visible
hrefTrack.setEnabled(false);

// change track name to HREFTrack
UserData userData = hrefTrack.getUserData();
String trackName = "HREFTrack";
QTPointer namePtr = new QTPointer(trackName.getBytes());
userData.setDataItem (namePtr,
                      QTUtils.toOSType("name"),
                      0);
```

Run this example with ant run-ch09-hreftrackbuilder.

When run, this demo creates a file called *buildhref.mov*. However, HREF tracks work only in the QuickTime plug-in—i.e., in a browser. In the book's downloadable code, the HTML file *src/other/html/embed-href-movie.html* has a simple web page that embeds this movie.

Figure 9-2 shows the page with the embedded *buildhref.mov*. If you click when you're on the first text sample (QuickTime for Java), a new window opens up and goes to Apple's QTJ home page. The other text samples each have a different corresponding HREF. The last one launches its page automatically.

To embed a QuickTime movie with HTML <embed> and <object> tags, see Chapter 1.

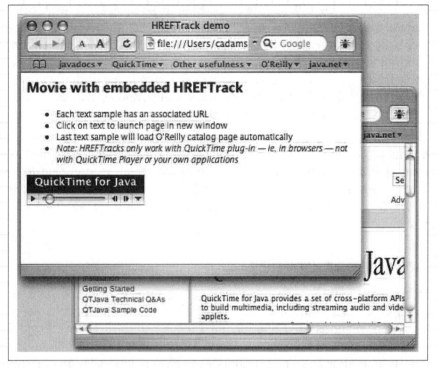

Figure 9-2. Browser showing movie with an HREF track; the page opened by clicking the movie is shown in the second window

---

TIP

Note that the arrangement of HREF samples to other tracks and samples in the movie is totally arbitrary—it depends only on when and for how long the HREF text sample appears. If you wanted to link a certain segment of video to a URL, you might add the sample at the time the video begins and make it have the same duration as the segment. This example makes the URLs correspond exactly to the text samples in the other track because that makes sense when you're playing with it, but it doesn't *have* to work like that.

What just happened?

As QuickTime parses each URL in the HREF track, it enables a link to that URL. However, the URLs can be specially formatted to achieve different behaviors. Here's what the demo's URLS array looks like:

```
static String[ ] URLS = {
    "<http://developer.apple.com/quicktime/qtjava/> T<_blank>",
    "<http://devnotebooks.oreilly.com/> T<_blank>",
    "<http://www.oreilly.com/> T<_blank>",
    "A<http://www.oreilly.com/catalog/> T<_blank>"
};
```

As you can see, the URL itself is enclosed in angle brackets. In each case, there's a second entry, T<_blank>, which is used to indicate a target frame. By using the special value _blank, clicking these URLs will always open them in a new window. However, you could also use a consistent name to open URLs in a single new window, or a frame. If the T<...> is absent, the URL will be opened in the current window (which will, of course, exit the page that contains the movie).

The last sample shows another interesting syntax. By preceding the URL and its angle brackets with an A, you can force the URL to be opened as soon as it is read, either by playing up to that point or scrubbing to it. There are lots of interesting uses for this approach, like an introductory movie (titles and credits) pulling up another movie, or automatically refreshing another frame on the page.

Adding Timecodes

In the professional realm, videotapes often have a *timecode* track in addition to their audio and video tracks. This track enumerates every video frame, and is used typically for various purposes: editing, logging what's on a tape, etc. Professional tape decks usually have an LED or LCD display of the timecode, and optionally can display timecodes on-screen.

You might think the text track provides a convenient way to embed timecodes—they're string values—you can have one for every frame of video (or many, if you set your time scale really high), you can read them from the TextMedia object, you can turn their display on and off by enabling and disabling the track, etc.

And this would be fine. But fortunately, QuickTime has a real timecode track that goes much further. Adding timecodes to a movie, in a format and resolution suitable for professional work, is a snap.

How do I do that?

No surprise, once again the key is to create a new track with a specific kind of media and to add samples to it. This time, the desired media class is `TimeCodeMedia`.

What's really interesting is that you don't actually write a sample for every video frame. You need to write only a single sample to define the timecode format and a start time, at the beginning of the period for which you want to provide timecodes. Because QuickTime already is measuring time in your track, at an arbitrary precision (i.e., the time scale you set for it), it can figure out the timecode for any time later in the movie.

To create the sample, first you need a `TimeCodeDef` object, which defines the timecode standard in terms of frames per second, duration per frame, and a time scale, each set with a method call. You also need a `TimeCodeTime`, which defines the starting point for your timecodes. Its constructor takes four arguments: hours, minutes, seconds, and frames.

Next, you need a `TimeCoder`, which is a `MediaHandler` for `TimeCodeMedia`. This object allows you to set flags to determine whether the time code is displayed and to set display options (font size, style, color, etc.) by passing it a `TCTextOptions` object. It also can generate a frame number, given the `TimeCodeDef` and `TimeCodeTime`, which is the data you need to pass to `addSample( )`.

You would think this would be called a Time-CodeHandler, wouldn't you?

The application in Example 9-2 takes an existing QuickTime movie and adds a visible timecode track.

Example 9-2. Creating a timecode track

```
package com.oreilly.qtjnotebook.ch09;

import quicktime.*;
import quicktime.std.*;
import quicktime.std.image.*;
import quicktime.std.movies.*;
import quicktime.std.movies.media.*;
import quicktime.std.qtcomponents.*;
import quicktime.io.*;
import quicktime.qd.*;
import quicktime.app.view.*;
import quicktime.util.*;
import java.awt.*;

import com.oreilly.qtjnotebook.ch01.QTSessionCheck;

public class TimeCodeTrackBuilder {

    public static final int TIMECODE_TRACK_HEIGHT=24;
```

Example 9-2. Creating a timecode track (continued)

```
public static final int TIMECODE_TRACK_WIDTH=120;

public static void main (String[] args) {
    try {
        QTSessionCheck.check();
        // open a movie
        QTFile file = QTFile.standardGetFilePreview (
                            QTFile.kStandardQTFileTypes);
        OpenMovieFile omf = OpenMovieFile.asRead(file);
        Movie movie = Movie.fromFile(omf);
        // add a timecode track
        addTimeCodeTrack (movie);

        // create GUI
        Frame f = new Frame ("Movie with TimeCode track");
        MovieController controller = new MovieController(movie);
        Component c = QTFactory.makeQTComponent(controller).asComponent();
        f.add(c);
        f.pack();
        f.setVisible(true);

    } catch (QTException qte) {
        qte.printStackTrace();
    }
}

public static Track addTimeCodeTrack (Movie movie)
    throws QTException {
    int timescale = movie.getTimeScale();

    TimeCodeDef tcDef = new TimeCodeDef();
    tcDef.setTimeScale (2997); // ntsc drop-frame
    tcDef.setFrameDuration (100); // 1 frame in 30 fps dropframe
    tcDef.setFramesPerSecond (30);
    tcDef.setFlags (StdQTConstants.tcDropFrame);

    // first record at 0 hrs, 0 min, 0 sec, 0 frames
    TimeCodeTime tcTime = new TimeCodeTime (0, 0, 0, 0);

    // create timecode track and media
    Track tcTrack = movie.addTrack (TIMECODE_TRACK_WIDTH,
                            TIMECODE_TRACK_HEIGHT,
                            0);
    TimeCodeMedia tcMedia = new TimeCodeMedia (tcTrack, timescale);
    TimeCoder timeCoder = tcMedia.getTimeCodeHandler();

    // turn on timecode display, set colors
    timeCoder.setFlags (timeCoder.getFlags() |
                    StdQTConstants.tcdfShowTimeCode,
                    StdQTConstants.tcdfShowTimeCode);
    TCTextOptions tcTextOptions = timeCoder.getDisplayOptions();
    tcTextOptions.setTXSize (14);
```

Example 9-2. *Creating a timecode track (continued)*

```
        tcTextOptions.setTXFace (QDConstants.bold);
        tcTextOptions.setForeColor (QDColor.yellow);
        tcTextOptions.setBackColor (QDColor.black);
        timeCoder.setDisplayOptions (tcTextOptions);

        // set up a sample as a 4-byte array in a QTHandle
        int frameNumber = timeCoder.toFrameNumber (tcTime, tcDef);
        int frameNums[ ] = new int[1];
        frameNums[0] = frameNumber;
        QTHandle frameNumHandle = new QTHandle (4, false);
        frameNumHandle.copyFromArray (0, frameNums, 0, 1);

        // create a timecode description (the sample to be added)
        TimeCodeDescription tcDesc = new TimeCodeDescription( );
        tcDesc.setTimeCodeDef (tcDef);

        // add the sample to the TimeCodeMedia
        tcMedia.beginEdits( );
        tcMedia.addSample (frameNumHandle,
                           0,
                           frameNumHandle.getSize( ),
                           movie.getDuration( ),
                           tcDesc,
                           1,
                           0);
        tcMedia.endEdits( );

        // now insert this media into track
        tcTrack.insertMedia (0, // trackStart
                             0, // mediaTime
                             tcMedia.getDuration( ), // mediaDuration
                             1); // mediaRate

        // move the timecode to the bottom of the movie and
        // set a transparent-background GraphicsMode
        int x = (movie.getBox( ).getWidth( )/2) - (TIMECODE_TRACK_WIDTH / 2);
        int y = movie.getBox( ).getHeight( ) - TIMECODE_TRACK_HEIGHT;
        QDRect moveFrom = new QDRect (0, 0,
                                      TIMECODE_TRACK_WIDTH,
                                      TIMECODE_TRACK_HEIGHT);
        QDRect moveTo = new QDRect (x, y,
                                    TIMECODE_TRACK_WIDTH,
                                    TIMECODE_TRACK_HEIGHT);
        Matrix matrix = new Matrix( );
        matrix.rect (moveFrom, moveTo);
        tcTrack.setMatrix (matrix);
        timeCoder.setGraphicsMode (new GraphicsMode (QDConstants.transparent,
                                                     QDColor.black));

        return tcTrack;
    }
}
```

Run this example with ant run-ch09-timecodetrackbuilder.

When this is run, the user is prompted to open a QuickTime movie. It adds the timecode track and opens the movie in a new window, as shown in Figure 9-3. Notice that the timecode stays accurate whether you play the movie, jump to a specific time by clicking the time bar, or scrub back and forth.

Figure 9-3. Time code track added to a movie

What just happened?

The addTimeCode( ) method begins by creating a TimeCodeDef object and setting its time scale, frame duration, and frames per second. Then it creates a TimeCodeTime for 0 hours, 0 minutes, 0 seconds, and 0 frames (typically represented in the form 00:00:00;00, though you need to remember the digits after the semicolon are in frames per second, not hundredths of a second, so in this case they'll run from 0 to 29). It also creates a new Track with TimeCodeMedia.

With these objects, you can create the sample you'll need for the track, so you need the MediaHandler, namely the TimeCoder, which you get from the TimeCodeMedia via getTimeCodeHandler( ). But some things are worth setting up on the TimeCoder first, before you worry about the sample. If you want to make the timecodes visible, you need to set the tcdfShowTimeCode behavior flag. TimeCoder has a really weird syntax for behavior flags, requiring you to pass in two values, the new values of all the flags, plus a mask indicating which one you changed. So, to set tcdfShowTimeCode, you have to do this:

```
timeCoder.setFlags (timeCoder.getFlags( ) |
            StdQTConstants.tcdfShowTimeCode,
            StdQTConstants.tcdfShowTimeCode);
```

Use the TimeCoder to set any display options: font, size, style, and foreground and background colors. To do this, get the TimeCoder's TCTextDisplay object and make method calls to set each parameter.

Finally, you're ready to create the sample. The data needed for the addSample() call is just a 4-byte frame number, calculated by the TimeCoder from the TimeCodeDef and TimeCodeTime in the toFrameNumber() method. To get it into a QTHandleRef required by addSample(), put it in a one-element int array, create a 4-byte QTHandle, and use the handle's copyFromArray() method to copy the int's bytes into the handle. The addSample() call also needs a SampleDescription to indicate what's in the QTHandle—get this by creating a new TimeCodeDescription object and setting its fields with setTimeCodeDef().

See Chapter 8 for information on how to reposition tracks with matrices and composite them with GraphicsModes.

After adding the sample, and inserting the media into the track as always, the timecode is ready to display. However, it defaults to a position at the upper right of the movie, and it has a background box that obscures the movie below it. You can fix these problems by setting a track Matrix to move the timecode display to the bottom of the movie's box and by setting a transparent GraphicsMode to make the background color disappear.

What about...

...those weird values for TimeCodeDef? What's with the "2997"? This shows off the power of QuickTime's timecode support. Imagine you had perfectly normal, 30-frames-per-second video. In that case, you'd expect the values for the TimeCodeDef would be:

Time scale	3000
Frame duration	100
Frames per second	30

Notice how this is redundant: if the time scale is 3000 and there are 30 frames per second, of course each frame is 100 "beats" long. So, why did they define it this way?

Because "normal 30-frames-per-second video" isn't necessarily how things work in the real world.

In North America, most broadcast video is actually in a format called "drop frame," a misnamed concept indicating that two timecodes (but not actual frames) are dropped every minute, except for the tenth, to sync the color video signal with the audio. This format is defined by:

Timescale	2997
Frame duration	100
Frames per second	30

You can use these values with the `TimeCodeDef` methods `setTimeScale()`, `setFrameDuration()`, and `setFramesPerSecond()` to represent NTSC broadcast video in QuickTime. You'll also need to call `setFlags()` with the flag `StdQTConstants.tcDropFrame` to tell QuickTime you're doing drop-frame video. While you're at it, two other real-world flags to consider setting are `tcNegTimesOK` to allow negative times and `tc24HoursMax`, which limits timecodes to go up only to 24 hours (mimicking the behavior of analog broadcast equipment).

And by the way, what is the timecode system buying me, other than accuracy? One important consideration with QuickTime's timecoding is to support the way things are done in the professional realm, with both digital and analog equipment. There are many different schemes for timecoding media, and QuickTime is designed to support any such system. Also, one of the nice things you can do with timecodes is to capture the timecode from an original tape and maintain it in QuickTime, even through editing, so the user always has a frame-accurate representation of where his original material came from. There are even advanced techniques to "name" timecode tracks, presumably after their original tapes (or "sources," as we move to a tapeless media world), which would allow you to use QuickTime as the basis of a content management system.

Creating Zero-Source Effects

QuickTime comes with an extensive collection of video effects, which you use by making movies with *effects tracks*—i.e., a track whose media defines a video effect.

These effects are grouped based on how many sources they operate on.

Zero-source effects
> These effects are meant to be seen just by themselves. Apple includes a few of these, like fire, clouds, and water "ripples."

One-source effects (or filters)
> These effects are applied to a single source. Examples of this kind of effect include color correction or tinting, edge detection, lens flare, etc.

Two-source effects (or transitions)

These are effects that apply to two sources at once. Typically, they're used to visually change the display from one video source to another. Examples of these include dissolves and wipes.

The simplest of these are the zero-source effects, because they don't require wiring up the effect to sources. Instead, you just put an appropriate effects sample into a video track and you're done.

How do I do that?

An effects track is really just a video track (literally, a track with VideoMedia), whose samples are descriptions of effects: the ID of the effect and any parameters it might take. In QuickTime, these are passed in the form of AtomContainers: tree-structures in which each "atom" can contain children or data, but not both. Each atom has a size and a FOUR_CHAR_CODE type, and can be accessed by index and/or type (i.e., you can get the *n*th atom of type *m* from a parent). For effects, you basically need to pack an AtomContainer with an Atom to specify the desired effect and possibly other Atoms to specify behavior parameters. This AtomContainer is the QTHandle you pass to the addSample() method. Fortunately, you can get a properly structured AtomContainer from a user dialog, instead of having to build it yourself.

Almost everything you do in QuickTime involves atom manipulation, but most of the time the API isolates you from it. Not this time, though.

To generate the user dialog, use an EffectsList object to create a list of installed effects—remember, the user could have installed third-party effect components, so you want to get the list of effects at runtime. Pass to ParameterDialog.showParameterDialog(), which will return an AtomContainer of the selected and configured effect.

The sample program in Example 9-3 shows how to create a zero-source effect movie, which is saved to disk as *effectonly.mov*.

Example 9-3. Creating a zero-source effect

```
package com.oreilly.qtjnotebook.ch09;

import quicktime.*;
import quicktime.std.*;
import quicktime.std.movies.*;
import quicktime.std.movies.media.*;
import quicktime.io.*;
import quicktime.std.image.*;
import quicktime.util.*;

import com.oreilly.qtjnotebook.ch01.QTSessionCheck;
```

Example 9-3. *Creating a zero-source effect (continued)*

```java
public class EffectOnlyTrackBuilder {

    public static final int EFFECT_TRACK_WIDTH = 320;
    public static final int EFFECT_TRACK_HEIGHT = 240;
    public static final int TIMESCALE = 600;

    public static void main (String[] args) {
        try {
            new EffectOnlyTrackBuilder();
        } catch (QTException qte) {
            qte.printStackTrace();
        }
        System.exit(0);
    }

    public EffectOnlyTrackBuilder() throws QTException {
        QTSessionCheck.check();

        QTFile movFile = new QTFile (new java.io.File("effectonly.mov"));
        Movie movie =
            Movie.createMovieFile(movFile,
                                  StdQTConstants.kMoviePlayer,
                                  StdQTConstants.createMovieFileDeleteCurFile |
                                  StdQTConstants.
createMovieFileDontCreateResFile);
        Track effectsTrack = movie.addTrack (EFFECT_TRACK_WIDTH,
                                             EFFECT_TRACK_HEIGHT,
                                             0);

        int TIMESCALE = 600;
        VideoMedia effectsMedia = new VideoMedia(effectsTrack,
                                                 TIMESCALE);
        // get list of effects
        // StdQTConstants.elOptionsIncludeNoneInList)
        EffectsList effectsList = new EffectsList (0, 0, 0);
        // show list of effects
        // flags are in StdQTConstants.pdOptions...
        AtomContainer effect =
            ParameterDialog.showParameterDialog (effectsList, // effectsList
                                                 0, // dialogOptions
                                                 null, // parameters
                                                 "Pick an effect", // title
                                                 null //pictArray
                                                 );
        // find out the effect type by getting the "what" atom,
        // whose data is a FOUR_CHAR_CODE
        Atom what = effect.findChildByIndex_Atom (null,
                                                  StdQTConstants.kParameterWhatName,
                                                  1);
        int effectType = effect.getAtomData(what).getInt(0);
        effectType = EndianOrder.flipBigEndianToNative32(effectType);
        System.out.println ("User chose " +
                            QTUtils.fromOSType(effectType) +
```

Example 9-3. Creating a zero-source effect (continued)

```
                            " effect type");

        // make a sample description for the effect description
        ImageDescription imgDesc = ImageDescription.forEffect (effectType);
        imgDesc.setWidth (EFFECT_TRACK_WIDTH);
        imgDesc.setHeight (EFFECT_TRACK_HEIGHT);

        // add effect to the video media
        effectsMedia.beginEdits();

        effectsMedia.addSample (effect, // QTHandleRef data,
                            0, // int dataOffset,
                            effect.getSize(), // int dataSize,
                            1200, //int durationPerSample,
                            imgDesc, // SampleDescription sampleDesc,
                            1, // int numberOfSamples,
                            0 // int sampleFlags
                            );

        effectsMedia.endEdits();

        // now insert this media into track
        effectsTrack.insertMedia (0, // trackStart
                            0, // mediaTime
                            effectsMedia.getDuration(), // mediaDuration
                            1); // mediaRate
        System.out.println ("inserted media into effects track");

        // save up
        System.out.println ("Saving...");
        OpenMovieFile omf = OpenMovieFile.asWrite (movFile);
        movie.addResource (omf,
                            StdQTConstants.movieInDataForkResID,
                            movFile.getName());
        System.out.println ("Done");
    }
}
```

When run, it presents the user with an effects dialog, as seen in Figure 9-4.

This allows the user to choose the effect and configure it. For example, the fire effect allows the user to set the height of the flames, how quickly they burn out and restart, how much "water" is doused on them to vary their burn, etc. The resulting movie is shown in Figure 9-5.

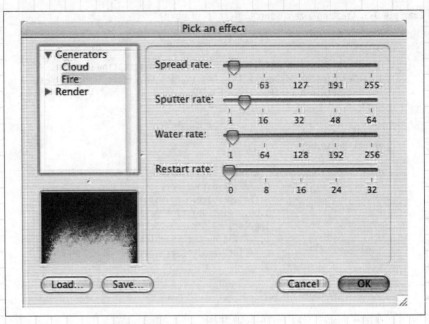

Figure 9-4. ParameterDialog for a zero-source effect

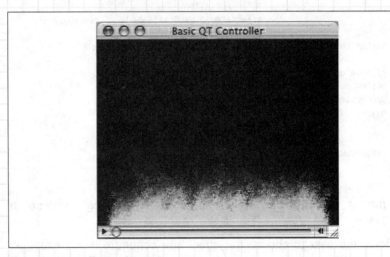

Figure 9-5. An effect-only movie

What just happened?

After setting up an empty movie, track, and video media (effects tracks are actually a special case of video), ask QuickTime for a list of installed effects:

```
EffectsList effectsList = new EffectsList (0, 0, 0);
```

To specify which effects are returned, this call takes a minimum number of sources, a maximum number of sources, and a flag. To signal that you want only zero-source effects, set the first two parameters to 0. elOptionsIncludeNoneInList is the only flag that can be passed to the third parameter, because it causes a no-op "none" effect to be included.

Then pass this to ParameterDialog.showParameterDialog() to present the user with the list of discovered effects, as well as controls to configure each one. This call takes five parameters:

- The EffectsList.
- A dialog options int, which alters the dialog for effects that have "tweening" values—in other words., those that change the effect over time (like how much of a transition is actually performed). pdOptionsCollectOneValue causes tweenable options to not be tweenable, while pdOptionsAllowOptionalInterpolations puts tweenable parameters into a more advanced user-interface mode.
- A "parameters" AtomContainer, which contains canned values for an effect. You could create such an AtomContainer by carefully studying the QuickTime native docs and constructing it manually with AtomContainer calls, or by getting an AtomContainer from this dialog and "canning" its bytes for future use. By passing null, you get the default values for all effects.
- A String title for the dialog.
- An array of Picts to use for previewing the effect. If none is provided, default images of the letters A and B are used for showing filter and transition effects.

When the user selects and configures an effect, it's returned as an AtomContainer. This is what you need to use for the addSample() call on the VideoMedia object. What's tricky is getting the SampleDescription to tell addSample() what to do with the effect AtomContainer. ImageDescription.forEffect() will create such a description, but you need to pass it the FOUR_CHAR_CODE of the effect—easy to do if you built the AtomContainer by hand, less easy if you got it from the dialog. The effect type is in an atom whose type is "what", so you can retrieve the AtomContainer by calling findChildByIndex_Atom() and asking for the first instance of the type kParameterWhatName. Atom.getData() will return an AtomData object, from which you can get an int with getInt().

There's an interesting concern with this int, because you must account for "endianness." QuickTime structures are defined as being "big-endian," meaning that in a given 32-bit value, the most significant 16 bits come first. That's convenient for 680x0 and PowerPC CPUs, which Macs run on, but not

Intel CPUs. On Windows, when you get this int from the AtomContainer, it's big-endian, making it wrong for use with calls to any QuickTime method that takes an int. You fix this with the self-describing convenience method EndianOrder.flipBigEndianToNative32( ). On the Mac, this call does nothing, because the native endianness is already big-endian.

Finally, you have everything you need to add the sample. It's interesting to note that zero-source effects aren't necessarily "played" in the same sense that other movie data is. When you open the resulting movie, the flame starts immediately, regardless of whether the movie is playing, and it keeps burning even if you stop the movie.

What about...

...the simpler version of showParameterDialog( )? Because this example just wants default values for everything, why not use that? Unfortunately, as of this writing, it's buggy. The native API has separate calls for creating the dialog, getting an event from it, and dismissing it. QTJ is supposed to catch the event and dismiss the dialog for you if you click OK, whereas a "cancel" throws an exception, like with other QTJ dialogs. Unfortunately, *clicking OK* also *throws an exception*, meaning you don't get the returned AtomContainer, and because there's not a ParameterDialog instance you can hold on to—the showParameterDialog( ) call was static, after all—there's no way to go back and find out what the user selected. Oops.

Always file bugs at bugreport.apple.com when you find things that are obviously wrong. This one is #3792083.

Anyway, the fancy version of the dialog doesn't have the bug, so that's what I've used here.

Also, what can I do with these zero-source effects other than just look at them? Remember, they're normal video tracks, so they can be composited with other tracks, as shown in Chapter 8. For example, you could take the fire effect, put it in the foreground by setting its layer to a lower value, use a transparent GraphicsMode to punch out the black background, and *voilà*, the contents of your movie are on fire! And that's always a nice way to spice up your boring home movies.

Creating One-Source Effects (Filters)

Filtering a video track by applying an effect to it is a critically important tool for doing color correction, adding special effects like lens flare, or offering novelties such as converting the video to black and white or pseudo-antique sepia tone. The technique of creating the effect is effectively the same as with zero-source effects, although in this case you need to create an object that tells the effect where its video source comes from.

How do I do that?

You create a one-source effect just like you do the zero-source version—create a track, create video media, get an EffectsList (this time of one-source effects), and get an AtomContainer describing an effect from a ParameterDialog.

But before adding the AtomContainer as the effects media sample, you need to map it to a video source, which is another video track in the movie. You do this by creating an input map, which is an AtomContainer indicating the sources that are inputs to an effect. Next, create a track modifier reference to redirect the track's output to the effect. You use the reference in building up the Atoms in the input map. Once built, the input map is set on the effect's media with setInputMap( ).

Example 9-4 exercises this technique by opening a movie, getting its first video track, and applying a user-selected filter to it.

Example 9-4. Creating a one-source effect (filter)

```
package com.oreilly.qtjnotebook.ch09;

import quicktime.*;
import quicktime.std.*;
import quicktime.std.movies.*;
import quicktime.std.movies.media.*;
import quicktime.io.*;
import quicktime.std.image.*;
import quicktime.util.*;
import quicktime.qd.*;

import com.oreilly.qtjnotebook.ch01.QTSessionCheck;

public class FilterTrackBuilder {

    public static final int EFFECT_TRACK_WIDTH = 320;
    public static final int EFFECT_TRACK_HEIGHT = 240;
    public static final int TIMESCALE = 600;

    public static void main (String[ ] args) {
        try {
            new FilterTrackBuilder( );
        } catch (QTException qte) {
            qte.printStackTrace( );
        }
        System.exit(0);
    }
    public FilterTrackBuilder( ) throws QTException {
```

Example 9-4. Creating a one-source effect (filter) (continued)

```
QTSessionCheck.check( );

QTFile movFile = new QTFile (new java.io.File("filter.mov"));
Movie movie =
    Movie.createMovieFile(movFile,
                StdQTConstants.kMoviePlayer,
                StdQTConstants.createMovieFileDeleteCurFile |
                StdQTConstants.createMovieFileDontCreateResFile);

Movie sourceMovie = queryUserForMovie( );
Track sourceTrack = addVideoTrack (sourceMovie,
                                movie,
                                0,
                                sourceMovie.getDuration( ),
                                0);

Track effectsTrack = movie.addTrack (EFFECT_TRACK_WIDTH,
                                EFFECT_TRACK_HEIGHT,
                                0);
effectsTrack.setLayer(-1);

int TIMESCALE = 600;
VideoMedia effectsMedia = new VideoMedia(effectsTrack,
                                TIMESCALE);

// set up input map here
AtomContainer inputMap = new AtomContainer( );

int trackRef =
    effectsTrack.addReference (sourceTrack,
                                StdQTConstants.kTrackModifierReference);
// add input reference atom
Atom inputAtom =
    inputMap.insertChild (null,
                        StdQTConstants.kTrackModifierInput,
                        trackRef,
                        0);

// add name and type
inputMap.insertChild (inputAtom,
                        StdQTConstants.kTrackModifierType,
                        1,
                        0,
                        EndianOrder.flipNativeToBigEndian32(StdQTConstants.videoMediaType));

inputMap.insertChild (inputAtom,
                        StdQTConstants.kEffectDataSourceType,
                        1,
                        0,
                        EndianOrder.flipNativeToBigEndian32(QTUtils.toOSType ("srcA")));
System.out.println ("set up input map atom");

// show list of effects
```

Example 9-4. Creating a one-source effect (filter) (continued)

```java
// flags are in StdQTConstants.pdOptions...
Pict[] previewPicts = new Pict[1];
previewPicts[0] = sourceMovie.getPosterPict();
// get list of effects
EffectsList effectsList = new EffectsList (1, 1, 0);
AtomContainer effect =
    ParameterDialog.showParameterDialog (effectsList,
                                   0, // dialogOptions
                                   null, // parameters
                                   "Pick an effect", // title
                                   previewPicts //pictArray
                                   );
// find out the effect type by getting the "what" atom,
// whose data is a FOUR_CHAR_CODE
Atom what = effect.findChildByIndex_Atom (null,
                              StdQTConstants.kParameterWhatName,
                              1);
int effectType = effect.getAtomData(what).getInt(0);
effectType = EndianOrder.flipBigEndianToNative32(effectType);
System.out.println ("User chose " +
                    QTUtils.fromOSType(effectType) +
                    " effect type");

// make a sample description for the effect description
ImageDescription imgDesc = ImageDescription.forEffect (effectType);
imgDesc.setWidth (EFFECT_TRACK_WIDTH);
imgDesc.setHeight (EFFECT_TRACK_HEIGHT);

// give the effect description a ref to the source
effect.insertChild (null,
                    StdQTConstants.kEffectSourceName,
                    1,
                    0,
                    QTUtils.toOSType ("srcA"));

// add effect to the video media
effectsMedia.beginEdits();

effectsMedia.addSample (effect, // QTHandleRef data,
                    0, // int dataOffset,
                    effect.getSize(), // int dataSize,
                    sourceTrack.getDuration(), //int durPerSample,
                    imgDesc, // SampleDescription sampleDesc,
                    1, // int numberOfSamples,
                    0 // int sampleFlags
                    );
effectsMedia.setInputMap (inputMap);

effectsMedia.endEdits();

// now insert this media into track
effectsTrack.insertMedia (0, // trackStart
                    0, // mediaTime
```

Example 9-4. Creating a one-source effect (filter) (continued)

```
                                        sourceTrack.getDuration( ), // mediaDuration
                                        1); // mediaRate
        System.out.println ("inserted media into effects track");

        // save up
        System.out.println ("Saving...");
        OpenMovieFile omf = OpenMovieFile.asWrite (movFile);
        movie.addResource (omf,
                            StdQTConstants.movieInDataForkResID,
                            movFile.getName( ));
        System.out.println ("Done");

    }

    public static Movie queryUserForMovie( )
        throws QTException {
        QTFile file =
            QTFile.standardGetFilePreview (QTFile.kStandardQTFileTypes);
        OpenMovieFile omf = OpenMovieFile.asRead (file);
        return Movie.fromFile (omf);
    }

    public static Track addVideoTrack (Movie sourceMovie,
                                        Movie targetMovie,
                                        int srcIn,
                                        int srcDuration,
                                        int targetTime)
        throws QTException {
        // find first video track
        Track videoTrack =
            sourceMovie.getIndTrackType (1,
                                StdQTConstants.videoMediaType,
                                StdQTConstants.movieTrackMediaType);
        if (videoTrack == null)
            throw new QTException ("can't find a video track");
        // add videoTrack to targetMovie
        Track newTrack =
            targetMovie.newTrack (videoTrack.getSize( ).getWidthF( ),
                                    videoTrack.getSize( ).getHeightF( ),
                                    1.0f);
        VideoMedia newMedia =
            new VideoMedia (newTrack,
                            videoTrack.getMedia( ).getTimeScale( ),
                            new DataRef(new QTHandle( )));
        videoTrack.insertSegment (newTrack,
                                    srcIn, // 0
                                    srcDuration, // videoTrack.getDuration( )
                                    targetTime);
        return newTrack;
    }
}
```

Run this example with ant run-ch09-filtertrackbuilder.

When run, this application queries the user to open a QuickTime movie. Then it opens a dialog to choose and configure the effect, as seen in Figure 9-6. Notice that a frame from the movie is used in the preview section of the dialog.

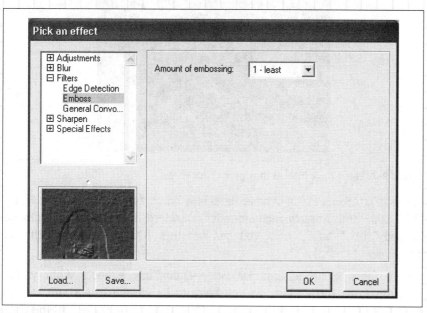

Figure 9-6. ParameterDialog for a one-source effect

After the effect is chosen, the new movie—consisting of just a video track and an effects track—is written to *filter.mov*. Figure 9-7 shows a video that is modified by the emboss effect.

What just happened?

After grabbing the source movie's first video track and adding it as a video track in a new movie, the example creates an effects track. The video track's output is redirected by adding a reference to it to the effects track, via the addReference( ) call.

Next, you need to set up the input map. This is a normal AtomContainer, into which you'll insert child atoms. First, create the "track modifier" atom, with the four-argument version of insertChild( )—this creates and returns a parent atom (the five-argument versions all create leaf atoms). To work, this atom requires two children: an atom of type kTrackModifierType whose data is the type of track being modified (videoMediaType in this case), and an atom of type

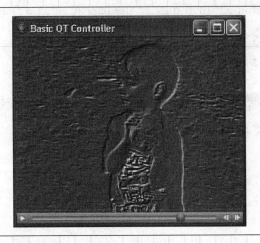

Figure 9-7. Video track filtered through emboss effect

kEffectDataSourceType whose data is a name for the track as a FOUR_ CHAR_CODE int. Apple's recommended standard is that source tracks be named "srcA," "srcB," etc.; you can get this 4CC name with QTUtils. toOSType ("srcA").

Again, there is an endianness issue—QuickTime expects what you're building to be big-endian, so you have to be careful to account for the endianness of the data you insert. In this case, the videoMediaType constant and the srcA name are native ints, so they need to be flipped to big-endianness with EndianOrder.flipNativeToBigEndian32( ).

Now that it's initialized, set this atom aside while creating the effect and adding its sample to the effects media. Two important to-dos for filters are to ask the EffectsList constructor for only one-source effects (by passing 1 for the minimum and maximum number of sources to get effects for) and to provide the ParameterDialog with a Pict[ ] that contains an image from your source movie for previewing the effect. Once the effect has been added, provide the input map with a call to Media. setInputMap( ).

What about...

...applying the filter to just part of the source track? Ah, this will turn up a nasty surprise...go ahead and make the effect cover just half the length of the source video, by changing the duration parameters in effectsMedia. addSample( ) and effectsTrack.insertMedia( ) from sourceTrack. getDuration( ) to sourceTrack.getDuration( ) / 2. You might reasonably expect that halfway through your movie, the filter simply would go away, because the duration of the effect would have expired and the video would be the only valid media at that point. Instead, the display goes blank!

Here's the deal: using a track for an effect makes it usable *only* by the effect. Setting up the track reference redirects the output of the source video track into the effect.

So, what can you do about it? One option is to use two different video tracks in addition to the effect. The first is the source to the effect and the second is all the source media not to be used in the effect. In adding this second track, you set its in-time (the "destination in" argument of `Track.insertSegment( )`) to come after the end of the effect. A somewhat cheesier alternative is to add another, "no-op" effect, like a color conversion configured to not actually do anything, allowing the source video to get to the screen by way of the effect.

The next lab shows this first technique.

Creating Two-Source Effects (Transitions)

Effects that combine two sources are called *transitions*, such as dissolves and wipes. You've probably seen wipes on TV and less frequently in film, although they're considered somewhat artificial in film because they call attention to themselves (the *Star Wars* films are probably the most prominent films to use wipes, perhaps as a nod to old black-and-white adventure films and weekly cliff-hangers).

To show off a transition, this lab will open two movies and create a user-selected transition between them.

Technically, a cut from one scene to another is also a transition, but that doesn't involve any kind of effect.

How do I do that?

In coding terms, the only significant difference from a one-source effect is, predictably, that you need to set up an input map that references both source tracks for the effect.

But in terms of practicality, although you might apply a filter to a long sequence of video, a transition will be very short typically—only a few seconds at most. Because a video track used as a source to an effect is shown only as part of that effect, to show all of one video source transitioning into all of another, you need *five* tracks:

- All of source A, up to the beginning of the transition (i.e., its last n seconds)
- The portion of source A to be used for the transition

- The portion of source B to be used for the transition
- All of source B after the transition (i.e., everything but its first n seconds)
- The effects track

So, to change the previous filter example into a transition example, ask for two source movies and create the new target movie:

```
Movie sourceAMovie = queryUserForMovie();
Movie sourceBMovie = queryUserForMovie();
QTFile movFile = new QTFile (new java.io.File("transition.mov"));
Movie movie =
    Movie.createMovieFile(movFile,
                          StdQTConstants.kMoviePlayer,
                          StdQTConstants.createMovieFileDeleteCurFile |
                          StdQTConstants.createMovieFileDontCreateResFile);
```

Next, add the four video tracks, with the addVideoTrack() convenience method from the last lab, which grabs the first video track from the source, creates a new track, and inserts the specified segment of video media into the new track:

```
Track preEffectTrack = addVideoTrack (sourceAMovie,
        movie,
        0,
        sourceAMovie.getDuration() - TRANSITION_DURATION,
        0);
Track sourceATrack = addVideoTrack (sourceAMovie,
        movie,
        sourceAMovie.getDuration() - TRANSITION_DURATION,
        TRANSITION_DURATION,
        sourceAMovie.getDuration() - TRANSITION_DURATION);

Track sourceBTrack = addVideoTrack (sourceBMovie,
        movie,
        0,
        TRANSITION_DURATION,
        movie.getDuration() - TRANSITION_DURATION);
Track postEffectTrack = addVideoTrack (sourceBMovie,
        movie,
        TRANSITION_DURATION,
        sourceBMovie.getDuration() - TRANSITION_DURATION,
        movie.getDuration());
```

After this, create the effect track as before, except that:

- You ask the EffectsList constructor for two-source effects.
- You provide two Picts to ParameterDialog, one from each source.
- You create the input map with two track modifier atoms, each of which refers to a different track reference (as returned by calls to

addReference( )). Their contents differ only by name: one is srcA, and the other is srcB:

```
int trackARef =
    effectsTrack.addReference (sourceATrack,
                            StdQTConstants.kTrackModifierReference);
int trackBRef =
    effectsTrack.addReference (sourceBTrack,
                            StdQTConstants.kTrackModifierReference);

// add input reference atoms
Atom aInputAtom =
    inputMap.insertChild (null,
                            StdQTConstants.kTrackModifierInput,
                            trackARef,
                            0);
inputMap.insertChild (aInputAtom,
            StdQTConstants.kTrackModifierType,
            1,
            0,
            EndianOrder.flipNativeToBigEndian32(StdQTConstants.
videoMediaType));
inputMap.insertChild (aInputAtom,
            StdQTConstants.kEffectDataSourceType,
            1,
            0,
            EndianOrder.flipNativeToBigEndian32(QTUtils.toOSType
("srcA")));

Atom bInputAtom =
    inputMap.insertChild (null,
                            StdQTConstants.kTrackModifierInput,
                            trackBRef,
                            0);
inputMap.insertChild (bInputAtom,
            StdQTConstants.kTrackModifierType,
            1,
            0,
            EndianOrder.flipNativeToBigEndian32(StdQTConstants.
videoMediaType));

inputMap.insertChild (bInputAtom,
            StdQTConstants.kEffectDataSourceType,
            1,
            0,
            EndianOrder.flipNativeToBigEndian32(QTUtils.toOSType
("srcB")));
```

Because you have two input atoms, you need to make two calls to insert them into the effects description:

```
effect.insertChild (null,
        StdQTConstants.kEffectSourceName,
        1,
        0,
        EndianOrder.flipNativeToBigEndian32(QTUtils.toOSType ("srcA")));
```

```
effect.insertChild (null,
            StdQTConstants.kEffectSourceName,
            2,
            0,
            EndianOrder.flipNativeToBigEndian32(QTUtils.toOSType ("srcB")));
```

Run this example with ant run-ch09-transitiontrack-builder.

When run, this example queries the user twice for input movies, then shows a dialog of all installed two-source effects, as seen in Figure 9-8.

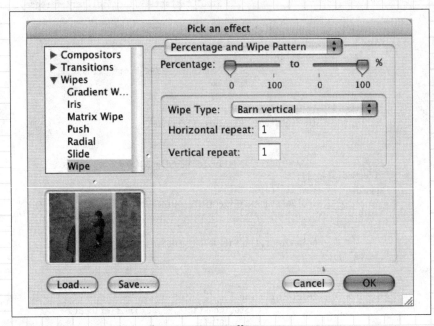

Figure 9-8. ParameterDialog for a two source effect

Once an effect is selected, the resulting movie is saved as *transition.mov.* Figure 9-9 shows an example of a movie in mid-transition, using a vertical "barn door" wipe with 5-pixel-wide borders.

What just happened?

In general, this isn't very different from the one-source case: an effects description defines the effect, and an input map indicates where the sources come from. Probably the biggest hassle is that because an effect by itself isn't very interesting, this example rips out the pre-effect and post-effect video as separate tracks so that you can actually see the one video clip transitioning into another.

Figure 9-9. Two video tracks as sources to a transition effect

What about...

...all these tracks? Who sends out QuickTime movies with five tracks, one of which QuickTime Player identifies by the name of the effect, like "Wipe"? Fair enough—this is the form you would want your movie in while editing it so that you can make changes easily, tossing the effect or reworking it on the fly, with minimal CPU or I/O cost to do so (because, as always, you're mostly just copying pointers). For end-user delivery, you probably would want to export the movie. Even if you export to another QuickTime movie (as opposed to a foreign format like MPEG-4), the export process will render and compress each frame of the transition, leaving you with just a single video track.

Also, is there a list of all the effects I can check out? Sure, but there are more than 100...too many to list here. If you look in *Inside Macintosh: QuickTime* (on Apple's web site or installed by developer tools for Mac OS X), the section "Built-in QuickTime Video Effects" lists all the effects provided by QuickTime, with examples and information about the parameters each one takes. Several dozen of them are defined and standardized by the industry trade group SMPTE (Society of Motion Picture and Television Engineers) and will be familiar to anyone who's worked with a television switcher. Remember, though, the user may have installed third-party effects, so it's important to be able to use the EffectsList to do runtime discovery of what's available to your program.

Index

We'd like to hear your suggestions for improving our indexes. Send email to *index@oreilly.com*.

S

SampleDescription objects, 160
  customizing with setter
      methods, 161
  timecode samples, 201
samples, 63
  building video track from raw
      samples, 173–186
  HREF, arrangement of, 195
  key frame or sync sample, 184
  raw, building audio track
      from, 156–163
  sample size, setting for audio
      track, 161
  sampling frequency, 159
  text, 188
    display flags, 189
saveAsPicture( ) (GraphicsImporter), 89
saving movies
  with dependencies, 59–61
  to a file, 54–57
  flattening, 57–59
scale( ), 169
scaleSegment( )
  Movie class, 50
  Track class, 65
scanForDifference( ), 134
screen capture, 100–103
screen size, 47
  movie editing and, 48
self-contained movie, 55
SequenceGrabber class, 113
  grabPict( ), 135
  idle( ), 118, 134
  prepare( ), 123
  startPreview( ), 118
  startRecord( ), 122
  stop( ), 118, 122
  update( ), 134
session handler for QTJ (example), 11
sessions, opening and closing, 11–13
setBalance( )
      (AudioMediaHandler), 148
setCompressionMethod( ), 82
setDataHandle( )
      (GraphicsImporter), 96
setDataOutput( ), 129
setDataReference( )
      (GraphicsImporter), 96
setDepth( ), 82
setDevice( ) (SGSoundChannel), 120

setEnabled( ) (Track), 65
setExportSettingsFromAtom-
      Container( ), 77
setFlags( ), 202
setFrameDuration( )
      (TimeCodeDef), 202
setFramesPerSecond( )
      (TimeCodeDef), 202
setFrequency( ), 152
setGraphicsMode( )
  GraphicsImporter class, 109
  VideoMediaHandler class, 172
setGWorld( ) (GraphicsImporter), 183
setInputGraphicsImporter( ), 82
setInputMap( ), 209
  Media class, 214
setInputPixMap( ), 103
setInputPtr( ), 109
setLayer( ) (Track), 169
setLightweightPopupEnabled( ), 22
setMatrix( ) (Class), 168
setMovieController( ), 37
setOutput( ), 123
setOutputFile( ) (GraphicsExporter), 82
setPlayEveryFrame( )
      (MovieController), 26
setProgressProc( ) (Movie), 56, 73
setSoundBassAndTreble( )
      (AudioMediaHandler), 148
setSoundEqualizerBands( )
      (AudioMediaHandler), 152,
      156
setTargetDataSize( ), 82
setTime( ) (Movie), 28, 34
setTimeCodeDef( ), 201
setTimeScale( ) (TimeCodeDef), 202
settingsDialog( )
  SGSoundChannel class, 121, 123
  SGVideoChannel class, 126
setUsage( ), 123, 134
  SGSoundChannel class, 117, 121,
    129
  SGVideoChannel class, 129
setVolume( ) (SoundChannel), 118
SGDeviceName class, 120
SGSoundChannel class, 129
  setDevice( ), 120
  setUsage( ), 117, 121
SGVideoChannel class,
      settingsDialog( ), 126

Chris Adamson is the Editor of O'Reilly's ONJava site and the Associate Online Editor for java.net, a collaboration between O'Reilly, Sun Microsystems, and CollabNet. He also writes about Java and Mac topics online and speaks at conferences such as ADHOC and the O'Reilly Mac OS X Conference. He develops media applications under the guise of his consulting company, Subsequently and Furthermore, Inc. He has an M.A. in Telecommunication from Michigan State University and a B.A. in English and B.S. in Symbolic Systems from Stanford University. He lives in Atlanta with his wife, Kelly, and their son, Keagan, and he has thus far managed to own seven and a half Macs.

About the Author

Our look is the result of reader comments, our own experimentation, and feedback from distribution channels. Distinctive covers complement our distinctive approach to technical topics, breathing personality and life into potentially dry subjects.

The *Developer's Notebook* series is modeled on the tradition of laboratory notebooks. Laboratory notebooks are an invaluable tool for researchers and their successors.

Sarah Sherman was the production editor and the proofreader for *QuickTime for Java: A Developer's Notebook*, and Audrey Doyle was the copyeditor. Marlowe Shaeffer and Claire Cloutier provided quality control. Ellen Troutman-Zaig wrote the index.

Edie Freedman designed the cover of this book. Emma Colby produced the cover layout with QuarkXPress 4.1 using the Officina Sans and JuniorHandwriting fonts.

David Futato designed the interior layout, with contributions from Edie Freedman. This book was converted by Joe Wizda to FrameMaker 5.5.6 with a format conversion tool created by Erik Ray, Jason McIntosh, Neil Walls, and Mike Sierra that uses Perl and XML technologies. The text font is Adobe Boton; the heading font is ITC Officina Sans; the code font is LucasFont's TheSans Mono Condensed, and the handwriting font is a modified version of JuniorHandwriting made by Tepid Monkey Foundry and modified by O'Reilly. The illustrations that appear in the book were produced by Robert Romano and Jessamyn Read using Macromedia FreeHand MX and Adobe Photoshop CS. This colophon was written by Colleen Gorman.

Colophon